A HARD LOOK
IN THE MIRROR

A HARD LOOK IN THE MIRROR;

FIXING AMERICA'S CRISIS OF CHARACTER

(AND OUR LEADERSHIP CRISIS)

Patrick F. Walsh

*To my precious wife Awilda, whose consistent encourage-
ment and belief, made ME a believer...*

CONTENTS

INTRODUCTION

THE BOOK

The extraordinary journey of our people and our country continues, amidst financial crises, leadership crises, and moral and ethical crises within our government, our media, and our society. We face unusual and unprecedented challenges and most times we feel powerless to effect the change we feel is so desperately needed to set the right course for our people and country. Our so-called political leaders continuously offend our sensibilities and disappoint us in their behavior, in their conduct of our nation's business, and in their general lack of integrity and moral fortitude, focused most times on what is in their own best interest and not that of the American People.

Of course we can change the names and faces of the leaders who occupy the highest offices in the land. But the real crisis seems to be that we don't seem to be able to attract people of character, intelligence and integrity to seek these offices. We seem to be on a constant search for answers, with no one we can trust to provide them. We feel that our politicians are more concerned with assuming leadership for the purposes of lining their pockets (and those of their cronies), rather than leading our people with integrity and vision through the rough and treacherous seas we find ourselves in.

PATRICK F. WALSH

I have written this book because of my passion and admiration for our great country, our Founding Fathers, and for the extraordinary courage, determination and character of our people of every race, gender, sexual preference and ethnicity. It may be an unsettling book to read, as I have directly challenged us to take a hard look in the mirror at ourselves, because like it or not, liberal or conservative, man or woman, black or white, straight or gay, if we are disturbed by what we see in our social and political leadership today, we must admit that it is a direct reflection of us. If we do not like what we see in our political leadership, the responsibility is ours, together. In this book, I have provided real-life examples of the problems, challenges and outrages we face today, and I have also provided real-life solutions to address them.

This is not a book full of complaints, but solutions. This is a book full of love and compassion for our people, full of great admiration for our heritage and our journey together and full of pride in our ability and our commitment to evolve and change and become better people and a better society.

This book is about today, about the state of our current society and the direction we now need to take, together. It is also my love-letter to my country and to my brother and sister Americans, celebrating the vision, courage, conviction and sacrifice of our Founding Fathers and of all Americans of every race and gender, who have sacrificed of themselves, first to win our freedom, then to abolish slavery and thereafter to protect and preserve those freedoms and our heritage on a global scale. In these pages I demonstrate how we must apply these values to set a new course today.

This book encourages us to appreciate and continue our journey toward perfection, which never ends. It calls upon all of us to reflect and understand the meaning of the values and the magnitude of the sacrifices that have made our country truly great and to pull together as a people to make new changes that are called for, **immediately**!

Is it also, however, **"A HARD LOOK IN THE MIRROR"**? Absolutely! From the first chapter, I have endeavored to concisely and accurately capture the anger and frustration of the American people with our current political and social leadership on both sides of the aisle and to clearly identify the causes across all party lines and across major issues of concern, affecting Americans today.

This book captures the genesis of that frustration and gives rousing voice to America's Silent Majority of every race, preference and gender. It captures the visceral reality of today's moral outrage in America, from a people's perspective. From the Wall Street bailouts by both American Presidents and Congress, to our overwhelming national debt, to our failing educational system (once a model for the world), to the use of our military in multiple foreign wars for the wrong-headed purpose of nation-building, this book outlines the abdication of responsibilities by our government officials towards integrity, truth and civility, in the responsible and honorable execution of their duties as trusted representatives of our people.

This book measures the behaviors, attitudes and actions of our current political leaders, as well as our society, against the gold-standard of our Founding Fathers and speaks to ALL Americans from the heart, with compassion and pride in who we are as a people and what we need to do today to address and correct these problems, together.

In these pages we tackle the obligations we have to those who are most precious to us, our children, our young Americans who will become tomorrow's leaders. We discuss what we must do to give them back that most important gift which most of us enjoyed and so very much needed;

a childhood that allows them "an age of innocence", a childhood that does not prematurely force upon them the abuses and exploitation that today's world heaps upon them, from early exposure to drug use, to the sex, violence and degradation that today's multimedia machine batters them with daily, driven mostly by greed. We also discuss the example we ourselves, as parents, are called upon to set in order to give them a chance to grow up as whole, fully-formed adults and happy, contributing members of society, including the obligation we have, as responsible adult Americans, not to saddle them with the shameful debt burden that our generation has and continues to create for them.

This book identifies the media elite of the "Media Industrial Complex" and clearly outlines the strategic approach they have all taken to play upon the emotions of the American People, in order to inflame our sensibilities for the purposes of ratings and revenue generation, and demonstrates how the media on the right and the left play a similar game designed, not to report the news or to be "fair and balanced", but to **make** the news and to **make** public opinion, rather than report on it. Why? Because generating emotions on either side of the issues, sells!

There is no subject too sensitive to tackle, from frank discussion about 911 and the Ground Zero Mosque and the real motives, agenda and politics that drove that effort, to the related strange and loud silence of the Muslim world, here and abroad, in never publicly condemning that horrific act of terrorism, even to this day.

We discuss matters ranging the sensitive subject of our openly Gay brother and sister Americans serving in the military, to the politics behind respected journalist Juan Williams being publicly attacked, humiliated and terminated from employment in a manner so ruthless, even Corporate America would recoil, and what all of these events say about our society, our media, and our political leaders of today.

A HARD LOOK IN THE MIRROR

In these pages, the politics of immigration are frankly examined and discussed, in the light of what is sensible and fair, as well as morally and economically responsible, tying our policies again, to the gold-standard of our Founding Fathers, recognizing the value and importance of supporting *legal* immigration as part of the DNA of our country and as a critically important component of our national vitality. It recognizes *legal* immigration and the welcoming of future Americans to our shores as inherent to our culture and our heritage and as lifeblood to our nation, constantly refreshing and revitalizing us as a country, as a people, and as a leader in the global economy.

This book identifies the reasons for the cultural shift in the quality, integrity and leadership of our national and local political leaders, as well as our business leaders and provides frank and sometimes frightening perspectives about the decline in character taking place before our eyes, as demonstrated by the likes of Tony Hayward (ex-BP CEO) and many like him.

This book is also about **intelligent solutions**! In identifying and giving voice to the moral outrage of our people and in being direct in identifying both the perpetrators and the root-causes. It also discusses the need for the American People to take **ownership** of **our** problems; essentially to accept that our political leadership is a reflection of us, WE THE PEOPLE, and if we don't like what we see, then we'd better change things, starting first with frank, self-examination, asking ourselves the hardest questions of all.

As each subject is addressed and each well-known party, group and individual is frankly and directly "called-out"; reasonable, sound, common-sense solutions are then discussed and identified. This book inclusively calls **all** Brother and Sister Americans back to our roots. It addresses politicians, media, citizens (adults and children) and prospective citizens in its observations and assessments.

PATRICK F. WALSH

In this book, I call upon us to come back together as a people and to solve our problems as Americans and I outline how to accomplish this. These pages may provoke anger, laughter, sentiment, reflection and pride...but in the end, I hope it inspires in you and in us, determination and confidence in our country, our heritage, and in each other, and that it sets in motion the actions required to get us back on track with the vision of our Founding Fathers in our shared journey together.

CHAPTER 1

IT'S UP TO US,
NOT THE POLITICIANS...

Black or White, Man or Woman, Straight or Gay...regardless of gender, ethnicity, or sexual orientation, we are *all* Americans. Each of us, individually and collectively, as disappointed and disgusted as we may be with the status-quo today, bear complete responsibility together, for our country's present, its future, and our shared destiny. We must have the vision and the courage to accept those responsibilities that our Founding Father's fully intended for us to **own**. We can no longer afford more excuses and finger-pointing at the politicians **we** elected. **We** are the ones responsible for setting our country back on the right course and only **we** can do it...and since 1776, "WE THE PEOPLE" have been the only ones charged with the **responsibility** to do it.

So, where do we start you ask? When in doubt, reflect upon the Founding Fathers of our country, who started it all. Reflect upon the frustrations and angst that they and our colonial citizens felt. Reflect upon the document that embodies their decisions for principled, decisive action and embodies what we represent as a people and as a nation. Keep the analysis simple and go back to the beginning for guidance. Reflect upon the profound and powerful vision and upon the just and challenging principles expressed by our Founding Fathers, from which our proud, free American soul and spirit was born and upon which our free and independent nation was founded...

*"We hold these truths to be self-evident, that **all men are created equal**, that they are **endowed by their Creator** with certain unalienable rights, that among these are **life, liberty and the pursuit of happiness**. That to secure these rights, governments are instituted among men, **deriving their just powers from the consent of the governed. That whenever any form of government becomes destructive to these ends, it is the right of the people to alter or to abolish it, and to institute new government**, laying its foundation on such principles and organizing its powers in such form, **as to them shall seem most likely to effect their safety and happiness**. Prudence, indeed, will dictate that governments long established should not be changed for light and transient causes; ... **But when a long train of abuses...evinces a design to reduce them under absolute despotism, it is their right, it is their duty, to throw off such government, and to provide new guards for their future security. --Such has been the patient sufferance of these colonies; and such is now the necessity which constrains them to alter their former systems of government.** The history of the present... is a history of repeated injuries and usurpations, all having in direct object the establishment of an absolute tyranny over these states. To prove this, **let facts be submitted to a candid world..."** ... **And for the support of this Declaration, with a firm reliance on the protection of Divine Providence, we mutually pledge to each other our Lives, our Fortunes, and our sacred Honor.***

- From the Declaration of Independence, July 4, 1776

When in doubt, look to the words of our Founding Fathers. Let the reality and facts of our current state of affairs be submitted to a candid world, indeed! Republican or Democrat, Conservative or Liberal, right, left, or middle; it doesn't seem to matter so much anymore, which of the existing political parties each of us identifies with. At the foundation, to many of us, all appear rotted and decayed at their core; bankrupt of principles and corrupt, and no longer connected to the majority of regular, everyday Americans they represent.

To many of us, the recent crops of politicians in Washington do not represent, in any meaningful way, the values and principles that our forefathers sacrificed so much to establish and in many cases laid down their very lives to defend. These are the same values and principles that countless other brave men and women have fought so hard and paid so dearly to preserve, through many painful and costly wars. White or black, man or woman...at the foundation, we all share similar dreams, hopes and aspirations for our families, for each other, and for our country; a country where we pride ourselves on being free, independent, fair-minded and supportive of each other and where we can maintain a reasonably level playing field of opportunity for all, and then succeed or fail, based *not* upon what political candidate we bought or influenced, but instead upon the results of our personal effort, ideas, ambition, skill and drive.

This is why people still try to come to our country at all costs; to simply have a fair opportunity to achieve their dreams and goals and to build a better life for themselves and their families. This is why being an American, or becoming an American, is an idea born of the human condition and should not be restricted to where you were born, what color you are, or what gender you are. *It is about what is in your heart. It is about what ideals and principles you hold dear and what you are prepared to pledge, sacrifice and commit yourself to as a citizen of this great country, or in lawfully becoming an American, and in embracing and defending America, our ideals and our way of life.*

As the melting pot of the world, we are constantly renewed by the passion, the creativity and the vitality of those who crave freedom and independence and who believe in the idea and principles of America, and who are prepared to take their turn at the oars to continue to drive our "Great American Experiment" in liberty, independence and a "government of the people, by the people and for the people", forward through constantly churning seas. *Without this, America stagnates. With it, America continues to renew and revitalize itself.*

Citizens of the United States have fought hard and died for these principles, from our battle for independence, to the Civil War, through WWII and beyond. The truth of these principles is written on our hearts, they burn in our souls as Americans and they are our heritage, our legacy and our birthright. These American principles, so gallantly fought for, are principles that we have a sacred obligation to defend, so that we may pass them on to our sons, daughters and descendants, intact, as we ourselves received them, at such a heavy cost.

As a people of all races, genders, ethnicities and sexual orientations, if we do not preserve and defend these principles and our freedoms, against even our own politicians and our own apathy, then we will have failed as a generation, as a society, and as a people. We will have squandered for pennies what was secured by a treasure of courage, honor, sacrifice and blood.

Whether we choose to accept or believe it, we were and still are a bastion of hope for the world; a place where freedom and opportunity still exists for those who are simply willing to sacrifice, work hard and apply their God-given intelligence and skills to bettering the situation for themselves and their families. If other, regular Americans of every gender and ethnicity feel as I do, then they must also inherently feel, in their hearts and minds, that our principles and our way of life are in jeopardy and that, as we passively work and move through each day and take in the events, that our freedom is gradually being eroded in front of our eyes; the freedom for which such a heavy price has been paid and which is the most important element of our culture, making us and our country that beacon of freedom and hope that still exists in a world that is becoming ever-more polarized, ever-more more dangerous, and ever-more intolerant and less civilized, as it supposedly "evolves".

As we watch the present crop of politicians jeopardize the values, the freedoms and the economic prosperity, philosophy and infrastructure of our great nation, we are called upon, through the responsibilities placed upon every American by our Founding Fathers, to peacefully and legally fulfill our obligations as active, fully participating citizens in this Democratic Republic.

While we still have a chance to remain a great nation of people, when I see where we are today and I look at our government and our representatives and see the way we treat each other as Americans, I am appalled. In truth, our representatives and our political parties have become repugnant to me over the last ten years and if it's affecting me this way, I have to believe it's affecting a large majority of people similarly, because I'm a pretty regular Joe and there's not much out of the ordinary when it comes to me. I have a wife, two kids and a job and I'm more and more disgusted and disturbed by what I see each day in our government, in our media, and in how we treat each other.

In college, I came to study, understand and identify with conservative American principles (Democrats, please don't stop reading, you will be surprised as you read on). I was in a vast minority in those days, just prior to the Reagan Revolution. I embraced those ideas because they appealed to my logic, my common-sense and my ideals; ideals which I felt this country was built upon, namely, independence, self-reliance, liberty, justice and a love of country and our fellow-man, and most especially, our fellow Americans. It didn't matter what color, gender, or national origin they were.

Being a conservative at the time, I embraced what I believed and still believe are a set of living ideas and principles that were the basis of a foundation on which to build and maintain true freedom, in the sense that it genuinely freed people to succeed and pursue their dreams, again, regardless of race, gender, or national origin. These were not a set of principles that existed in a vacuum, but principles and ideas that grow and evolve and both reflect and celebrate the vision, courage and commitment of our Founding Fathers, as expressed in the Declaration of Independence, our Constitution, and our Bill of Rights; a set of ideals and beliefs that seemed to me clearly inspired by our Creator, the ultimate provider and supporter of free will.

After being a longtime, eco-Republican (from the time I decided in college that this party's beliefs and economic principles mirrored many of my own), I left the Republican party and re-declared myself an Independent and I have remained an Independent, since. This took place during the Presidential re-election campaign of George W. Bush, whom I voted for in his first term. GW, of course, then proceeded to abandon many of the economic principles of the conservative Republican agenda he purported to represent, and went off in a direction all his own...which is where he completely lost me. I don't know about you, but when the guide I hire tells me he's taking my family east and then he heads west, well, I figure he either doesn't know where he's going, or he's intentionally trying to mislead me...Either way, he's fired and I'm heading in my own direction.

By the way, the term I coined above, eco-Republican, stands for economic-conservative Republican, **with a social conscience**. Who says you can't design a budget to be true to conservative economic principles (by which regular citizens like me and you have to run our households), while creating programs and safety nets for those brother and sister Americans in our society who truly and profoundly need them? I have an accounting degree, I've constructed multi-million dollar budgets and

A HARD LOOK IN THE MIRROR

I've run multi-million dollar business units for some of the largest global companies. With the right team, the right plan, the right budget and some strong discipline in executing to the plan and budget, anything can be accomplished. Social programs are not evil or irresponsible, people who conceive them poorly, who are economically irresponsible in their administration, or who abuse those programs are the ones that give social programs a bad name and reputation in some political, economic and social circles. This is the fault of politicians, not the programs themselves.

In my view, the true economic differences between the two parties (Democrat and Republican), have become so blurred, that neither represent my basic beliefs anymore. Whether you're Republican or Democrat, I think it's reassuring to know that the candidates you are supporting actually have some intention to execute to the principles and platform they tell you they stand for in their election campaigns. Silly me...as such has not been the case; not with Bush, not with Obama, and certainly not with the Senate or House of Representatives.

In President Obama's case, I'm sure if you ask the folks who steer left-of-center if he's stayed true to them, they'd probably say no and might punctuate it by telling you to go do something unnatural to yourself. Likewise, if you ask the folks in the middle who voted for President Obama, if he's stayed true to the middle-ground he represented to them during the election campaigns, well, they'd probably respond by telling you that he's done something unnatural to them.

The reason for this (and I'm not talking about President Obama, but our entire political community), is the absence of character and integrity in the majority of the elected officials holding positions within the parties today; both Republican and Democrat. Know that I have always respected both parties and admired our system of government,

7

as I still do. The first President that I was ever exposed to was John F. Kennedy, whom I have great respect for, both in the execution of his duties as President and as a patriot and war veteran, who put his life on the line for all of us. When I was very young, I vividly remember my mother worshipping the ground he walked on, thinking he was a cross between Cary Grant and St. Francis of Assisi, as I'm sure most moms did at that time, Republican or Democrat. I know my father admired him greatly.

From Eisenhower, to Kennedy, to Reagan, there was a certain GRAVITAS (read *CHARACTER*) to these men that went beyond political parties and purely self-serving politics. In these men, you simply knew that, regardless of the political differences, their moral and political American compass and beliefs led in a straight line directly back to those of our Founding Fathers, to our roots. It didn't matter whether they were Democrat or Republican. In the end, they espoused the beliefs and embodied the principles and ideals which, as born or naturalized Americans of any race, gender, national origin or sexual orientation, we all cherish in our hearts and hold most dear; or at least should.

Today we have politicians like... well... like Nancy Pelosi...I'm sorry, but if you're looking for a contrasting comparison to the aforementioned political giants, she has to be the poster child. Democrat or Republican, one must agree that having had her as third in line for the Presidency seemed a bit like having Edith Bunker (the beloved "dingbat" of "All in the Family" fame), as third in line for the highest office in the land.

A HARD LOOK IN THE MIRROR

Edith Bunker – The beloved "ding-bat"
["All in the Family", image courtesy of Sony Pictures Television]

Look to the right and you see Sarah Palin having been chosen by John McCain to be second in line for the Presidency. One needs look no further for a reason to be afraid...very afraid, to have voted for Mr. McCain...

You thought ding-bats were fictitious eh? Not in Washington. I don't know about you, but just the thought of having had Nancy Pelosi as third in line for the Presidency and Sarah Palin as (potentially) second in line, makes me want to run like hell for the bottle of Kaopectate! Just as Tom Hanks said there's no crying in baseball...there can be no ding-bats in the Oval Office. This Pelosi-Palin duo, both drew the legendary "Benny Hill" reaction from me...

PATRICK F. WALSH

[The always lovable, Mr. Benny Hill (courtesy of FremantleMedia Ltd.)]

Let me add that this has nothing to do with the fact that they are women. If a woman with the intelligence, character and courage of Margaret Thatcher had been running for the U.S. Presidency at any time from 1988 to the present, she'd have had my vote over all of the male candidates that have run since.

Today's politician, Democrat or Republican, is a different animal. They seem more guided by political polls, greed and by the direction of the prevailing wind of public opinion, than by a strict moral code and patriotic compass. They are in it to line their pockets and take a power-trip, designing a political agenda to achieve those ends, while letting the means about how they get there and the purpose of why they have been put there, become secondary (if considered at all). They are willing to say anything and do anything that's expedient, to get into office and stay in office.

How else can one possibly explain pushing through and voting on bills to control vast, unimaginable sums of *our money*, **without even having read the bill** (e.g. the two bailout bills and the healthcare bill), knowing only at the 20,000 ft. level, what the bills may really do and **caring only that it will give them access to the money and the economy they so desperately**

seek to control? For this type of blatant irresponsibility, arrogance, and some may say larceny, those who operate in this way should be fired by the American voters (Democrat, Independent and Republican). This is absolutely <u>not</u> how we expect our elected representatives to operate and we should not permit it.

Democrat and Republican, our political representatives have come to resemble political hyenas fighting over the carcass that is fast-becoming the bankrupt U.S. economy, by the strictest definition of bankrupt. The dirty little secret is that our politicians, with our full cooperation, have us living not off our assets, but off of our liabilities and our cash-flow. They have us operating off the biggest credit-card account on the planet, while they are lining their pockets and doling out political favors, and it's us, our children, and our children's children, who are being saddled with the debt they are ringing up and <u>we</u> will have to pay the bill.

Unfortunately, there's no "800" number to call for a debt remediation company that's going to come to our rescue and settle with our creditors for 10 cents on the dollar, as much as we might blindly hope this could go on forever, without consequences. Democrat or Republican, we know this to be true in our heart of hearts. But it seems we're unwilling or unable to take political control of our situation and "just say no".

PATRICK F. WALSH

The American Economy in the near future...

Don't get me wrong; *we want to say "no", we know it's the right thing for us and for our children.* But the only way we have of saying "no", is to throw these hyenas out on their collective rear-ends, by going to the voting booths and electing...umm...who...?

Ahhh, there's the rub... We appear to have gotten ourselves into a zero-sum game, where the outcome is rigged no matter which Republican or Democrat we put in office. It always seems that the results are pre-arranged with what today has become one of two, very similar alternatives. **We are aching to "just say no" in a big way. I can feel it, you can feel it; hell, we, the silent majority of every race, gender, ethnicity and orientation can all feel it. But there is no Dwight Eisenhower out there warning us of the Military Industrial Complex. There is no John F. Kennedy out there telling us: "Don't ask what your country** can do for you, ask what you can do for your country!" We don't have a Ronald Reagan out there challenging the oppressors of our time, saying: "Mr. Gorbachev, tear down this WALL!"

Instead, what we have for the most part is a bunch of educated opportunists looking to make a lot of coin in politics. *So where and to whom do we turn?*

CHAPTER 2

WHERE AND TO WHOM DO WE TURN?

Where do we turn? To whom do we turn? We turn to where we have always turned when crisis strikes...*we turn to each other*, as Americans. We have done so in the past, from the War of Independence, to the Civil War, through two World Wars and beyond. These were times when everyone, to a greater degree at least, put aside race and gender and worked together as a people-united. Whether it was the integration of the military, or "Rosy the riveter", we put aside much of our preoccupation with these differences and worked alongside each other **as brother and sister Americans**.

Today, we must face hard truths about our government and our society and we must start fixing both, together as one. We must be certain to put aside any media-hyped, obsessive focus on race, gender, orientation, and our respective national origins and on obsessive personal agendas revolving around such matters. We must realize that we need to lift ourselves above these oft-times divisive considerations and from this point forward simply work together as "Americans", who are color-blind, gender-blind and ethnicity-blind.

To effectively fix our country's problems as a people-united, requires a wholly "American Perspective" from all of us.

We must begin to face the mess that has been created by our own distractions, apathy and lack of attention to what's been going on in our government and in our society and we must remember one very important thing, my brother and sister Americans, *our government is the "business" that runs our communities, our schools, our armed forces, our country! If we don't like what we see, then we need to collectively look in the mirror to take a hard look at the people responsible for what we're saddled with...US! You see, the politicians are the executives and management team that run the business of our country. We are the Board of Directors that put them in charge. If we don't like how the business is running, we need to fire the executives and management team WE put in charge. That's the simple logic of it. So if we want to point fingers, then we must walk to the nearest mirror and point our fingers directly at the person(s) looking back at us!*

This seems to be one perspective that both the conservative and liberal talking-heads seem to repeatedly leave out of the equation. They seem to want to solely blame our government representatives for the mess we've created as a society, in order to polarize us as Americans by pointing fingers, because doing this creates TV ratings. Well, I've got news for you my brother and sister Americans... *"We"...you and me...are responsible for the mess, because we planted the recent crops of clever jackasses in office.* Now, while they may not all be jackasses, a majority of those so-called leaders are, and if we put these leadership and ethically challenged people in office, then what does that make us? At the very least, it makes us **responsible**, and perhaps even a little lazy and apathetic. At most...well, I'm sure each of us can fill in the blanks.

That's about the best thing I can say about it and I'm as guilty as anyone else. I think we all have to start by admitting this serious error, this negligence of which each of us is guilty, and then resolve to work together as Americans to fix the problems. But we can't move forward to the "fixing phase", if we don't first, collectively, own-up to the fact that we, you and me, are fully responsible for it in the first place.

Now, for a lot of years, we've put some pretty irresponsible people in-charge, thinking we could trust them to make good decisions in running the business of our country. We've let them run things right into the ground and we've let them grow fat and happy on the money that's been generated through greed and personal avarice. Why do you think many, if not most, leave office as millionaires? Most didn't come into office with the kind of wealth they leave with...

Republican, Democrat, it doesn't matter. There's a myriad of examples. From George W. Bush growing the government and the spending exponentially (while the debt piled up), to Barney Frank and his cohorts telling us that the housing market was good and strong, while he and his cronies instructed Fannie Mae and Freddie Mac to loosen-up their lending requirements, regardless of whether any of our fellow brother and sister Americans could realistically pay for the mortgages they were doling out like free liquor, because *supposedly*, they felt it was each person's inalienable right to the American Dream; **conveniently forgetting of course that the American Dream is not a house (as they might have us think), but rather, the American Dream is Freedom and Liberty and Self-Determination, and a Government of the People, by the People, and for the People. The American Dream, you see, is a free society, which has always had to be earned and maintained through enormous sacrifice. In fact, if you review the excerpt of the Declaration of Independence, which I quoted above, *NOWHERE* will you find it stated that;**

"...they are endowed by their Creator with certain unalienable rights, that among these are life, liberty and the pursuit of happiness, **along with a house and a mortgage they can't possibly afford.***"*

A HARD LOOK IN THE MIRROR

But hell, rhetoric like Mr. Frank's sounded good enough to get votes and stay in office, despite his colossal failure of oversight, responsibility and stewardship. And as we've seen, when the dust cleared, he disappeared like magic. Suddenly, he wasn't responsible...right? Meanwhile, all of us citizens watched the economic disaster develop in relative indifference, even though we saw the handwriting on the wall. ***Come on!*** **We all saw what was going on and we all knew, at a common-sense level, that it made no sense!** If we can't be honest with ourselves about that, there's really no hope to move forward and escape the mistakes we've made. Let's admit it to ourselves that we all had an ominous feeling in our collective guts, when we saw the skyrocketing home prices and saw many of our fellow Americans putting no money down and actually getting cash back in their hands, as they purchased homes that we all knew they couldn't afford.

Why did we watch this happen with no reaction whatsoever? I'll tell you why, but you may not like the answer! **It's because many of us said to ourselves (me included), "What's good for the goose is good for the gander**!" For those citizens who owned homes, they were getting ridiculous windfalls by selling, and sure, if things continued to loosen up like this, *we saw ourselves maybe going out and purchasing a house that we had no business buying either!*

It was all good, though. We were like drunks on a binge. The banks, the regulatory agencies, the Congress, even President Bush (by his quiet and "apparent" indifference), were all cooperating together to hand out the high-cost, tainted booze (on credit), and guess what? **"WE THE PEOPLE", along with the rest of them, turned into sailors on a weekend pass in sin-city, consuming the tainted booze together in droves.**

PATRICK F. WALSH

["On the loose on Easy Street..." Pictured above:
Some Wall Street Bankers, the Regulatory Agents,
Congress, the President, and "We the People"]

Let's admit it. Everyone involved was making money, a lot of people were getting fat and many people were living the high-life in homes which, as little as 5 years earlier, they couldn't have possibly sniffed. The sad part of it is they did it on my nickel and your nickel. They didn't pay for it; we did, when the bailouts came. And I don't know about you, but I didn't partake of the tainted booze while it was going on and I'm pretty damned furious about bailing out billionaire bankers and people with poor judgment, while the bankers continued to make millions in commissions and bonuses. To my knowledge, not a single person has gone to jail or had to hand back a nickel in those bonuses they collected! Certainly no bank executives have, as I understand it. What about the regulatory agency heads? Why is not a single one in jail for criminal negligence for their dereliction of duty? Why wasn't someone impeached, or a Congressman like Barney Frank censured by Congress? How does that happen?

It happens because of who **WE** put in office and because, like docile servants, **WE** allow it to happen. Remember, they work for us, not the other way around, my brother and sister Americans of every race, gender and ethnicity.

Ok, we can't do anything to change the past, but we can take action to straighten things out moving forward. First and foremost, let's recognize what went wrong and what we did as citizens to allow it to happen. Then let's send a message to Washington that we're no longer sleeping (as we did in the last mid-term elections that took place in 2010, if anyone still remembers). We're going to fulfill our constitutional responsibilities as citizens and take control back from the conniving horde in Washington that has taken full advantage of the situation.

Sticking with the theme of this chapter and before getting more specific about what went wrong and what we can do to take control back and correct it, we first need to recognize that we need to trust one another as brother and sister Americans. We need to see each other only as brother and sister Americans, putting ourselves above any other considerations and be honest with each other and most importantly, honest with ourselves.

Now, I'm going to run the risk of sounding contradictory. We can take a lot of constructive things from President Barack Obama's election. It demonstrated how far we've come as a people and as a country and it spoke volumes about our ability to look beyond race and ethnicity and to look instead at the important things we value most; character, integrity and values and the ability of a candidate to communicate his or her message effectively **to us, the "Board of Directors" of the country**. I hope everyone has taken in what I've said! The President and the Congress may be the CEO and the executives running the business of our country, **but again, we are the board of directors; we replace them at our discretion**.

Now, getting back to my comments about the original election of Barack Obama, there are many constructive, positive things we can take from that experience as a society and as a unified people. As to whether President Obama was completely honest and forthright about his intentions with his election rhetoric, relative to both his first and second terms, well, that is a separate matter, and in that he may be just as guilty of disingenuous campaign rhetoric as the rest of the elected officials **we** have chosen to surround him with and elected over the years.

Additionally, I believe the original election of President Obama is an indicator that we can all feel good and take pride in our relationship with each other, as a whole. I believe that his original Presidential election milestone spoke volumes to us as brother and sister Americans, and to the world about what type of a people and nation we are and have become. It spoke to our long and continued evolution as a people and as a country.

I couldn't have been more proud of our country and people that night, after the results were in (regardless of how I voted). I think that there were few dry-eyes in the house when President Obama gave his speech. That's because, regardless of who you voted for, it spoke to our <u>very American hearts</u> and to our <u>very American souls</u>, and stoked the fires burning within each of us, reminding us of our proud <u>American</u> ideals and our uniquely <u>American</u> heritage, started by our Founding Fathers. I believe this important milestone touched us all very deeply, as a very special people and country, if you'll allow me to say so. This election allowed us to affirm, in a very loud, clear and profound way, that the connection to our Founding Fathers, to the Spirit of 1776, to our own Declaration of Independence, and to who we are as a people and a country, is alive and well in these United States, in these humble Colonies founded and established through such incredible courage, vision and sacrifice, which could only have been divinely inspired (in my humble opinion).

A HARD LOOK IN THE MIRROR

In so many ways, I believe that we love this country and each other as Americans and we need to assure that we again begin to trust each other and depend upon each other, so that we engage together in taking back control of *the business of our country* and in being responsible citizens and stewards of our shared and proud heritage, once again.

If Barack Obama's first election as President showed us one thing, it's that we can and do trust each other as Americans. All Americans elected President Obama, a man of African-American descent and with a middle name of "Hussein", with parents of mixed national origins and heritages. Clearly, we elected him based **not** upon prejudiced notions of race, religion, or his family's national origin. We elected him based upon our perceptions and conclusions about the content of his character and his ability. So let's have some honest dialogue with each other, as responsible brother and sister Americans, regardless of race, color or sex.

How can we establish and continue to maintain consistent UNITY with each other as brother and sister Americans, without all of us having the foundational knowledge and common understanding of our rich history as a nation and as a people, in order to truly understand the shared Principles, Sacrifices and Ideals that bind us together as Americans in this Great American Experiment?

In loving our country together as Americans, we have to love what our country represents, and each of us has to feel that we have something in common with each other, something important and profound that we share; something that goes beyond race, gender, national origin and even family. It's what allows us to look at each other and appreciate each other as Americans first, and our many cultural origins, second. We must take care to properly educate ourselves and our children about this nation's origins, its rich human history and what it represents to us. We're not doing that sufficiently today.

We must also require the proper education of those who want to become citizens of this nation, as to precisely what the history of this nation really is and all that has been sacrificed to see it born. All must know of the many wars that have been fought, not only to win these liberties and freedoms that we enjoy today, but to sustain them and build upon them (e.g. the Civil War, WWII, etc.). If we do not, then how will we ever expect them to see themselves as Americans first and foremost, and to understand and carry what America really means in their hearts and souls, thereby continuing to bind us, each to the other, as new Americans arrive on our shores (legally, of course)? How can we expect them to know and understand why what we have is so very precious, why it works, and why we must be prepared to fight for it, if we do not do this?

This country was born in brother and sisterhood, in Unity and in Blood, at great cost, by people willing to die for each other, willing to risk everything they had and everything they had achieved for themselves and their families, for a concept, a dream really, a vision only of what could be. WE THE PEOPLE lost entire generations to war and suffering, first to achieve and then hold onto our freedom and independence and our American Dream.

First and foremost, we must assure as a people, for the preservation of our country and our ideals, that everyone who is born here, or who applies to become an American citizen (and therefore an American) and who wishes to share in the American Dream, both understand and appreciate exactly what being an American really means (in their own context, of course). To gain that understanding and context, they must know how our freedom was purchased, and re-purchased again and again by our citizens of all races, genders and origins, at a great human cost.

A HARD LOOK IN THE MIRROR

There is a fire that burns in my heart and in each American's heart. It is the fire that causes us to well-up with tears at the sound of our National Anthem, and that fills us with national pride when we see our military defending our freedoms. It is the fire that caused tears to well-up in every real American's eyes and swelled every real American's heart with pride (and a certain sense of justice), when we elected our first African-American President and heard his speech. Whether we agreed with President Obama's politics or not or whether we voted for him or not, we all felt the pride in our country, in our People, in our President, and in our shared Heritage. At that moment, we again lived up to the greatest ideals of our country and our Founding Fathers. Together we wrote another chapter in our journey as a people and as a nation, when we "<u>walked-the-walk</u>" of our Founding Fathers, delivering on their promise that we consider ourselves a nation and a people where "all men are created equal." We all felt a deep pang in our hearts and in our souls that traced its way back in time, all the way to July 4th, 1776.

We shared this feeling and sentiment together, only because we understood the rich history, heritage, and extreme sacrifice behind what it took for our nation, our people of every race, gender, orientation and origin, to take this journey together and to reach this milestone **together**. It required a shared understanding and appreciation of our American history and our continuing fight for freedom and justice for every American.

This, by the way, is all part of the same fire that also causes us to take so personally the insults and jabs of foreign powers at our way of life and what we stand for; the fire that causes us heartache when we see our troops fighting and laying down their lives for peoples in foreign lands, who do not appreciate the fact that, while our troops are certainly fighting for our national interests, that included in the fight's end-game is also a fight for their personal and national freedoms, as well.

So, we come back to the question of how can we make certain that we are properly educating our children and those who want to immigrate to our nation and become citizens and have a stake in the American Dream, in such a way so that they can truly appreciate in their heart of hearts, what it means to be and to become an American. Isn't this so very important and central to our existence as a people and as a nation? Don't we owe this to those who long to become Americans and risk their lives in some cases to get to these shores? Don't we owe this to each other, to those who died in every war, and to our forefathers? Yes, of course we do.

If we love each other as a people and as a country, we can be honest about this dialogue with each other. We may disagree on many things, but I think we all agree that this country and our ideals and the ever-evolving discourse we engage in, is all possible because of that which has been fought for and paid for at such great human cost and which is put into unforgettable words by our Declaration of Independence. It is the foundation of our freedoms and cements our connection to our Founding Fathers, our Creator and to each other.

Our sacred obligation to our children and to anyone who wants to become an American is to educate them about what it means to be an American. Anyone who is properly taught about this uniquely American journey, surely understands as well, that their national origin and heritage adds to the richness of who we are as a people and as a nation and renews our vitality. But their individual national origin also takes a back seat to the bigger meaning of what they are engaging in and committing themselves and their children to.

For as we know, they are not coming here and applying for citizenship, solely to take advantage of an economic situation or opportunity, but instead to become an American, in every sense of the meaning, and to share in the richness of what that means and in the obligations it requires and to likewise be willing to sacrifice and lay down ones life for their country, *our country*, should America call upon any of us to do so. And if this education has been accomplished correctly, then the issue of bilingualism in the public schools and insistence on a separate but equal national identity, well, that becomes moot.

They instead understand that their heritage adds great value to our culture, but that they are becoming Americans, first and foremost, and that this is a conscious and intended decision that they are making that will tie them and their heritage to a Country, a People and an American Dream, going all the way back to July 4, 1776, which they will share in equally and completely, as brother and sister Americans.

Therefore, requiring intense and thorough education in our heritage, our rich history, our American values, ideals and our national sacrifices and the obligations this places upon them as Americans, in addition to the rights they will enjoy, is absolutely one of the most important foundations that our country must mandate for our children and for those applying to become citizens. This is an educational process that should take significant time and should require successful completion of examinations, which will assure that the education has been properly, appropriately and successfully administered and completed. This should be non-negotiable, for it is at the core of who we are. I will discuss this further in another chapter about immigration and what I believe is a fair, just, and necessary immigration policy. This will be a policy that will preserve and continue our heritage of welcoming to our shores those seeking freedom, while assuring they are also truly committed to becoming productive, contributing Americans, while also striking a balance with what is fair, reasonable and necessary to protect our country, our people and our economy.

PATRICK F. WALSH

We have accomplished so much together as a people and we should be so very proud of how far we've come. But we're facing challenges today that are new and can erode the American foundation that has been built. We must put aside pettiness and distrust. We must trust each other; trust that we have reached a point in our maturity as a nation and as a people to put aside Political Correctness and instead, look into each others eyes and agree on the priorities and "be real" with each other; real enough to have logical, mature adult conversations about our present and our future as Americans of every gender, ethnicity and preference. Otherwise, instead of **making things happen** as a people-united, we'll be asking ourselves **"what the hell happened?"**, when the damage has already been done. And there will be no solace or satisfaction for anyone who wants to say "I told you so", when that day comes. That day is on the way, so which position do we want to be in as a people-united? I don't believe any of us want to in the position that's asking "what the hell happened"...do we?

CHAPTER 3

BEWARE THE MEDIA INDUSTRIAL COMPLEX...

Where and to whom do we *not* turn?

Part of our responsibility to each other, is to stay informed. We can't afford to stick our heads in the sand any longer. We need to shut-off the reality TV and ESPN for a few hours a week, for our country and for each other, at least long enough each day to stay abreast of events and the things that influence our society, our families, our businesses, our economy, and most importantly, **our values**. For without solid foundational values, societies erode and disintegrate over time. History is replete with examples of this and if we allow it to continue here, with us, our society and our **Great American Experiment**, comprised of liberty, freedom, and a government Of, By and For the People, will pass the way of other failed societies that lost sight of what truly made them great.

First and foremost, we need to communicate forcefully and directly with the people we elect, whether to the President, the Congress, or the local school board. It's all equally important. So let's stop looking suspiciously at each other, as if based upon race, gender, origin, or sexual preference, we each have some sinister agenda in place to profit at the expense of each other, or hold each other back based upon such things. It's ridiculous and a waste of otherwise productive energy to live and think that way.

PATRICK F. WALSH

Let's stop allowing the media, both liberal and conservative; to drive wedges between us, which they make their living doing. Let's instead turn our eyes towards THEM and look at THEM suspiciously, recognizing that they are all clearly pursuing an agenda of conflict, primarily for commercial gain (ratings and money) and political influence, knowing full-well that by creating friction and animosity amongst and between us as a people, they create buzz, viewership and listenership for themselves. This has become a methodology they use to divide us, segment us into groups, and draw us into their respective folds, thereby creating ratings and $$$ for themselves. By preying upon us and using us (the American People) in this way, they feed their media money machine, which they believe in-turn, justifies their behavior.

Now, I don't doubt that some of them think they're doing us a service by opening-up our eyes, and to a degree, one could argue that these developments have served some useful purposes, making us more aware of the sleaze and graft in our politicians and the hypocrisy and toxic pollution that needs to be cleaned up from our political landscape. But the media's strategy is still based upon driving wedges between us. We have to see it for what it is and know it isn't going away, unless we "watch it away". Sooner or later, they need to change the childish, combative, disingenuous and divisive strategy that they pursue purely to drive ratings, and start communicating and reporting in a way that doesn't continuously offend us, demean us and tire us out, making us numb.

Whether we're talking about MSNBC, Bill Maher, Fox News, Rush Limbaugh, et al, we need to start using them instead of them using us. Let's first realize they all have a common agenda (no, I'm not crazy...they do). Let's frankly recognize what that agenda is. That agenda is drive ratings, make money, and peddle a philosophy and set of positions that speaks to their viewer's constituency.

A HARD LOOK IN THE MIRROR

The process by which they do this is to seize upon an emotional political or social topic, simplistically create a two-sided set of positions (e.g. for or against), framing the issue in a favorable light towards their position, and then take their own side, based upon the particular network's right or left-leaning philosophy. Then they promote the hell out of that side and sell that side to their network's viewer constituency, again, in order to drive emotions (which drive ratings) and to make money, as well as to manipulate our thinking and wield some measure of political influence.

This method also leaves them no shortage of guests to invite on their programs, guests who wish to push an agenda, for or against the particular topic. And the deck is always stacked properly to the appropriate side of the network's individual, political-bent.

I say let's play the B.S. card and let's take the information they provide us with through the process I've described, and let's manage it ourselves and be intelligent enough and discerning enough to filter it through the logic of our minds and not simply accept it and parrot it. Let's filter it through the lens of our basic American Values and those of our Founding Fathers and ask ourselves if the information they are reporting, or the viewpoints they are espousing and peddling, are in-line with our values as a unified people, as brother and sister Americans of all races and genders. Let's take advantage of *them* and the exposure we are getting from *them* (to multiple points of view) and filter that through the lens of what it means to be an American, as defined by our Founding Fathers.

Let's view and evaluate that information, relative to laws required to protect and govern and not to rule the people; and relative to a *Limited* Government Of, By and For the People, to provide for the common good and not interfere with our freedoms, our successes, or our failures. Let's view and evaluate that information relative to our <u>RIGHT</u> to keep most of what we make under our Capitalist system and spend it as we see fit, which alas, is not the case today, at least not when you add up federal income tax, state income tax, sales taxes, property taxes and various municipal taxes. Most of us in the middle class today, end up paying in excess of 50% of our income to the government, after all. What kind of nonsense is this?

Most of these media talking-heads on the right and the left are agenda-driven blowhards in any case (in my humble opinion). If you listen closely, most of their arguments are based on pure rhetoric, with minimal data or analysis to support their points, or their positions. They're mostly coming at us with bluster and loud screeching, trying to expertly push our buttons to get an emotional response out of us. But in most cases, experts they're not. Frankly, I personally find them to be less skilled at it than my daughter and my wife. You want to talk about expert button-pushers, the blowhards in the media are pikers compared to my ladies.

So, we need to recognize the blowhards in the media for who they are, and what they are trying to evoke from us. We need to be firm in our values and in our understanding of our own American history and heritage. We cannot let them divide us and "dumb us down". We need to view the Media Industrial Complex with a balanced and always-suspicious perspective these days and with a heavy dose of skepticism, understanding that their priority is to make money, manipulate, and generate ratings, through controlling the political discussion. We need to understand that, by allowing them to polarize us emotionally, we allow them to accomplish that.

It's a pretty simple formula when you think about it and they expertly use it on us every single day. We need to view them through the lens of our American values and discard all the noise, gibberish and fanaticism of the left and the right, as well as discard the fanaticism of those who espouse almost no values at all, who simply attack anything that represents belief in God, country and each other.

Keep in mind that the left, and more seldom the right (when it works to their respective advantages), also try to marginalize and dismiss the perspectives of those who believe in God and embrace religion. They do this by labeling them "religious fanatics", as if their opinions do not matter or count, because of their beliefs. Now, I'm certainly a strong believer in the separation of church and state and always have been. I believe it is one of the basic foundations that have allowed our Democratic-Republic and our freedom to last. But make no mistake about it, this is a clear strategy designed to neuter this segment of our society in the political discussions of the day and disqualify them from having any legitimate input or voice.

In my opinion, those who try to do this to them are the real fanatics, the **"secular fanatics"** who believe that people who hold religious beliefs and who believe in God and a God-based moral and spiritual code of ethics and living, have no right to any legitimate societal voice in our national, political, social and economic debate. These **"secular fanatics"** are the ones who scare me the most, as an American. They strike me as the real extremists, as people who would deny legitimate segments of American society a voice and their just-rights in the political discussion, based upon their "secular dogma". When I hear these "secular fanatics" speak, scary thoughts of Lenin and Soviet Russia flash across my mind. I get the impression that they would like to completely control the discussion and if possible, the rights of the people participating in it and, as I said, this strategy exists on the left and the right, depending upon the issue at hand.

The Media Industrial Complex's greatest fear should be an informed American public, which dismisses the rhetoric and extremism of the left and the right and embraces those things that our Founding Fathers taught us about being Americans. Their greatest fear should be a public that realizes that seldom do complex political, economic and social questions come down to only two possible positions or perspectives (for or against). That is, after all, how they get the hook into us.

The politicians and news media alike, try to set up complex issues (like healthcare or the federal bailouts) as a two-position question, yes or no, for or against, rather than consider the myriad of other potential solutions, plans and perspectives available to solve our problems, because they do not want us to consider anything but their agendas and they don't want us to complicate the "either/or" outcomes they desire, by opening up the discussion to the other, sensible universe of solutions and alternatives that exist. They simply want to dumb-us-down in order to control the conversation.

Know that when they successfully employ this strategy on us, they have us! They have us because we fall for it hook, line and sinker. This is how the politicians get away with not reading the highly complex healthcare bill, or the bailout bills, prior to voting on them and still remain in office, rather than us cleaning house and firing them all, if for no other reason than for not reading these highly complex bills, which will so dramatically affect our future and our children's future (yes, it really is appalling!). Even though the majority of the politicians didn't read the bills before voting, they still knew the financial outcome of where the money will be controlled and where it will go, which is all that is truly important to them. Their attitude is, "Details? Ha, not important!"

I use the term "Media Industrial Complex", not so much to suggest an unholy tie between media and industry, but instead to describe the media **as an industry unto itself**. They are no longer just reporting the news in the interests of informing the public, but crafting the news around their own, respective political agendas and ratings strategies, always with the formula in place to manipulate and divide us, in order to create conflict, buzz and emotion between us, to generate predictable behavior, ratings and revenue. If you don't think there's a formula in place, then you are either not paying attention to the programming, or you are naïve as hell.

Information and analysis does not drive the news any longer. Political agendas, personalities, and ratings strategies drive the news. The media outlets (e.g. Fox News, ABC, NBC, CBS, CNN & MSNBC) shape the way the information is crafted, portrayed and broadcast to us for our consumption, in a manner designed to generate in us pre-determined reactions, emotions, perspectives, opinions and conclusions, before it is ever delivered to us.

You see, their success in getting us to watch, depends upon the predictability of our reactions and emotions, within the viewer constituency they are targeting. Therefore, it is in their best interests to prevent us, to the greatest degree possible, from freely interpreting and digesting the news, unencumbered by their spin. I don't care what network it is... if we believe "the spin stops here" with any of them, right or left, we are simply naïve, and/or stupid. To trust any of them today to be fair and balanced is simply ludicrous.

What does it mean to be an American and what impact does it have to view ourselves, our society and the Media Industrial Complex through that lens?

To answer this, we need to know in our hearts, what it means to be an American. Let me try to define what it means to me. I believe that before we are Black, White, Latino, Asian, European, Middle-Eastern or some other descent, that we are Americans, first and foremost. That we embrace and share our love for, and dedication to the values and uniquely American ideals for which so many have fought, struggled and laid down their lives, throughout America's history; whether fighting for freedom and independence, or against injustice and slavery, or against Nazism and tyranny; they all sacrificed and many died to establish and defend our way of life and they only asked that we be prepared to do the same in return, so that the legacy of freedom, independence and self-determination continues.

From Columbus, to the Pilgrims of the Plymouth Colony, to several of our Founding Fathers who signed the Declaration of Independence, many of us were not born here in America. So no single American, who is legally an American, has a superior claim to being American over anyone else, whether your ancestor was a signatory to the Declaration of Independence, or whether you became an American citizen, yesterday.

Those who came before us risked everything, fighting for a set of ideas and principles meant for **all** Americans; those of us here today and those of us who will arrive in this country (legally), tomorrow. They fought for themselves, their countrymen and for all the kindred spirits around the world, who come to this country in search of a better life and the freedom to pursue it, provided that those who come in search of it are willing to truly understand it and to make the same commitment to it that our Founding Fathers and those who came after them made.

This country belongs to those who believe in the ideas and ideals of 1776, to those who are willing to struggle and work hard and to lay down their lives (if called upon to do so), to preserve and defend our liberty, our freedom of speech and ideas, our freedom of religion, our belief in equality, our justice system and our government; a government charged with protecting our rights and not curtailing them. It belongs to those who embrace and defend this government Of the People, By the People and For the People. It has nothing to do with a person's national origin, race, religion, gender, sexual preference, or anything else. *It has everything to do with having the Heart and the Soul of an American.*

Turning the Tables on the Media Industrial Complex; the "We're Americans First Filter"

If we think and feel as Americans first, before we think and feel as people of Black, White, Hispanic, Asian, European, Middle-Eastern or other descent, then we can easily turn the tables on those engaging in the battle going on for our minds and our emotions.

From a purely American perspective, their formula is insulting to every real American's intelligence, regardless of race, gender, or preference. We've got a bunch of hyperactive, obnoxious news personalities, writers and pundits, with the disposition and manners of teenagers, most of whom don't appear to have the intellectual discipline to thoroughly educate themselves on the issues and the data, yet who nevertheless try to convince us that they know precisely what they're talking about and precisely what we should think.

Most of them behave like pompous jackasses, as if they are the owners of the keys to truth and only they have the wisdom and judgment to understand the burning issues of our time. Meanwhile, they speak to us lowly, middle-class common-folk, as if we're a bunch of under-educated hillbillies, who just fell off the turnip truck, who they must deign to educate.

It really doesn't matter who you're talking about. Pick a few...how about the two Bill's? Bill Maher? OMG!...Sorry, I have to use a teenage social media expression when referring to someone who I believe has so little wisdom, knowledge and intellectual firepower, yet seems to yap the loudest about what people should think or believe, while at the same time demonstrating world-class arrogance in doing so. I've dubbed him *"The Chihuahua"* (barking constantly, but with nothing of much value behind the barks). He's the absolute trifecta: (1) lack of intellectual horsepower; (2) telling people with absolute certainty what they should believe; (3) and being world-class arrogant.

How did he ever get into a position of being a commentator/pundit on news, events and social policy? Well, in today's world, he's one of the little attack-dogs from the left, specifically cast to be the foil of the little attack-dogs on the right.

He seems to me to have a higher degree of contempt for **some** American values, as viewed through the "We're Americans First Filter", than just about anyone I've seen on the popular scene. That's fine, in that this is what our Forefathers, in-part, fought for, namely his freedom to yap.

But when viewed through the "We're Americans First Filter", his methods take us down a path designed to have us become intolerant of one another; sniping at each other and polarizing us as a people, rather than inspiring a rational, goodwill discussion or debate and allowing for good-natured disagreements. He garners ratings through pursuing a strategy that is designed to marginalize those who disagree with him, while attempting to make them look foolish by stacking the panel he presents on his show, against those whom he disagrees with.

He's free to do as he and his network please, but it's important to recognize the strategy he employs for what it is, which is to push our emotional buttons, polarize us, and espouse a clear left-wing, liberal perspective, while doing everything to intellectually marginalize and declare war upon those who believe in God. He's the epitome of the **"Secular Fanatic"**.

A HARD LOOK IN THE MIRROR

How about Bill O'Reilly? Now this is hard, because as a person and personality, I happen to like Bill O'Reilly, like many Americans. I can't tell you exactly why, except that he's like that family member, Uncle Bill, who shows up at family gatherings from time-to-time, who is warm, amiable, and always says the damndest things that just make you smile in amusement, *or flinch in horror.* He's the life of the party. But to continue the task at-hand...

Uncle Bill has simmered down a bit since he came bursting out of the gates and has changed-up his strategy over time (whether that's his doing, or Roger Ailes' doing, is anyone's guess). That's fine, though I found him more interesting in his original, non-watered down version of O'Reilly. While I didn't agree with some of the things he had to say, he and his product were more genuine back then. He also did better homework and was more in command of facts and data.

Now he's more subtly manipulative and more a caricature of himself, doing what he thinks is commercially smart to maintain his appeal to the widest possible audience. To me it appears to be just another commercial strategy. But aside from his very annoying lack of basic good manners, in not letting anyone other than himself speak without interrupting and talking over them (to the point that his so-called interviews are almost unwatchable), he has turned into someone who doesn't provide us with nearly as much pertinent data and information supporting his opinions. He has even regressed to engaging in the narcissistic practice of analyzing his own body-language on his show and providing post-show self-critiques of his own performance, I hear, if one wished to subscribe to his website package, that is (I've never seen it).

The premise and design of the show is still clearly aimed at pushing our emotional buttons, polarizing us, and espousing a clear right-wing, conservative message and creating divisiveness, disguised as news, just as MSNBC does from the left. It also shapes the news and makes it conform to its agenda.

Those of you who are alert may be saying, "Hey, he just contradicted himself". Nope, not really...while I may have given the impression that the current strategy of media personalities jumping down our throats with extreme views is wrong, well, that's not what I said. I find the battle of ideas to be at least interesting, even if delivered by a hyper-active bunch of teen-agers who are all over 40, trying to hoard as much cash and fame as they can before they retire to their own, respective islands in the Caribbean. The challenge is in filtering these ideas, making sense of them, discarding the chaff and identifying the valuable ones.

These ideas, presented in the extreme by design, motivate or excite by setting Black Americans against White and/or Hispanic Americans against Caucasian and/or Asian Americans against some or all of the above, based upon perceived leanings of each group, relative to the subject matter at hand. For the Media Industrial Complex, this is little more than child's play. For you see, they underestimate us and take us for little more than children, at best, or a conglomeration of fools and dingbats, at worst.

Through the "We're Americans First Filter", though, we recognize these cheap, petty, tactics for what they are and we discard the emotion they are trying to evince and instead, we focus on the questions posed and the ideas discussed. If we look at the hot-button topic of illegal immigration, for example, it's very easy to get side-tracked and emotional. The Media Industrial Complex is intentionally making it a race issue, first and foremost (remember, two sides, for or against?).

But through the "We're Americans First Filter", we can look at it a different way, regardless of our race, gender, national origin, etc. We can ask ourselves what is best for our people and our country, as a whole, as brother and sister Americans, based upon our shared "1776" ideals, based on our shared obligation to our Founding Fathers, to each other, to our children, and to the economic and social well-being of us all. You see, we start to ask the questions that way, instead of the way the Media Industrial Complex would like to frame the question, and now it's not a race issue at all, and there is a whole universe of considerations, perspectives and therefore solutions, not just two.

We certainly know it's a worthy topic that needs discussing amongst us, the American People. We, The Board of Directors of this country, must decide how the President, Congress and Courts should deal with this, based upon our values as Americans first, not as Black, White, Male, Female, Gay, Straight, or national origin related criteria. That's right, WE need to decide and WE decide by voting into office the people who will represent our ideas and values through the "We're Americans First Filter", based upon what is most important for the good of our nation, each other, our children and the future of our country.

In a later chapter, we'll fully cover the immigration subject and more, including the state of the educational system in our country today and very specifically what to do about these issues. But I want to stay focused on the Media Industrial Complex and our need to turn towards each other, not away from each other.

Our greatest responsibility is to preserve our freedoms, our democracy, our moral foundation, our system of government and our Capitalist system, put in place by our founders, which we are owners and caretakers of and bear the highest moral responsibility to pass along intact to our (hopefully) well-educated and deserving children. We cannot do this if we are a divided people, who because of all of the vitriol spewed by the Media Industrial Complex and their $$$ inspired strategy, cannot communicate and work together effectively for the well-being of our country and **all** of our People.

So, we must listen to the issues, educate ourselves about the most important ones, consider their multiple sides and decide what's in the best interest of our country, our people and especially our children. In doing this, we must reflect upon what positions are most in-line with our basic foundational principles. If we put our narrow self-interests, our national origin, our color, our gender and our sexual orientation aside and decide as reasonable Americans with goodwill towards each other **first**, then we'll know what to do.

Turn the tables on the Media Industrial Complex! Take from it. Use THEM to get multiple perspectives and diverse information on the issues of the day. Make the time to read more than one newspaper or online media outlet, both conservative **and** liberal, and let's educate ourselves.

When the vitriol from the Media Industrial Complex gets ugly; when you hear Sean Hannity going off the deep-end, to the point of resembling a petulant child, as opposed to an educated, mature adult; when you hear Bill Maher with his non-holier than thou attitude, talking down to all who embrace Judeo-Christian-based religion, beliefs and faith, as if we're a bunch of unwashed, under-educated rabble who don't deserve to be politically represented, or to even vote in a civilized society, just remember that it is you and me and each fellow citizen who represents the values of our Founding Fathers, so long as we keep the best interests of our nation and each other at the heart of our thoughts and motivations.

CHAPTER 4

OUR ECONOMY & THE AMERICAN DREAM - THE REAL BATTLE OF OUR TIME AND A SHAMEFUL BURDEN ON OUR CHILDREN!

Bailouts, Obamacare, the Debt & Taxes

I get angry just thinking about this subject. How did we allow ourselves and our elected representatives to deviate so far from our common-sense principles upon which this country and its economic system was built?

As you may have surmised by now, I don't like mincing words and I prefer to put the cards on the table. So, let me start by inviting those who have a problem with our Capitalist system and society to kindly re-locate to France, or Germany, or any number Scandinavian countries. Because if anyone has a problem admitting that our Founding Values and our Capitalist system have worked to make this country an economic powerhouse (until recently, at least) and that Capitalism has been the economic engine upon which this great country of ours was built, then you have a problem in dealing with reality and understanding some basic, common-sense facts about America and our history.

Remember, I'm the voice from the middle. I'm the middle-class Joe, in a middle class job, who is center-to-conservative in my political leanings, an independent, and who left the Republican Party for its G. W. Bush-allowed betrayal of its own economic principles.

Note that I also think that the economic principles of some well-centered Democrat Presidents served our country very well in the past and it would behoove current Democrats not to dismiss or forget that fact, and to learn about it, if they haven't already. I believe that Presidents Eisenhower, Kennedy and even Bill Clinton delivered solid economic results for us. Ronald Reagan, of course, did a magnificent job, both understanding and freeing America's economic engine to produce great prosperity during much of his two-terms, after an initial, challenging start. But, of course, he could have done a better job down-sizing government (contrary to popular belief, government actually grew under President Reagan). I also believe he could have focused more on the environment, without sacrificing in any significant way our economic recovery.

There are some economic lessons there that bear examination and re-learning. There were also mistakes made that we need to reflect upon. But all-in-all, some principles of economic reality became pretty clear through some of these Presidents' time in office and demonstrated what can be accomplished by embracing and sticking to some basic economic principles that work.

Now, I warn you, these principles are in stark contrast to what we see happening today, in President Obama's Presidency, and they are likewise different from what we saw happening during President G.W. Bush's two terms. Observing what has transpired, I believe we are headed for disaster over the next several years, unless something changes. I'll tell you why and what I think President Obama should have done. Remember, I don't claim to be an economist, or an expert. I'm just a guy from middle-America with a fair amount of business experience, who may have some reasonable powers of observation regarding cause and effect, and hopefully, a little business common-sense, having managed multi-million dollar budgets and business units of a couple of recognizable companies, and having received my degree in accounting from college.

WHAT ECONOMIC PRINCIPLES GOT US INTO THIS MESS?

First, it started with President George W. Bush, a fellow I voted for in his first term and didn't vote for in his second. He portrayed himself as a Republican with conservative economic principles and ended up spending our money like a sailor on a Las Vegas lost weekend. The only problem is that the lost weekend lasted eight years and ended up spending us into oblivion. Certainly he had terrorism and the Iraq/Afghanistan wars to contend with, but it was his decision to initiate and hitch our collective wagon to those wars and allow government spending to run wild, while paying little more than lip-service to regulatory oversight of the financial markets, which is what has really gotten us into this mess, and I'm afraid he has to take full responsibility for that. After all, there were viable alternatives. Certainly there were strategies other than military invasion and nation-building that could have been pursued, and in my humble opinion, should have been pursued (a subject that I will discuss in a later chapter and will fully explain the viable alternatives, supported by actual cases).

But in addition to those sources of spending, he increased spending in so many other discretionary areas, with money we didn't and don't have, that it completely alienated me, along with what I'd say is a fair portion of the American people.

Second, of course, the S.E.C. failed to do its job of policing the financial industry, either not knowing, or not caring to know about the abuses going on in the financial markets; more specifically in speculation in the petroleum markets, and of supreme importance, the regulation of the banks involved in the housing markets.

Third, Mr. Barney Frank and his cohorts in congress, as alluded to earlier, were mandating that Fannie Mae and Freddie Mac loan money to people who clearly had insufficient income and assets to support their loans. Mr. Frank, evidently, thought that *EVERYONE* has a right to the American Dream, which of course they do. The glaring problem though, was that he incorrectly defined the American Dream as home ownership (which it's not, as I've explained), whether they can afford to pay for it or not.

Talk about sailors on a booze-fueled binge...this guy and his cohorts were on an all-out jag, long enough to bring the most prolific economy the world has ever known to its knees, right to the brink of economic destruction...with the full participation and cooperation of the Wall Street bankers, the U.S. Treasury and...I'm sorry to say...**ALL OF US!** [Remember the earlier photo?]

"Yes, they're back again...they just can't get enough..."
[Left to Right: The Usual Suspects...the S.E.C. under Bush, the Treasury under Bush...and...I do believe that looks like Barney Frank (former Chairman of the House Financial Services Committee, during the housing collapse)...

A HARD LOOK IN THE MIRROR

That's right, I said "ALL OF US". We're the ones who put these **economically irresponsible** incompetents in office, directly, and of course, indirectly. The problem I have is that we did it with our eyes wide open, or perhaps intentionally shut may be more accurate.

Barney Frank has been involved in as many scandals over the years as any NFL star player. Yet, his constituents continued to re-elect him, time and time-again. You know, I thought with all of the top-notch Universities and the great education system that Massachusetts is known for, that our fellow citizens there might apply at least some of what they've learned to their choices in the voting booth. But I suppose it's not all about education. Sometimes, it's simply about common-sense, which as I've learned in life, is not all that common, particularly it appears, in Massachusetts. I'd ask my brother and sister American's up there to just put on your "We're Americans First Glasses" and do the right thing for yourselves and for the rest of us, moving forward, will you? Throw any remaining irresponsible, out-of-touch yahoos who behave like Barney Frank, out of office. Fortunately, Barney did us all a favor and retired.

Also, just to be clear, please don't think my comments have anything to do with Mr. Frank being gay. They do not. An economically responsible and morally upright gay person should be as inflamed as I am over the conduct of politicians like Frank.

Speaking plainly, if Frank was straight and conducted himself the same way he has over the last 20 years, he'd have probably been in a lot more trouble, because the press would not be afraid of having the Political Correctness Grenade thrown at them, blowing up their career goals, and they'd be saying precisely the same things that I'm saying about him, only more so. This is one reason why we've got to get over and past the whole black, white, gender, gay, straight, national origin stuff, so that we can focus in a *real* way upon the behavior of irresponsible politicians, who are supposed to represent our interests, regardless of their race, gender, national origin, or sexual preference, etc.

These are the numbskulls representing us to the world, after all. We have every right to insist that they at least be responsible custodians of American values, American freedoms and the American legacy of our Founding Fathers.

I think we can all agree that the most important role of the President and the Congress is to preserve this Democratic Republic in a manner that is true to those Founding Values, that is economically and morally responsible, and that provides for the education of our people, our common defense against those that would act against us and our interests, and preserving and maintaining our physical and social infrastructure.

Let's ditch the Political Correctness Crowd and recognize that America was founded on *Political Incorrectness*, and I'm happy with it staying that way. This Political Correctness stuff drives me crazy and should drive every American crazy. It flies in the face of our natural, ingrained spirit of revolution; and a little revolution now and then is healthy for our country, after all. It reminds us of who we are and where we came from and the long journey we've taken together. Now, we can have at least reasonably good manners in voicing our opinions and still damn the political correctness. But I, for one, am politically incorrect and loving it.

Fourth, Mr. Bush, seeing what was coming, didn't take forceful enough or decisive enough action to reign-in Mr. Frank and his cronies, and at the same time, he didn't go to the whip on the SEC, in order to control the reckless investment banks that were operating with no common-sense rules, oversight or restraint, while the barbarian hordes on Wall Street (the Financial Services Companies and the Mortgage Industry), were all collecting big, fat commission checks and setting themselves up for life, regardless of what happened to the economy or the American People, as a whole.

A HARD LOOK IN THE MIRROR

No one can tell me that the people in power didn't know. Let's face it, the head of the Federal Reserve and the Treasury Secretary were, and are, hooked into Wall Street and the financial services industry at the hip. They are some of the best educated and most financially savvy people in the world, and they knew very precisely what was going on. We're talking about some of the most brilliant people in the game, after all, and they came from inside Wall Street...way inside (e.g. Goldman Sachs-it doesn't get any more prestigious or "inside" than that), and we're to believe they didn't know what was going on? Excuse me, but I'd have to take an overdose of stupid-pills to believe that, and so would every other American.

Let's just admit that, since they did come from inside Wall Street, they absolutely knew what was going on and they weren't about to blow the whistle on anyone or send anyone to jail, because it would be tantamount to blowing the whistle on themselves. *They just kept watching the drunks get drunker by-the-day and continued to open the spigot to keep the booze and the economy flowing, putting off the inevitable "morning after" that would surely come. They were just hoping the hangover would come during the next administration and not theirs, in my humble view.*

Fifth, as I stated earlier, all of us Americans, or at least most of us, were watching our friends, or people whom we knew damn well couldn't afford the mortgages on the homes they were buying, finance 110% mortgages, while in many cases not putting up a dime of their own money, and in some cases, getting money back at closing. They were completing applications with false information, because there were loans out there that required no verification of income or assets. You don't think that the highly educated Wall Street insiders running the Treasury, and a President educated at Yale, who also ran businesses, could figure out there was something wrong with this? If you don't, then you really did fall off a turnip truck, or were dissolving and mainlining the aforementioned stupid pills.

Let's face it, *everyone* had three-sheets-to-the-wind, drunk with visions of grandeur and flush with free-flowing money, and they couldn't have passed an economic breathalyzer if they wanted to. Many of us saw the handwriting on the wall and, let's be honest, many of us simply thought that, hell, one of these days, we might just benefit by joining in the soirée ourselves, taking full advantage of the system just like others whom we were witnessing. After all, people were getting record money for selling their homes and were getting into homes which, a few years earlier, they couldn't have sniffed in their wildest dreams...Then they used the money they got back at closing for down payments on expensive cars, boats, jewelry, or whatever, so that they could fulfill their own version of "The American Dream"...Hell, they were the stars in their own reality T.V. shows.

People were signing interest-only loans and all manner of financial instruments, which years before, common-sense might have kept them from seeking, or responsible banks would have kept them from obtaining (and getting in over their heads), or the S.E.C. might not have allowed to exist in the first place, had they done their job.

The problem occurred when, somewhere along the way, people and corrupt or indifferent politicians and bureaucrats forgot that *the American dream means having the freedom, liberty and security to live in a free society and to thereby compete in the American economy, in order to have the <u>means</u> to own your own home, as opposed to simply having the ability and the option to sign a document that would put you in a home, <u>whether you had the means to pay for it, or not</u>.*

That crucial distinction and unavoidable reality got lost somewhere along the way. So the inevitable day of reckoning came and a lot of people settled instead for becoming reality stars in what ended up being their own, sadly personalized version of "Queen for a Day" (substitute "King" if you want), the old television sob-series where whomever shared the greatest personal tragedies and failures with the audience, won a washing machine or dryer, or something...Only in the case of the financial crisis, instead of telling of their personal tragedies on the front-end of the TV show to win the prize, they instead won the prize first (the homes they couldn't possibly afford), then lost the prize, and then told of their personal tragedies on the back-end of the show, to their mortgage banks, as their mortgages were foreclosed upon...Sad indeed.

So, when common-sense is thrown overboard by people and politicians, who or what is supposed to rein all of "us" in?

When I say "rein all of us in"...I mean you, me, the banks, the financial industry, the SEC, the Congress, the President, <u>all of us</u>. When we're all behaving like liquored-up Romans at a "Financial Orgy", who or what stops us and returns us to our senses?

"It's Toga Party Time in Washington and on Wall Street, baby!" [Center: Isn't that Henry Paulson, former Treasury Secretary, and the gang from the SEC?] (Image courtesy of Universal)

Well, the final economic vice-cop that puts a stop to our financial intoxication and public humiliation (when all of us go financially mad), is the incredibly complex, yet paradoxically beautiful and simple system that our Founding Fathers, after 1776, ultimately set up for us, through their choice of our financial system and our system of government.

These choices, while providing for an environment of maximum financial freedom, creativity and entrepreneurship in supporting business, commerce, risk-taking and individual freedoms, are also extremely effective in reining us in and correcting the markets, when we make serious mistakes and behave in irresponsible or negligently risky behavior (or simply make very poor decisions). Indeed, when that happens, the marketplace moves quickly to self-correct the failed behavior by imposing sometimes swift and painful consequences, which can be both painful and humiliating, as it puts those of us who engaged in the failed behavior and decisions, in what amounts to the economic drunk-tank to dry out. Who is this economic vice-cop, you ask?

This economic vice-cop and final authority is "Capitalism" and the free-market system.

The Capitalist, free-market system is the logical result of our form of government, chosen by our Founding Fathers. It was specifically designed to be minimally invasive to our freedoms. It was to provide maximum freedom, along with maximum individual responsibility and, through later laws establishing corporations, provided for limited liability and certain protections, to go along with those freedoms, so that we wouldn't get too conservative and so that we would not shy away from reasonable risk-taking.

The system encouraged calculated (and hopefully intelligent) risk-taking and boldness. Meanwhile, it provided that our mistakes and our excesses would come to their own, natural, and sometimes abrupt end, *if the system is allowed to work as designed.* If it is allowed to work as designed, it causes the markets to correct themselves fairly quickly and to punish poor decision-making or irresponsibility, while minimizing the duration of the negative impact on both the economy and the individuals. It is truly the best economic invention that the world has ever seen, in my humble opinion.

So, getting back to continue my original thought, when all of us go slightly mad, including WE THE PEOPLE, and including the financial institutions, the President, the Congress, etc., it is our Capitalist system that, unfailingly, takes us out to the woodshed and puts the paddle to our collective behinds, forcing us all to face reality and to come back to earth and regain our sanity...***BUT THIS ONLY HAPPENS IF IT IS ALLOWED TO OPERATE AS IT WAS DESIGNED!***

Capitalism, having just taken us to the Economic Woodshed...
[left to right: Capitalism, Us (holding our behind...)]

While we may get paddled, it's over pretty quickly (relatively speaking) and we're usually the better for it, having learned a valuable lesson that we can apply, moving forward. Then we're free to continue on our way. Our Capitalist system is a fail-safe system. A person, a business, a corporation, a government, a people, or a President makes a bad economic decision and the Capitalist free-market system swiftly takes them (and us) out to the woodshed and puts the parties responsible over its knee.

Now, you and I may initially say that WE THE PEOPLE were not responsible for the financial crisis and then ask the next logical question as to why WE THE PEOPLE, rather than just the politicians representing us and those in the government regulatory agencies (charged with protecting us), as well as the Wall Streeter's who took full advantage of us, got taken out to the woodshed with them?

Well, the consistent and correct answer of course, is that **we are *all* fully responsible for the acts of our politicians and government entities, as well as our own acts.** It's why it's so important that we take the time, the ownership and the full responsibility to get to know who we're electing, to assure they are financially/fiscally responsible people and that they represent solid American values and understand what the Founding Fathers tried so very hard to teach us about this nation they built for us. *WE THE PEOPLE <u>own</u> the government, its victories and its mistakes, and we'd better understand and accept that reality, and we'd better take that responsibility very seriously and very personally, because in the end, WE THE PEOPLE bear the ultimate consequences, good or bad, like them or not.*

In many cases, if any of us (or our leaders) makes terribly poor business or personal financial decisions, our Capitalist system swiftly punishes us for those poor decisions and corrects the market rather quickly, while teaching us a lesson not to do it again. It does this by imposing financial hardship, through a poor economy and unemployment in the case of a government's poor decisions, or through loss of financial principal placed in poor investments, or even bankruptcy, in the case of poor individual or business decision-making.

In cases where laws are broken, jail time may result; unless of course you are a modern-day politician, in which case you are forgiven and sometimes even named to a high, cabinet level position, just like past Treasury Secretary, Timothy Geithner. But for us normal folk, it can include all of the above and, generally speaking, it is also *supposed* to be the great equalizer amongst us. It doesn't matter whether you are Senator Grift-a-lot, or Mr. or Ms. John Q. Public, or if you are Bear-Sterns, AIG, General Motors, or...Oops...something's just not adding up here...

See where I'm going? It's not supposed to matter who you are, or which company you are, when it comes to the long-arm of Capitalism. If you make bad personal financial decisions, or bad business financial decisions, you are supposed to pay the price in our Capitalist, free-market system. It's the great equalizer and it teaches those who make irresponsible or very poor financial decisions, a stern and sometimes severe lesson. It allows those involved and those outside the situation to watch, learn, and not repeat the mistakes, or take advantage, because they know they will get similarly punished by loss of investment, bankruptcy, business failure, or worse. But at least they will learn from their mistakes and make better decisions moving forward.

Now, in our tumultuous Bush/Obama financial crises, certainly the great and storied financial institution, Bear-Sterns, paid the price. They went belly-up. But they were thereafter acquired by J.P. Morgan, and a new, blended entity was born. Those who made the poor, irresponsible business decisions were punished. Hard lessons were taught and hopefully learned. Stockholders paid the appropriate price, as did the board of directors, as our Capitalist, free-market system (our economic vice-cop) did its job, imposed its justice, punished the offenders, and did its part to correct the market in that particular case. That's how it's supposed to work.

The crisis there did not last overly long and some folks were properly, financially set-back for making poor decisions. But it worked out and people learned a very valuable lesson (in the limited Bear-Sterns example), and no one had to be bailed-out by the American taxpayers.

Now, that didn't happen with AIG or GM. Yet it should have. The administration said these companies were "too large to fail". Now, if you'll excuse me for saying so, and even if you won't, **that's a lot of CRAP!** If we stick to our Capitalist, free-market system and let the markets dole out reward and punishment, as they were designed to do, we'd see the same type of economic fluctuations that the U.S. has seen throughout its history; sometimes severe, but mostly short-lived, lasting only a few years.

The Capitalist, free-market system is the most reliable, resilient, and healthy economic system the world has ever seen, and we have always been the better for it. *Further, when Capitalism and the free market is allowed to operate as it should, and imposes consequences and correction on those who should receive it and we then don't have to entertain government bailouts of hundreds of billions of dollars at the taxpayers expense.*

But alas, instead, Presidents Bush and Obama supported significant government intervention into the free-market, by way of the massive bailouts funded by us, the taxpayers, which perverted the system by sparing those responsible (banks and others) from the consequences and correction that the free market system would normally impose, thereby creating an unbearable and unimaginable burden on our children (and on our children's children), while setting this nation up for longer-term economic failure and inflation, on a grand scale in the future, in my humble opinion.

A HARD LOOK IN THE MIRROR

These government behaviors that I have outlined, from lack of regulation and oversight, to Barney Frank and Company, to the George Bush/
Secretary Paulson and Barack Obama bailouts, to creating an unimaginable debt-burden on our children, are what got us into this mess, in
my view. As a guy from middle-class America, I've watched in disgust as
these events have unfolded.

**SO, WHAT HAVE OTHER PRESIDENTS DONE IN THE MIDST
OF FINANCIAL PROBLEMS AND CRISES OF THE PAST AND
WHY DIDN'T BUSH, OBAMA AND CONGRESS TAKE SIMILAR,
PROVEN MEASURES?**

I started this chapter by talking about some great Presidents of my time,
mentioning Presidents Eisenhower, Kennedy and Reagan, in particular.
Although I was only a new-born during Eisenhower's administration, all
I have read about him has me include him in this group.

I can tell you that they believed in the basic principles of our system and
they both understood and believed in freeing the economic engine that
drives our country. That engine is *us*, the American people and our
Capitalist free-market system. They believed in letting us keep most of
the money that we earned and in allowing us to use that money freely,
to drive the economy.

Both Kennedy and Reagan used tax-cuts to stimulate economic growth.
They both understood that the money was ours to begin with, not the
government's money to confiscate and dole back out to us as they see
fit, in any manner they see fit. In each case, this philosophy and practice worked. WE THE PEOPLE worked, spent and saved our way out of
economic doldrums. We kept more of what we made and we spent it on
our families, on buying goods and services and on giving to charity in
huge numbers. *We put ourselves back to work* by working hard and working

smart and by simply being able to generate, keep and spend more of our own money.

It's a pretty simple set of principles and is in-line with my uncomfortable habit of putting the cards on the table. Despite what the politicians and economic conjurers may try to tell us about its complexity, *it's no bloody mystery!* The politicians all know it, or should know it. They would know it if they had any business background, training or experience, which in my opinion should be a prerequisite for serving in Congress. But let's also admit that they didn't get to Washington by being stupid. They certainly didn't get to Washington having just fallen off the turnip truck. After all, Kennedy knew it, Reagan knew it and each time it has been tried, it has worked. What am I talking about? Well, every time taxes are cut and WE THE PEOPLE get to keep more of WHAT WE THE PEOPLE earn (more of what is ours to begin with), the economy benefits and more jobs are created and the stock market takes off.

So, what's the problem and how come no one tried this route during this economic crisis, along with allowing our Capitalist free-market system to work as designed and punish the aforementioned Wall-Streeters, corporate giants, and irresponsible citizens, along with some other prudent measures when the current financial crisis hit, rather than going with a combined trillion-dollar bailout?

Other than Obama acquiescing to extend the Bush tax-cuts, and only then under great duress, no one has been talking about that which I believe is absolutely necessary. Let's face it, the current administration and congress, which does not seem to believe very strongly in the Capitalist free market system and its aforementioned principles (as evidenced by their actions and not by their words and rhetoric), wanted to go another route, *so that they could get their opportunistic hands on our money (not their money) and control the hell out of it.*

Simple? YES! The truth usually is. Oh, they knew better alright, but they just didn't (and don't) particularly care. They saw the money, they wanted the money, and they felt entitled to grab the money (as they always do), because they hold the political reins of power today to do so and operate under the arrogant and deluded position that it is *their money*. Simple!

To paraphrase Julius Caesar... "We Came, We Saw, We Looted!"

They saw, alright. They saw the opportunity to loot and pillage the Treasury and get their hands on our money and they took the opportunity and ran with it!

...and guess what...they got it all and they doled it out as they saw fit, on programs and entities and healthcare and spending bills and corporate bailouts and takeovers of union-friendly companies (GM), and ACORN-like beneficiaries...They'll spend it on whatever they want to spend it on...! Why? Because they can! Because they see it as **their money, not ours**, and once they get their hands on our money, they're about as arrogant a bunch as you'll find. Think about Barney Frank and Nancy Pelosi and the arrogance you saw in their defiance of the concerns expressed by the American people.

Hell, Pelosi, while generally exuding the aura of a Queen-Dingbat, didn't even want the contents of the Healthcare Reform Act to be known or digested by anyone, until after it was voted upon by Congress. She especially didn't want the American People to know what was in it. We must remember her now infamous and head-scratching words:

*"But we have to pass the bill so that you can find out what
is in it, **away from the fog of the controversy."***

[Nancy Pelosi speaking in Dingbat, on the Healthcare Reform Act]

You know, what's really sad is that we, the American people, actually let her get away with that remark. Dingbat? You betcha! Smarmy and arrogant Dingbat? Absolutely! This of course begs the question, are our brother and sister Americans who elected her in California, also Dingbats, or is the Queen-Dingbat Pelosi just a very skilled politician who put one over on them? Well, I have no doubt that she's a skillful politician. But I've concluded that she's definitely a Queen-Dingbat and her constituents in California are going to have to prove to us in the future that they are not from the same brood.

A HARD LOOK IN THE MIRROR

Keeping the Faith with America: "Moving Forward...We the People of California, shall Vote No Dingbats into Congress..."
["All in the Family"- base image courtesy of Sony Pictures Television]

Make no mistake about it, if you were to follow the money-trail all the way through to its destination, through the cracks and crevices to where it ends-up, my bet is that you'll find distasteful political and personal business interests there, benefitting from it. This is just one man's view.

WHAT SHOULD PRESIDENT OBAMA AND CONGRESS HAVE DONE TO DEAL WITH THE FINANCIAL CRISIS?

In my own humble, middle-class-American point of view, they should have immediately:

1. Cut income taxes to individuals and businesses to put more money immediately into people's individual paychecks. This would have immediately stimulated consumer and business spending

in the economy. This in-turn, would have immediately inject-ed our own, taxpayer-generated and business-generated stimu-lus money into the economy, producing demand for products, homes, goods and services, and would have given confidence to people, businesses, and overseas partners, *without getting us all into a mountain of debt, through the government spending our money, which by the way, we don't have to spend.*

2. The government should have come out with a statement saying that these tax-cuts were going to be in place for at least the next four to five years and that they would look to extend them lon-ger, if necessary, so that the businesses and people could plan accordingly and spend accordingly, not having to worry that this was going to be reversed in short-order, so that the stimulus to the economy could be sustained and business investment in ex-pansion, capital goods and equipment could also be sustained.

3. Rather than bailing them out with our taxpayer funded, com-bined trillion-dollar bailouts, the government should have allowed the financial institutions that made poor business deci-sions in the mortgage industry and elsewhere, to go into bank-ruptcy, stepping in to guarantee only people's deposits, not the continued survival of the financial institutions or bad invest-ments. Certainly other financial institutions and investors, who did not make such bad decisions, would have come in and likely purchased the troubled ones, similar to J.P. Morgan taking over Bear-Sterns at a bargain price. And if they didn't get purchased, then let them close.

4. They also should have let the individuals who borrowed the mon-ey for mortgages they couldn't afford, take the full consequences of living beyond their means and making the poor decisions they

did, and likewise let the investors who purchased the mortgage tranches in the financial markets take the full consequences of their poor investment decisions.

This would have created a free-market correction and re-structuring, which may have been steeper in magnitude, but shorter in duration than what we have been experiencing and what we are experiencing now (which I think will have much more serious consequences in the future). It would have dealt the just consequences of their actions to those who deserved them, rather than propping up the banks, financial institutions, their directors and management, and their financial advisors, with hundreds of billions of taxpayer dollars, putting the next three or four generations of young and old Americans into hock up to their eyeballs, with dire consequences which, as yet, cannot even be imagined by the average American.

Make no mistake about it, this is a razor's edge we now walk, which requires only a very slight economic downturn, a rise in interest rates, or a natural or political disaster in one of the world's hotspots, or an unfavorable decision by one of our large creditors, to push us into a depression, the likes of which has not been seen since the 20's, and which may be accompanied by rampant inflation through the devaluation of our currency, in my humble, middle-class, middle-America opinion.

5. They should have cleaned house at the S.E.C. (pursued legal prosecutions, if possible) and likewise censured or forced Mr. Barney Frank to resign at the time. You see, the S.E.C. is one of the chief culprits in all of this. They were asleep, or drunk behind the wheel, as the high-powered economy went careening out of control, with Mr. Frank, intoxicated with financial power,

applying more and more pressure to the gas pedal by demanding that our financial institutions, led by Fannie Mae and Freddie Mac, provide more and more money to support mortgages for people who could not possibly afford them, under the guise of promoting **"The American Dream for all Americans"**, while leaving out of course, the unspoken second-half of that statement**... "Whether they can afford it or not..."**. As mentioned previously, owning a home is not what the "American Dream" is. This will be discussed further, a bit later.

Amazingly, outside of a brief period of finger-pointing and some negative press, nothing whatsoever has happened to these culprits. It's the most amazing thing of all to me. It suggests that these have been the errand-boys to a much more powerful contingent of banking special interests, who had most, if not all of congress in their pockets, exerting significant influence over those politicians and institutions whose job it is to protect America's economic system, its investors, and us, its citizens.

I believe that there is a bigger story here that still needs to be told. That's the only reason I can come up with as to why there was absolutely no punishment doled out to almost anyone...They were all dirty, and our elected officials and regulators weren't about to implicate each other when it all hit the fan. Either that or they were all grossly incompetent.

How could so many college-educated people, many with advanced degrees and backgrounds in finance and law, be so consistently incompetent on such a massive scale? If you believe they could not, then the other most likely answer is that they were in bed together with the special interests in the banking industry. If that's so, then it's quite logical that, even today, they all have remained protected and continue to protect each other. Either way, it simply says one thing to me...**CLEAN HOUSE AND IMPLEMENT TERM LIMITS!**

6. With regard to General Motors and companies like them (A.I.G.), the government should have let GM find its own way back. They should have simply stayed out of the mix. GM ultimately declared bankruptcy, as it should have anyway. So the government intervention and bailout money did not prevent the inevitable. The company needed to be rebuilt and restructured from the ground-up, and there was no reason that this could not happen without the government coming in to prop-up the company with billions of dollars of taxpayer money, in the form of federal loans.

The dirty little secret that didn't get near enough publicity, was that the U.S. Government (that is us, the taxpayers), in selling the last of the GM bailout stock we held in 2013, lost $11 billion dollars on the investment. So, who still thinks that was a good idea? Not me, a U.S. taxpayer. GM could have found its own way out through the bankruptcy it filed, and/or been acquired by another manufacturer.

Now, even if GM ends up stabilizing itself long-term, **IT'S STILL NOT OK**. It's just not the way our Capitalist system is supposed to work and it's a risk that should not have been taken with **my money** and with **your money** and with **our money**! We wasted $11 billion dollars that we don't have, unnecessarily.

Now, do you think that if you, John Q. Public, had a business in trouble, that President Obama and his team would swoop in to rescue you in a similar manner to G.M. and A.I.G.? Of course not.

You may say the comparison is silly...apples and oranges, and that a lot more was at stake. But you see, I don't think so. I have abiding faith in our Capitalist, free-market system and I believe that it works equally well for large and small companies, alike.

7. I did mention tax cuts, above, but I must add to this that no economy, not even the U.S. economy, can flourish when the government, in one form or another, is confiscating more than 50% of every dollar the middle-class makes, and supports corporate tax rates on business that are too high and no longer competitive in the world market (why do you think businesses are going overseas?). I don't know about you my friends, but just a few simple calculations tells me we're not even keeping half of what we make. Want to challenge me on that? Ok, let's see:

<u>An Admittedly Rough Calculation</u>:

A. 33% Federal Income Tax Rate for a Middle Class Family
B. 8% Average State Income Tax Rate (they range from under 6% to over 12%).
C. 6% Sales Tax in most states (+/-)
D. 3% Average Property Tax in my state (based upon Median Florida property taxes)
E. 5% Social Security and Medicaid taxes

Total of the above: 55% in taxes on dollars that you make and spend.

Now, having an accounting background, I know that the above does not mean that you are taxed at a 55% rate on your total income, but when you add up what you get taxed on what you make and on what you spend (and in the case of property taxes, on what you own), I'm going to tell you that it's still nuts. Note that I did not include taxes on what you earn on investment income.

Published reports indicated that a formal figure back in 2005 was 54%. Therefore, I am certain that my rough calculation today may even be low. How can a nation like ours, founded on the rights of the individual, condone taking more than 50% of what each of us in the middle-class makes, so that the government, in it's infinite wisdom and capacity to buy $2,000.00 hammers and pay $1,000,000.00 to buy and ship a bag of screws (cited on 60 Minutes), can be handed our money to spend as it see's fit?

What we need to understand and accept is that a radical re-evaluation of government taxing and spending is needed, starting first and foremost with a re-evaluation of the people who are spending it. We need to take back our rights and take back our money and elect people who will not simply expect us to accept such things, as if we are a bunch of children and they are our parents. We must demonstrate that we are not a country of simpletons, who will sit still for any fleecing the government wants to give us, as long as we have our Cable TV, our NFL Football and our all-important remote controls to pacify us and numb our minds.

WE THE PEOPLE *need to put Washington on a budget* and tell **them** what they will be ALLOWED to spend of our money and how much we will VOLUNTARILY PROVIDE to them for our infrastructure, our common defense, our social programs and our environment, etc., etc. I'm sure Nancy Pelosi would like to have a commoner like me locked-up for suggesting such a thing. The audacity of me to even think such a thing!

Now, I also happen to be a flat-tax proponent, or a national sales tax proponent. I think I can speak with the majority of Americans who would love nothing more than doing away with the IRS in its' current form and implement a straight flat-tax, or a national sales tax, and flush the rest of it away. Taxes on business would be handled, separately. I will discuss this compelling solution in more depth, later.

8. AND FINALLY...If we really wanted to fix this thing long-term, the President and Congress should have gone forward in the same breath, with a balanced budget amendment, which would assure fiscal sanity and responsibility. This would have told the world that, at least if we're not on a gold-standard any longer, the balanced-budget amendment would go a long way toward guaranteeing that America will be financially stable and responsible, and for that reason, amongst many others, our financial system and our currency are sound and will remain sound in the future. But of course, who in politics has the guts to do that? Going back and putting on our "We're Americans First Glasses", our Founding Fathers would have had the guts to do these things, and we need to elect people more like them and less people like Barney Frank, Nancy Pelosi, Harry Reid and Lindsey Graham.

And as Forrest Gump might say... "That's all I have to say about that..."

CHAPTER 5

SENSIBLE POLITICAL REFORM VS. THE SEAN PENN OCEAN THRILL-RIDE

As I've stated, we have to turn towards each other first, in order to solve the myriad of complex problems we have today. But that does not address the issue of where we look for political leadership, which is the second most important answer after turning toward each other to accept our shared responsibility in having elected many of the bums and reprobates we have in office today. You see, to solve our problems, we must correct our mistakes by electing those who will replace them and who will implement effective solutions, tomorrow.

As I've mentioned, I'm a disillusioned former Republican, who feels that both parties and the people in them, have abandoned the successful, proven economic principles upon which this country was successfully built, and under which it has flourished over the long-term. This is despite the relatively brief periods of economic challenge, which all economies experience over time. The periods of economic challenge which we as a country have experienced, have been extraordinarily brief, when compared to the rest of the world's economies (for the most part). Economically, I'm still a Reagan conservative, who believes that Reagan went too far with deregulation. I felt he went too far then, and I feel that way today. Today, of course, under the Obama Administration, we have gone too far in the opposite direction and we are going a lot farther still, before this Administration ends its term.

As I mentioned, it was President G.W. Bush who caused me to change my political affiliation to Independent, and I think I'll keep it that way. The Republicans have become as freewheeling in their spending as the Democrats and both are taking us to an appointment with disaster, if we let it continue.

What many in the Democrat party don't realize, is that the ill-conceived, improperly supervised and negligently administrated social programs being implemented and administered today, are going to financially destroy the viability and existence of those very same and other programs tomorrow. It just doesn't have to be this way. If people with any sort of proper business experience and acumen were placed in charge of designing, implementing, executing and administering intelligent, targeted social programs and in putting together a proper budget, many of the social ills we are trying to fix, would be fixable. But I digress.

Regarding the whole Obamacare bill and debate, again, I believe that the current program is going to take us down a road to ruin, with rationed medical care and the government in the driver seat, trying to efficiently and effectively administer the largest single social program in history, while ultimately deciding for us if we will get the medical care we may desire and need in our old age (or in our particular situation), or if that care will be denied, whether through policy, or the logical reality of rationed care, which in my opinion will be the inevitable result.

Now I'm sorry, but I have a problem with that. Further, the government administering any program is usually always fraught with fraud and inefficiency. Just look at Social Security, as well as Medicare and Medicaid today. For the most part, these programs are broke. They continue to operate the way some households do today. They keep financing these programs with cash-flow not assets, with money that's not there, essentially charging up the debt on the American People's Credit Card, while fraud runs rampant through these programs. Now, ask me why I don't have confidence in the government running a national healthcare program! The healthcare reform underway represents an even bigger opportunity for fraud and waste and endless debt.

To give you even more of a feel for what I'm talking about, have you taken a drive down to your local Post Office, Passport Agency, or your Division of Motor Vehicles lately? How do you like the lines, the lack of efficient, responsive customer service, and the downright nasty and apathetic government employees you get to interact with, at least half-the-time? Have you ever had to try to reach someone in authority in a U.S. Government-run office, who could make a decision or sort out a problem quickly and efficiently? Ok, enough said about putting our government in charge of our money, healthcare, and retirement. Are you getting nervous, yet?

IF YOU THINK YOU'RE GOOD WITH IT, THEN LET'S HAVE SOME FUN AND TAKE IT FURTHER, AND LET'S TAKE THE "SEAN PENN CHALLENGE", TOGETHER...

So, if you really are comfortable with all of that, then be honest with yourself. What you really need to do to get a real taste and understanding of where this road can go, is to move to the old version of the Soviet Union, where the government provided for all of your needs and was your mommy, your daddy, and your friendly neighborhood Commissar. Where is that you ask? Well first, just buy a plane ticket, then leave your money behind, take a flight down to the Dominican Republic, and then hop a connecting flight into Cuba, and stay there for a couple of years. Either it will be exactly what you're looking for, while you're being thoroughly and practically educated about Communism/Socialism, or it will cure you of any delusions you may be suffering from about government-run programs and the wonders of a Communist/Socialist system, in general.

Don't pull a "Sean Penn" though, and just go down there for a quick visit, espousing the virtues of Cuba and its Communist/Socialist model, and then quickly return to your manse in Beverly Hills. That might give the impression that you are disingenuous (God forbid), and may suggest to people that you were just going down there, engaging in your own version of slumming for publicity purposes, and to endear yourself to a certain segment of the political population in this country. But of course, Mr. Penn, unlike regular Cuban "citizens", and with his political connections, he'd be one of the few "special citizens" in Cuba who could actually travel to the U.S., at his own discretion. His publicity value would make that a no-brainer for whichever Castro, or Castro-surrogate happens to be in-charge.

How nice for you, eh Sean? At last check, the "citizens" of Cuba don't have that freedom. They also don't have the freedom to <u>legitimately</u> elect a new government, if they are unhappy with the present one, nor do they have the freedom to permanently leave Cuba, if they decide they don't like the current government in power...unless of course they take to a raft and brave the dangers of crossing the open ocean to try and gain their freedom that way, with their chances of success ranging somewhere in the neighborhood of winning the Power Ball lottery.

Make any political noise inside of Cuba, or try to organize a peaceful campaign against the government in power, and you tend to either disappear, or die of lead-poisoning, usually by having a hunk of lead purposefully lodged in the base of your skull by a motivated and enthusiastic supporter of the current dictatorship...er...I mean government. Sorry for the slip-up in word usage there, Mr. Penn. God-forbid I use the politically incorrect term, dictatorship (no matter that it is correct). The citizens of the old Soviet Union, under Communist/Socialist rule, had it similarly.

Now Mr. Penn, why again do you feel the system there is so grand? Oh yes, they have nationalized healthcare for all, consisting of a few legitimate doctors (who dedicate much of their time to the ruling class and their minions in power), along with many other so-called Doctors, who are more closely the equivalent of glorified paramedics. They also have food rationing because, rather than a free-enterprise economic system, they have a system more closely resembling the old Soviet-style system, which depends upon the largess of the government and the relative amount of political pull one may have for himself and his family. No political pull and you'll have no need for any South Beach Diets or Jenny Craig there, Compadre. You'll get small rations of some bread and some rice and you'll remain very trim and svelte...not to worry! You see, I work with many American friends here in South Florida, either born in Cuba, or of Cuban decent, who have visited their families there, so I know of whence I speak.

If you were honest of course, Mr. Penn (and I'll extend this to Mr. Michael Moore, as well), you'd be prepared to put your money where your mouth is and move there and live under the system you think is so wonderful for EVERYONE. Of course that would include donating your money to their government and allowing *them* to decide how much money you'd receive each month, and what you'd do for a living, and must include assuming the lifestyle of a "real Cuban citizen", not a visiting dilettante.

Now, after spending some **real time there**, should you subsequently change your mind and decide it's just not for you and wish to return to the U.S., then you'd have to do so using the aforementioned leaky raft, of course. Why you ask? Well, because Mr. Castro and his minions would not wish for you to leave, after having changed yr mind about what a swell government he's got there. What's that you say? You thought freedom and freedom of speech exists there? Nope. It's a simple mistake though. You're thinking of the country 90 miles to the North...you know, the one you left, where you enjoyed freedom and prosperity.

Now, *if* you were fortunate enough to wash-up alive on a friendly shore, as opposed to becoming a high protein fish snack, or getting lodged in the gullet of a happy-to-see-you shark (admittedly, a big "if"), you would then perhaps admit that, in retrospect, it's not really such an awesome system to live under and it's not really all that it's cracked up to be and maybe, just maybe, it's not truly your cup of tea...What say you Mr. Sean Penn...hmmm?

A HARD LOOK IN THE MIRROR

[Sean Penn's California Home - Before Moving to Cuba]

[Cuban dwelling, similar to what Mr. Sean Penn might expect after moving to Cuba...as a regular citizen of course...Now we're talking!!]

And should Mr. Penn decide his digs in Cuba aren't quite up to his standards, he would of course, as a regular Cuban citizen, have the option to escape...er...I mean to return home to the good ole U.S. of A...

Pictured: Sean escaping...er...returning home to the good ole U.S. of A, courtesy of Divine Providence (along with a little help from our good ole U.S. Coast Guard)...

Now, all of this said, I do believe that there are reasonable compromises available to radical healthcare reform and the government taking over traditionally private sector functions. I firmly believe that we do need healthcare reform for those requiring a safety net, such as the truly poor, the elderly who cannot afford proper care, and those who are temporarily out of work (between jobs), as well as the permanently disabled who are not covered (etc.). But doing what the Obama Administration and Congress did, is like trying to take care of a roach problem in your house by setting off a hydrogen bomb; you get a lot of collateral damage and everyone's going to be hit and it's going to do more harm than good to the economy, the health care delivery system, and the people it's ultimately designed to help, which apparently is all of us, whether we like it or not.

Now, I don't know about you, but when it comes to healthcare, I am doing just fine right now. I like my present coverage and I don't need or want it from the government, at this time in my life, when I'm gainfully employed. Now, years ago of course, when I was out of a job and trying to find a new one, I certainly could have used some healthcare help for my family and me. Get the picture? I believe that many Brother and Sister Americans feel the same way I do. *Why go to the nuclear option, when a sensible, targeted approach will do?*

FIX WHAT NEEDS FIXING AND DON'T SCREW AROUND WITH THE REST OF IT, FOR GOODNESS SAKE!

How many other people feel just this way? I'm guessing, but I'd say the majority of Americans. Instead, the politicians decided to make a money-grab...the biggest in American history...to control as much of our money and the economy as possible. But I digress and find I am repeating myself. What we have, which appears to be a pattern with the current administration, is just an example of the politicians ignoring the true will of the People, **again**; a standard these days.

1. So, what do we do about the political problem of getting rid of the bums who don't really concern themselves with listening to us; the bums who see us as little more than peons? Peons, by the way, who happen to be their bosses and the people they are supposed to represent.

2. How do we assure that we keep the good ones (few that there are)?

3. How do we fix the system, which may have allowed us to initially put good people into office, but which has since allowed those representatives (who have successfully fought to stay in office for so long), to have their values compromised and degraded so completely, that they are presently more like rotting fruit on the vine? Let's face it, the system as it exists today, even for the good ones, well, it's got to be like sending Gandhi to live in the Playboy Mansion with Hugh and his Playmates. Initially he might be fine. He might even convert a few bunnies to his philosophies and way of thinking. But over time, even Gandhi would be tempted and would likely join in the orgy. Further, consider that most of the politicians are probably a lot more like Heffner to begin with, than Gandhi. Until we admit to ourselves that this is the true nature of Washington, we won't come to terms with the only logical solution to help resolve the problem...and I don't really think that the American people, as a whole, need much convincing about this reality...

So what then are our choices? Republican, Democrat, Independent, Tea Party? Since the reality is that we are not going to be able to dismantle the Democrat and Republican parties, and since I don't think that's a good idea to begin with, nor a solution, and since we know that, even if we could do such a radical thing, that whatever sprung up to replace them would be subject to the same endemic root-rot we have today, then we need to more carefully work on a solution to change the culture and eliminate the rotted portions of the root. But how can you change the culture of something that appears to be rotten to the core (read Republican and Democrat parties)? Well, since we've touched on healthcare a bit, let's stick with that imagery. If there's a cancer involved, you excise the infected tissue. Or, if you want to talk Mother Nature, if a tree is infected with a disease, you cut off or you cut out the portions that are infected, or alternatively, you take even the smallest portion of uninfected root and replant it. Yes or no?

You simply can't allow people to be corrupted by the political cesspool-type environment of Washington. You can't send Gandhi to the Playboy Manse and expect him not to become corrupt, over time. You've first got to clear out the corrupt Manse. Only after you eject Hugh and the Playmates and clear out the den of corruption, can you then turn the Playboy Mansion into a representative Capitol Hill that truly has a chance to represent the will of the people.

So, first and foremost, as soon as we have the opportunity, we as voters must IMMEDIATELY clear out the incumbents and only vote those people into office who will commit to the following, immediately upon entering office:

1. **Demand Term-Limits**. We must clear out the rotten, corrupt individuals, not get rid of the parties. The parties are not necessarily the problem. They are just the vehicle. The motor is the system itself and many of the people become corrupt over time, if they don't arrive there that way already. If they do arrive there that way, term limits will limit the damage they can do. No candidate for any elected political office should be allowed to hold that office for more than two (2) terms.

2. **Outlaw P.A.C. Contributions**: Demand that political contributions from PAC's (Political Action Committees) to candidates or parties, be outlawed in their entirety and prohibit them from financially supporting, directly or indirectly, any activities related to a politician's campaign or election, and require stringent

registration and disclosure requirements for PAC's, so that we know who is funding them and precisely where the money is coming from. The politicians should be beholden only to the American people, the citizens.

3. **Outlaw Lobbyist Contributions**: Demand that direct and indirect contributions from Lobbyists to candidates or political parties be outlawed and require stringent registration and disclosure requirements, similar to PAC's. Again, the politicians should be beholden only to the American People.

4. **Outlaw Corporate Contributions**: Demand that companies be prohibited from contributing to political campaigns, or to political parties, directly or indirectly. You want a government of the people, by the people and for the people, then get rid of the financial influence of the special interests, including the corporations, the lobbyists, and the PAC's.

5. **Implement Strict Campaign Financing Regulations**: Essentially, mandate that contributions to political campaigns can only come from individual taxpayers and limit those to a reasonable, maximum level.

6. **If we want the Best and Brightest, then Pay them like they are**: I'd imagine a fair amount of people may not want to hear this, but raise the salaries of those serving in the U.S. Congress, so that we attract some of the best and brightest, so that the effect of term limits does not make the job unattractive or impractical for those who wish to serve.

7. **No Freebies**: Prohibit those holding political offices from accepting trips, or participating in activities financed by private

individuals, organizations, or by corporations. The history of government "junkets" and "research trips", funded by private interests, more often to vacation-like and exotic destinations, is just another way for private individuals, organizations, or corporations to curry unsavory favor with politicians and is just another way to tempt those in office to become beholden to these organizations and their agendas and to set them on the course towards political corruption.

I WISH...

I wish it were possible to mandate that every politician have the experience of running a business, having to meet or exceed budget expectations, and having to make payroll. I personally believe we'd be better off having people in office with these skill-sets, who understand business principles, fiscal responsibility and economic principles, as they apply to businesses in the real world and the impact their decisions have on real people and their families, in real jobs, and the critical role it plays in our country's success.

This would also help them to understand just how important the decisions they make are, in impacting every man and woman on the street (you and me, in other words). They would ideally make the tough decisions, not for short-term popularity, political gain, or expediency, but for strategic, long-term success, which would position us competitively in the Global Chess Game of business and economics; that is, as long as we elect the right people.

As it is today, the business of our country is being run by a gaggle of corrupt lawyers in Washington (for the most part) and elsewhere, who left law school, practiced law (maybe) for a couple of years, or not at all, where all they had to do was generate billable hours, but never manage the strategic direction of a company, the revenues, expenses, the payroll or budgets. They got into politics, where all they had to do was demonstrate their literacy, basic intelligence, hand-shaking abilities and their golf-game, and demonstrate how they could maneuver, generate campaign funds, and buy and sell political favors, which would keep the special interests happy and keep them in office. They learned how to navigate and manipulate the system and the voters, like a skilled, sleazy personal-injury attorney who chases-down ambulances for a living and creates a lawsuit factory for a practice; the kind that has driven up insurance rates and tied up our legal system for years.

They become experts in practicing the politics of *"pull"*, buying and selling political favors, regardless of the impact on WE THE PEOPLE. And for most, in my humble opinion, it has become an embarrassing, destructive game that, among other things, is ultimately costing this nation its economic future.

From a human perspective, it's costing us the lives of our sons and daughters, fighting wars we have no business fighting and trying to nation-build, which has seldom been successful. It is costing us our credibility on the World Stage. It is costing us our educational system, which was once the pride of our country and an example to the world. Our educational system now turns out kids with test scores ranking last amongst the industrialized economies of the world, with some high school students of some means, unable to accurately articulate the participants in the Revolutionary War or the Civil War (believe it or not...I saw it with my own eyes on a television news program).

It is costing us our treasure, as well as our leadership position in manufacturing and production in the world, and it is costing us our honor, as a people. We are not upholding the values of our Founding Fathers today, with the representation we have in office in both houses of Congress.

A HARD LOOK IN THE MIRROR

This is why I suggest the above steps, as difficult to implement as they may sound. I see it as the only way to have a chance to get and keep much of the corruption out. We will never get it all out. But if we can get most of it out, that will be a good start.

I don't really have a lot more to suggest in fixing the political system. I simply figure that by limiting terms, limiting contributions, and by forcing candidates to generate their support from the grass-roots level and through volunteerism, we, my American brothers and sisters of every race, gender, origin and preference, stand to be the ones who will benefit the most, which is as it should be.

Some may argue that this may restrict the political messages getting out and may keep good people from getting the attention they should on the national stage. Well, the only thing I say to that is that at least it will be a more level playing field for everyone and the candidates who can generate the most grass-roots support, contributions, and volunteers, will get the most attention. I'm sorry, but I don't find anything fundamentally wrong with that and I don't think most average Americans like me will, either.

CHAPTER 6

ABOLISH OUR TAX SYSTEM, RE-DIRECT & RE-TARGET THE I.R.S.!

Earlier, I made reference to my preference for a straight flat-tax for businesses and a national sales tax for individuals. This would logically result in the end of the vast complexity of the U.S. Tax Code, and the filing of income taxes as they exist today. It would also result in abolishing much of the current activities of the I.R.S. as it exists today, while allowing us to positively redefine, redirect, and even reenergize the current I.R.S. organization, giving it, in-part, a new and different mission, which I believe it would be very effective at and which I believe would be both appreciated and valued by the American people and the I.R.S. personnel affected. Since I believe that many Americans (both in the low and middle income tax brackets) would feel positive about such changes, and since I believe the existing I.R.S. organization would as well, I thought I should devote some time to this subject.

One of the most complex manuals ever written was, and is the U.S. Tax Code. It requires armies of accountants and lawyers to understand and interpret it for businesses, and even for us, the "little people". It requires businesses to keep two sets of accounting records; one for financial reporting purposes and one for tax purposes, since income and expense is not accounted for quite the same way when determining what is taxable income and what is not, and what is a deductible expense to arrive at taxable income and what is not.

It also requires judges and courts that are separate and apart from the rest of the legal system (depending upon your perspective), by way of Tax Courts and Tax Attorneys, to interpret the laws and to adjudicate the cases. We as taxpayers of course, pay for these courts and these judges, and all of the related staffing and buildings and additional expenses that go with them, across the United States. We pay in excess of 10 billion dollars per year to run the I.R.S., and U.S. Companies pay billions upon billions each year, just to hire the attorneys, tax accountants and support staff to account for and determine their taxable income, their actual taxes, and to engage in the litigation that may go with it from time-to-time.

Then we of course, the middle-America, middle-income citizenry, have to putz around like schmucks every year as we hire accountants or H&R Block, or buy Turbo Tax, as we try to figure out the intricacies of that which even tax judges and legal minds have problems discerning and navigating through.

So we expend billions upon billions of OUR taxpayer's dollars to support an entire federal agency and a court and legal system that is impossibly complex to navigate, whose rules, regulations and loopholes change every year...and for what?

I'll tell you for what! For what should be the very simple purpose of collecting tax money for our national defense, education and our physical and social infrastructure. Oh, and of course, let's not forget that the money is also needed to support our bloated federal government, which absolutely lives to feast on our middle-class, middle-income, middle-American carcasses (read tax dollars), so that our hard-earned income can be lifted from our wallets and our families, with our full participation and cooperation, as law-abiding citizens, so that it can be re-distributed to pay for political favors and political hacks, as well as for healthcare, schooling, housing, and in some cases the arrest, adjudication and incarceration of illegal-aliens, who have entered the country illegally. Let's not forget that the money is also used to line the pockets of special interest groups and entities, who are all very well represented by lobbyists, more lawyers, and of course, by our elected representatives, as well.

And why is this complex IRS regulatory and tax structure in existence? To keep the accountants and lawyers employed? Well certainly. If you don't think that's part of the game, think again. They too have lobbyists.

But there is a much bigger reason, of course...Why to keep all of us common-folk from ever being able to figure it out and to keep us so bamboozled, so as to be able to lift 55% or more of our income from us, through multiple, combined taxes (state, local, federal, property, etc., as outlined earlier), in order to support this wasteful, bloated, and irresponsible bunch of stooges in Washington, along with their anointed and favored special interests. These "special interests", in-turn, end up enriching many of these elected representatives, so that by the time they leave office, many are millionaires many times over...while "WE THE PEOPLE", whom these representatives consider the real stooges, are fleeced in the process, while simultaneously wondering why we don't get better representation.

A HARD LOOK IN THE MIRROR

Pictured left & right: Our current Politicians reaching into our right pockets. Tax Lawyers & Accountants Lobbyist's reaching into our left pockets. Center: Us, the American middle-class Taxpayers

The purpose of this specific system is to keep this money-machine, this taxpayer-funded ATM, in perpetual operation, with our full financial support and cooperation, year-in and year-out, so that we DON'T get better representation, because if we did, the fleecing might diminish, or come to a near halt. And of course, the sickening irony of it all is that the only ones who don't have an ATM card for withdrawals...ARE US... "WE THE PEOPLE"! What a swell system, eh?!

Allow me to give you a graphic analogy...and I apologize in advance for those whom I offend. But this is akin to a prostitute servicing a client, and then paying the client, instead of the other way around. And yes my brother and sister middle-class taxpaying Americans of every race, gender and orientation, unfortunately we are the prostitute in this scenario and we are paying the politicians (the clients) to let them have their way with us, and boy, are they letting us have it, but good!

Of course, as I've outlined before, WE THE PEOPLE of middle-income, middle-America, are the root-cause of the reason we don't get better representation. Why? Because we don't demand it and do something about it by putting down our television remotes, bypassing Sports Center, game shows, and paparazzi/reality programs, and instead get informed and stay involved...but I won't revisit that again, or I shall digress...

So again, why do we need this extraordinary, multi-billion dollar IRS apparatus and system in place to simply collect taxes for our infrastructure, education and defense? *The answer and the dirty little secret is... WE DON'T!*

We have allowed Washington to dictate the system and it has been perverted to serve the real masters in Washington, along with their special interests, and it's interesting to note that, every time someone brings up a reasonable, sensible, efficient alternative, it is immediately dismissed with a derisive laugh and pronounced "ridiculous, impossible and unfair".

Of course it's pronounced "ridiculous, impossible and unfair"! It's pronounced "ridiculous, impossible and unfair", not by the majority of the American citizenry, but by our elected officials, the devious (and of course highly educated and highly skilled) crooks in the House and Senate, *those who benefit from the perversity of this system.*

Did you ever notice that almost every time one of these elected "representatives" makes the standard "ridiculous, impossible and unfair" pronouncement, that there is a nervous little laugh, or nervous little smile, or even a nervous little bead-of-sweat that appears on their forehead? That's because they are scared to death that if we, the middle-America, middle-income, middle-class stooges who elected them (as they see us), ever realized that we could come together in a moment of clarity, revelation and awareness and tell them that they either simplify this monstrosity of a tax system (according to our preferences and instructions), or we will throw them out on their collective keesters, then their elaborate, expensive, and intentionally-confusing system of granting economic favors to those who take care of them the most and make them rich, could become seriously transparent and thereby disrupted and, dare I say, abolished!

Now, what would be the fun and incentive in that for our elected, highly educated crooks-in-Congress? Then the only incentive would be to serve the people they represent, honestly, fairly, and for the right reasons. They would be aghast! After all, there's no "real money" in that! The law firms, accounting firms and lobbyists, who also love this convoluted, confusing, and arcane tax system AND WHO LIVE OFF OF IT, would never stand for it.

This is why we must forge ahead and proceed with shutting off the TV, bypassing Sports Center (more than occasionally), as well as the paparazzi/reality shows, and instead, read the real news of the day, get and stay involved with our local, state, and federal political system and school boards, educate ourselves about the candidates, and support term-limits and those representatives who will carry out our will as voters. We have an obligation to ourselves, our children and to **all** Americans to do this, for the most basic reasons (previously discussed).

But back to the tax system...My own personal preference is for a most simple, efficient, cost-effective, and fair option; that of a flat-tax on businesses and a flat consumption tax on citizen taxpayers. The latter would have some conditional exemptions for those at very low income levels, addressing the fairness issue.

The flat-tax on businesses would be applied to all income and profits, without exception and without exemption. In other words, there would be no special adjustments for tax purposes and no need to keep a second set of books for tax purposes. The percentage tax rate itself could be studied so that it could initially be pegged at a rate that, when applied to net income and using the standard P&L (profit & loss)/income statement for financial reporting purposes, according to GAAP (generally accepted accounting principles), it would result in a taxable income commensurate with what would have resulted under the old tax code (it could even be structured to be industry-specific, if appropriate and necessary). Such a process, at the outset, would help to guard against any wild fluctuations that could do damage to businesses and thereby the economy.

If any sort of special deductions need to be considered to incentivize companies in different fields of endeavor (e.g. oil & natural gas exploration, etc.), then don't do it through the tax code requiring two sets of books. Do it through the regulations related to standard financial reporting. Again, it could be industry-specific, if necessary.

I must add one caveat to the above. Today, our taxes on businesses and the laws surrounding them are out-of-step with the times. Our tax rates on businesses are much too high, relative to the rest of the industrialized world. If we don't do something about it, we're going to see the continued flight of businesses and capital to other countries and we may indeed end-up delivering pizza's to one another (as the Rev. Jesse Jackson once joked)...that is...assuming that pizza delivery can't also be outsourced to India like everything else (sorry, I couldn't help myself). We must then have some other incentives to go along with it, in order to encourage companies to keep the money earned here, in this country.

Regarding individual taxpaying citizens, as mentioned, I favor elimination of the current system and instead, implementation of a flat consumption tax (essentially, a national sales tax, if you will). If you want to call it a VAT, or value-added tax, go ahead. With this system, we would no longer complete IRS forms every April, paying attorneys, accountants, or software companies to support us in figuring out our taxes. Our taxes would instead be incurred and paid at the check-out counter, on every purchase. This would simplify everyone's life, eliminate loopholes and special considerations, it would keep the rich individual taxpayers from exploiting loopholes, and would keep the tax-cheats from cheating. There would be no way for one to avoid paying one's taxes and would encourage the type of behavior that is good for Americans; namely, encouraging savings.

Some would maintain that this would unfairly impact the poorest in our country and put them at an extreme, or unfair disadvantage, since the poorest in our society today are exempt, to one degree or another, from paying taxes (if they fall below a certain income threshold). That's a fair and logical criticism. However, just as we have food-stamps today for those who qualify for them, we could have a similar process for those very same people, right at the checkout counter, as we do today.

For those below the poverty-line, or for those who today would normally qualify for exemption from income tax, or reduced or minimal income taxation, we could have them apply for a program which, if qualified, would provide them with a government-issued card (with appropriate smart-chip technology protections), which they could present at check-out, or time of purchase, which would exempt them from the national sales tax, or alternatively, would allow them to pay a lower tax, based upon a graduated scale, essentially having the same net-effect as a reduced or eliminated income tax payment. The burden would be on those citizens to follow the appropriate qualification steps to obtain such treatment (as they do today for food stamps, for example) and would not impact the citizenry at-large. With nothing more than a swipe of a card at a checkout counter, they would receive a lower tax rate at time of purchase, or would pay no tax at all, if applicable

Well, what happens to the stimulating economic effect of certain income-tax deductions for mortgage interest and the like, you may ask? Good question. I have a couple of different thoughts about how to handle that.

First, my foundational belief in the power of Capitalism and the private sector, makes me say that it is not government's job (meaning your job and my job as citizens, since the government is supposed to represent us and since it's our money the government holds to begin with), to subsidize other peoples loans in the private-sector economy, in order to fund their purchases, whether it be an economy and/or business stimulating purchase like a home, or not. It is up to pure competition between the banks to provide the lowest interest rate incentives. If they want to attract home borrowers, they will need to simply reduce the interest rate to the most competitive levels they can.

Second, if we as a people decided it was in our economic and cultural best interests to provide incentives to first-time home buyers, which we all were, are, or may hope to be at some time in our lives, then it should be up to our elected representatives to identify and implement such incentives in the system I've described. For example, it occurs to me that we could simply provide reduced rates of taxation on certain classes of purchases by reducing the flat-rate national sales tax, or VAT, on those classes of purchases, and likewise we could provide reduced rates of taxation on banks for net-revenues earned on this particular portfolio of loans, providing them with a means to pass along lower interest rates, which would be appropriate, should they wish to take advantage of these lower taxation rates on the specific portfolio or class of loans, in order to remain competitive in the marketplace.

A HARD LOOK IN THE MIRROR

These solutions I have proposed may sound simple, at least when compared to our current ridiculous system, and in fact, those much more knowledgeable and wiser than I may be able to identify a few issues with what I have outlined. Of course I would expect my proposals to be met, as is customary by the usual Washington suspects, with the same reaction that we've experienced so often in the past; namely, that it is "ridiculous, impossible and unfair". Well, a sufficient number of wise and intelligent people have proposed similar taxing methodologies in the past, and I hope I've provided some tweaks that will help protect the poor and not negatively affect certain classes of job-creating purchases (e.g. homes). So...now what's the problem, hmmm? I'm sure the Crooks in Congress will think of something...But remember, you have the power to vote them out of office.

I believe that the majority of Americans favor such a simplified system. After all, with this system, we'd reduce the billions spent on the IRS and on the court and legal apparatus supporting the tax courts. We'd help to keep our citizens out of legal trouble and even jail, because there would be little to no interpretation required and little to no possibility to fool the system and cheat, and we'd provide a great deal of emotional relief to the taxpayer-citizens as a whole, who do not have to fret every year over dealing with a tax system that takes an army of judges, lawyers, accountants and IRS employees to figure out and interpret.

Further, our federal government needs to focus on efficiencies and streamlining and "leaning-out" their business processes. This is one sure-fire way to do that. It would increase revenues (by eliminating tax-cheats), reduce cost of collecting and enforcing tax laws, and would simplify the lives of every American and lift from them the burden of filing tax returns every year and worrying about potential problems with the biggest of perceived "Big Brothers", the IRS...!

Now, a fair number of the existing IRS personnel would still be required to administer this new tax program. But a fair number of them would no longer be required for investigation, enforcement and collection.

So the next step is to take these very qualified, patriotic government employees in the IRS, who are no longer required for these activities [excluding of course, those few who are under investigation for political abuses (e.g. Lois Lerner, etc.)], and turn this team into an aggressive enforcement arm to investigate fraud and waste in Medicare, Medicaid and government contracting & spending (including military contracts and contracting). These folks have a keen financial eye for fraud, and for people and companies cheating the system. Put them to work as an aggressive arm to uncover and punish the perpetrators who are stealing from us, the U.S. Government, who is in fact us, the American Taxpayer. "WE THE PEOPLE" would applaud them in their endeavors and they could feel quite proud about the job they'd be doing, directly benefitting themselves and all of us, for we're all U.S. Taxpayers. I'm sure they would feel re-energized and re-focused.

The only thing required to see this done, is for all of us middle-income, middle-America, middle-class taxpayers and citizens of every color and gender, to get our collective heads out of the sand, out of the TV, and out of our collective behinds, and to get involved and vote the right people into office. We must simply fulfill our responsibilities and our basic obligations as citizens, which are the basic responsibilities of our free society and our government By, For and Of the people.

Lest we forget, our forefathers fought to establish these privileges for us, and our citizen-soldiers fought (and continue to fight) to preserve these freedoms. So we must, as brother and sister Americans, fulfill these responsibilities that go with the freedoms we enjoy, which many sacrificed to achieve and preserve. We have

A HARD LOOK IN THE MIRROR

at least an obligation and responsibility to educate ourselves on these important matters and vote people into office who will carry out the will of the people and not the will of the special-interests and the "purveyors-of-pull", who are presently represented by our current batch of elected officials, which consist of a generous percentage of crooks, putz's and flimflam artists. Now, this is do-able, but only if we are willing to act, and act together.

CHAPTER 7

VALUES, LEADERSHIP AND MORAL GRAVITAS...PRECIOUS COMMODITIES GROWING SCARCE IN OUR SOCIETY?

It's a good thing that when key battles went poorly, and several did, that our then CEO of the Army, General George Washington, didn't whine that he wanted his life back and then head-off for a yachting vacation to get his mind off of his problems, as our forces got pummeled by the British.

There is something to be said about good, old-fashioned moral commitment, internal fortitude, courage and leadership that seems to be conspicuously absent from many in leadership positions today. Whether we're talking about our Congress, our local representatives, or multi-millionaire businessmen, it makes me think about what it was that we used to teach our kids and young people, that we're not teaching them today. That's not at all to say that there weren't corrupt politicians and business types in the past. That would be grossly naïve and ridiculous to suggest. But there sure seemed to be a lot less of them. There seemed to be a set of core traditional and leadership values that many in the Media Industrial Complex and media elite today consider obsolete, unnecessary, uncomfortable, or unfortunately, even foolish; this, while the American people seem to be crying out for these values today like never before.

A HARD LOOK IN THE MIRROR

We wonder why we have filth and corruption glorified on TV, in movies, and on the internet. We wonder why children must be forced to grow up so fast. We wonder why we are having trouble like never before with drug abuse, children dropping out of school at record rates, and the general dumbing-down of our country. Well, I'd only say look to the deterioration of our moral foundations, observe the drift away from religion, church and God. Note the worship of the fast-buck and the complete lack of focus on the values that might have the most to do with re-setting our moral compass, re-establishing our economic foundation, and regaining control of our society, which appears to be on the road to moral confusion and decline.

Let me start with an example. Take Mr. Tony Hayward and his handling of the BP oil spill disaster in Louisiana a few years ago. I ask you, what type of personality does it take? What are the moral underpinnings and characteristics that allow a well-educated, apparently adept businessman/CEO of a global organization, to make such selfish, self-centered, immature, and ethically questionable decisions, which would have him, at the height of an economic, environmental, and international disaster impacting millions of people and entailing billions of dollars in damages, decide to basically say the equivalent of:

"Hey, I know this is negatively impacting you "little people", but I'm under a lot of pressure and I'm trying to get my life back. Now, I'm going on holiday across the pond, to pilot my yacht in a sailing race, which I'm hoping should be jolly-good fun, so that I can unwind and relax a bit, you know, away from it all…while you "little people" worry about little things like your livelihoods and how you're going to support yourselves through this gi-normous economic and environmental crisis that my company and I have created.

Now, I know you all are suffering, but certainly not nearly as much as me, with all the enormous responsibilities I carry, and considering that your media is being terribly impolite, aggressive, and difficult with their questions. Hell, you're lucky I'm not going away for a month. The way you're all criticizing me and my company, it seems as if you expect me to take this thing personally, or something?

My God, do you seriously expect me to act like a responsible leader of my company and express true remorse and concern about this and vow to stay on the job and provide you with regular updates, telling you exactly what we're doing...daily if necessary, to address the multitude of problems this is creating for you? Do you expect me to demonstrate serious, mature leadership and sensitivity to the problems you "little people" are experiencing? Do you expect me to consider my stock-options and my millions irrelevant, and instead identify with you, the people? Do you expect me to work hard to fulfill the expectations of my position and office and to earn your trust? Do you expect me to come down off of my high horse and speak to you directly and spend time in your communities, facing you and your families, directly, while pledging myself and my team to be on the job until the job is done, and done correctly? Do you expect me to act like the mature, moral, committed, worldly, highly paid, well-educated and down-to-earth adult and business leader that I should be, and do the right things?"

The answer to all of the above "questions", of course, is a resounding "YES". Instead, his answer seemed to be more like:

"Hell, wake up and smell the coffee, little people. No one behaves according to those old-fashioned, moral expectations any more. That's passé. Now go back to the beaches with your Dawn detergent and collect some water-fowl, or crawfish, or whatever you call those crustaceans, and clean them up! Do something worthwhile with yourselves, while I jet-off to my yacht race and some well-deserved R&R..."

I must ask...where have the moral, stand-up people and culture gone; who would have answered those questions with an unequivocal "YES", and then backed it up with action? More importantly, why have they gone and when, if ever, will they return? Don't get me wrong. There are still plenty of business leaders and people who would conduct themselves in the proper and correct way, I believe. There are still serious and moral men and women of virtue out there. But we must ask ourselves (and eventually come to know) how people like Mr. Hayward are chosen, and then how do they make it into positions of serious responsibility, without the leadership skills and moral gravitas that is so absolutely necessary to be able to lead, and more importantly, lead by example!

Certainly, while he was on a developmental track to his CEO position, there must have been warning signs about his strength of character, his ability to manage in a crisis situation, and about his ability to relate to people in-general. I can assure you that, in most any ascendancy to a CEO role, these executives must manage through all manner of crises along the way and demonstrate that they can handle it. Generally, by the time they get to a position like Hayward's, there is little doubt about how they handle pressure.

In asking ourselves where the moral, stand-up people and culture have gone, it's easy to see that this is the very same question we might ask ourselves, relative to our elected leaders and representatives, most of whom don't lead, and most of whom don't represent or even listen to us any longer, but instead go to Washington or assume office locally, mostly for the purpose of making a quick-buck and lining their pockets, demonstrating in spades the maxim of "do what I say, not what I do… and by the way, don't dare to actually watch what I do, nor hold me accountable for it."

Whatever it is that has brought this pattern of behavior about, it appears to behave like a virus, spreading from elected officials, out to some business leaders, and on to other members of society. Unfortunately, we can't blame it on a bug. It's a set of values, or lack thereof (anti-values, if you will), which appears to manifest itself as a learned set of behaviors. Politicians seem to demonstrate these anti-values as if they are second nature to them; as if they were almost born to them. Could it be that politician-types, educated in business (e.g. Hayward), are making it into the corporate halls of power more pervasively?

You'd think on the surface of it that this would be impossible; that they'd be weeded-out and that people would not follow them, or their lead. Further, people of this ilk generally don't achieve the hard results demanded by business, results required to survive in such positions. Nevertheless, you see the arrogance and the assumed privilege breaking out from time-to-time, over the last decade or two. Look at Enron and WorldCom, two global giants that were headed by arrogant, unprincipled CEO's, who thought nothing of taking people to the cleaners to enrich themselves, while flimflamming their respective boards' of directors. Look at AIG, the insurance giant. There are abundant examples.

I choose Tony Hayward as an example, only because his example is still somewhat recent, relevant, and blatantly obvious to point out. The BP crisis was very well-known and the impact was extraordinarily devastating and widespread. Finally, his behavior was so arrogant and so representative of the "me-first and the hell with everyone else" mold of what we see daily in our so-called political leaders... strike that, not leaders...elected representatives in Washington, that it seemed absolutely appropriate to make my points about challenges to our society.

I keep attempting to capture the behavior in words, but I can't seem to find words to adequately describe the decay we all see daily, whether we are talking about elected representatives, administrators, local politicians, school-board members, or alas, even some teachers. Certainly not all of the people holding such positions are bereft of maturity, integrity, talent, good-judgment, leadership skills, and moral gravitas. But enough of them are that, as a people and as a society, I believe we recognize it and we are saying to the whole bunch who demonstrates the behavior: *"Enough already, we've had it with all of you. We're ready, willing and able to chuck the whole lot of you out of office and bring some real "regime change" to this country, to our states and to our local governments and school boards."*

Clearly, many of these individuals, while bereft of some of the qualities I have mentioned, are not bereft of talent. Look at the case of Hayward. You don't rise to the top of a global organization without being smart, experienced, and talented. So how could Hayward make such callous, unthinking blunders? My own answer is that he is revealing what's inside the man himself. Or more correctly, what's not inside the man himself. He's revealing what's missing, in other words.

We look at our representatives in Washington and at the state and local levels and we can see similar phenomena taking place. These individuals didn't rise to their positions of trust, responsibility, and leadership because they are stupid, after all. It takes skill, some hard work, and some ability to rise to these positions. So, what's missing?

What seems to be missing today is a solid moral and ethical foundation and the leadership qualities that lend themselves to an individual having the make-up, the convictions, and the skills to take him or her beyond their own private self-interest, vanity, and even narcissism, and instead keeps them grounded and focused in a way that impels them to consider a higher moral imperative and mission, and ties them morally and ethically to our people, our proud history, and our brave future together. Many of our leaders of the past had "it". Sadly, many, if not most of our leaders of today, do not.

As I implied previously, I believe that there are many things that drive us as individuals and as a society. There are also many complexities in the make up of each one of us. I believe that it is the combination of these elements, from birth to death, and how they combine and are influenced by the conditions and the people around us, that create in each of us a balance that makes up an individual, good, bad, or indifferent. I also believe that, amongst yesterday's leaders and citizens, there was a certain commonality and consistency in that uniquely American make up, which provided for the type of good leaders we used to experience in this country, in higher relative numbers and on a wider scale than we do today (in my opinion), which, make no mistake about it, was produced from the bottom-up, not the top-down.

What I mean by that is that these leaders did not emerge from their mother's womb, fully-formed and ready to lead. They, like us, were a product of their parents, their home-life, their communities, their education, and their understanding of our history, their moral upbringing, their imbued sense of duty to our country and to our people, and the inarguable impact of the sharing of a great many common sub-sets of our values, which were shared by society in-general, across a wide spectrum.

Society, in-turn, also became a product of these leaders, who emerged throughout our history, in fairly high numbers (proportionate to today), who led us from the birth of this nation, through a Civil War, and through two World Wars and more.

I'm suggesting that it was a symbiotic relationship. They were a product of their parents, their upbringing, their education, and American society. And their society, our American society, reflected-back these similar values and expanded or added very important new ones (e.g. Abraham Lincoln, Dr. Martin Luther King, Jr., and their leadership,

A HARD LOOK IN THE MIRROR

work and sacrifice in pioneering freedom, equal rights and an equal seat at the American Table for our brother and sister Americans of color). Each strengthened, expanded, and reinforced the other.

I believe that it is our society and our culture that has changed over time (part of the DNA of our society), and it is our society and our culture that is now producing the types of leaders we have today (e.g. Harry Reid, Nancy Pelosi for the Democrats) and non-leaders, as well (John Boehner and Lindsey Graham for the Republicans). As I outlined earlier, one way we can control our political and even social destiny (to a degree), is by throwing the current crop of bums out of office. Our vote and our constitution give us the power and right to do this. But if we don't get to the root of the problem, we'll simply continue to elect bum, after bum, after bum.

Sure, term limits will limit the damage any one bum can do. But we have to look deeper, I believe, to the root-cause of why we elect bums in the first place. We have to look at what we need to do to refocus our values, our morals, our priorities, and change this short-term, sound-bite-type of focus we seem to have on our federal, state and local representatives and, to a degree, on our families, and re-evaluate and change how we prioritize our time and manage our lives. We clearly need to focus more on our own self-development as a people again, and focus more closely on our families (in education, time-spent and values instilled), our schools, our school boards, our local governments, our state governments and our federal government.

Sure, we can throw the bums at the top out of office, but if we don't start focusing on what's immediately around us, first, we're not going to make and achieve any real, meaningful, consistent, and long-term change. It's like a pebble in the pond. *I believe we've got to start with what's around us and work our way out.* That's not to say that some change can't be simultaneous. Of course, research the candidates; consider running for local office yourself, if you've got the commitment. Let's also get the current crop of non-leaders out of office and get term limits in place and let's elect the best candidates we can. But let's face it, real, fundamental change is required to fix the foundation of our democratic republic. The foundation, after all, is people. It's that way with a business and it's that way with America. We're only as good as our people.

What good is reconstructing the top of the building going to do (the President and Congress), when all we do is to continue to replace it with a similar construct? Getting our country back on a solid foundation simply doesn't come from a single series of changes at the top, or a few changes in the middle. It comes from sustained change over time, which must include reinforcing, or re-constructing the foundation, with our children, our local school boards, and our local governments, and work our way up and out from there, simultaneously where possible.

This requires basic changes in the way we approach our daily lives. It requires, I believe, that we focus less on the immaterial-material things; like what we own; from the newest gadgets, to homes, to cars, and the latest "nice-to-haves", and instead focus more on our values, on our families, on our individual personal development, and on creating financial and social stability for us and our families. I believe we need to focus more on the most important people and issues immediately surrounding us, and eliminate the more empty and vacuous distractions in our lives. I think we need more focus on our families and loved ones, and the education and experiences we create for them. **Please process what I just said…the education and experiences <u>we create</u> for them. Not the education and experiences that the school system or society creates for them. But first we need to understand that what the school system** and society creates for them *is what we have created for them*. It is one in the same. It is a reflection of us! If we don't like it, it's up to us to change it.

If we take the position that we have no power...then guess what? **WE HAVE NO POWER!** The opposite is also true. *If we take the position that we have the power...then guess what?* **WE HAVE THE POWER!**

If we take the position that we influence our family members less than society around us, the same society we believe is eroding or betraying our principles and only looking out for number one, then we are simply wrong, and we are surrendering ourselves and our families to that which we are saying is wrong with our society. At that point then, we simply become a part of the problem that we are saying we are trying to correct. We are also taking the easy way, or the coward's way out, I believe.

No one has more influence on your family and on your immediate circle of influence than you do! It is the simple, daily interaction and experiences that fully engage us with those around us. It is these experiences that cause us to exchange thoughts about morals and values and what's really important, and also about what's not! It is also our daily conduct that speaks volumes to those family members, friends, and society around us. If we don't take time for self-examination and personal reflection and thinking each day, then we will not change what we see around us, either directly or indirectly.

It is my humble opinion that we need to focus less on what we own, less on T.V. and other daily distractions, and focus more on internal and external discussions about the quality of our character and our lives, and the REAL things that determine them. We need to focus more on what we're teaching in our schools, through involvement in the school board, involvement in school board elections, and even in volunteering to participate in such elections (for those who are qualified and committed).

We must insist upon the teaching of real, traditional American values, and a complete and thorough teaching and learning of American history in our schools, so that children can comprehend, value, and be proud of their rich, shared heritage, whether their family roots go back two centuries in this country, or two weeks in this country. We must insist upon the same, proper teaching and learning of this rich history to immigrants applying for citizenship, so that they understand the heritage they will share and the responsibilities that go with it. We all share the same rich heritage when we land on these shores (legally) and become citizens, or when we are born in this country. But we can't value it, embrace it, and knowingly make the commitments it calls for, and then pass it down to our children, if we don't teach it and if our citizens don't learn it, including the moral foundations, which underpin our heritage, our values and our history.

We must continue to reflect upon and talk about that, regularly (which happens through teaching, learning, and engagement), if we expect it to remain a part of our collective American DNA and if we expect our citizens and our children to embrace it and live it daily and be willing to defend it with their lives, in order to continue to preserve this country and the noble experiment that it represents for future generations of Americans.

Finally, I know I'll lose a few people here when I say this. We need to re-introduce ourselves to God. This is still, I believe, one nation, one people, under God. Our moral grounding, our values, and our country, descend from God. I'm not pushing one religion over another. Nor do I believe that someone's sexual orientation precludes them from being sons or daughters of God or loved any less by God. I just believe that, despite the misguided messages espoused by the bereft Mr. Maher and his ilk, it is the love of God, the love of each other, and the logical respect for human life and the beauty of the morals we are taught, which makes life (my life at least), worth living, and transcendent from the other beasts of the earth.

This is not to say that I decry science in the least, or its theories, or its magnificent discoveries on so many frontiers, or the proven facts it has uncovered and made known, including incredibly important historical discoveries about our universe, our solar system, our Earth, and about man. On the contrary, I celebrate and embrace it and am constantly amazed and thrilled by it. I have been in awe, admiration, and wonderment of science since I was old enough to perceive it. I celebrate science, as long as it is hard-science, not some of the social-political theories thought-up and taught to our children and to society today as fact, which rely more on social popularity, pull, and political persuasion, than they do on quantifiable, scientific analysis and proof.

This said, in my view, I believe that the greatest scientist that the universe has in it...is God. I see no conflict between God and science. I only see conflict in what we do not yet truly understand. I think that Albert Einstein implied this himself, in his own way, in some of his latter reflections:

> *"Every one who is seriously involved in the pursuit of science becomes convinced that a spirit is manifest in the laws of the Universe-a spirit vastly superior to that of man, and one in the face of which we with our modest powers must feel humble."*
>
> *"The scientists' religious feeling takes the form of a rapturous amazement at the harmony of natural law, which reveals an intelligence of such superiority that, compared with it, all the systematic thinking and acting of human beings is an utterly insignificant reflection."*
>
> *- Albert Einstein*

Now, anyone who wishes can go and look up a plethora of Albert Einstein's reflections, which may appear to contradict the inferences of the statements, above. This is fine. I'm not trying to tell anyone what to believe, or not believe. I am simply choosing quotations personally meaningful to me, which suggest that there is room for reflection in what I have stated immediately above the quotations. Clearly, Einstein's thoughts reflected a progressive, developing perspective, which I believe is true of most human beings, as their life experience grows and as they perceive and study the world around them, over time.

Further to my statement above the quotations, I only see conflict in how men sometimes choose to use their scientific knowledge; that is, when it is used to the detriment of the human spirit and the destruction of our fellow-man. But that is also part of our human journey.

CHAPTER 8

CHILDREN, ADOLESCENTS AND YOUNG ADULTS – WHAT ARE WE THINKING?

Freedom, as I think we all realize, is a two-edged sword. It is the foundation of our country, our government and our heritage and it is also one of the reasons that we are a nation of laws. Freedom, unrestrained by laws, is chaos (or anarchy, take your choice).

As our children grow up in today's society, they are inundated with messages all around them, which from what I have seen, basically tell them that "almost anything goes" (and glorify that message), whether it be unbridled access to the use of drugs, glorification of violence, all manner of messages related to any type of sex, with any type of partner, at any time, almost anywhere, from a very young age and all the other things that go with a free and open society, as well as active promotion of the excesses of various types of lifestyles in the media, on Facebook, My Space, etc.

There is also the so-called "Hip-Hop" generational message which, by appearances, and whether intentionally or not, seeks to reverse the gains that the Feminist and Women's Liberation movements of the 1960's and 1970's eventually achieved for women. Most messages that I have been exposed to from the "Hip-Hop" crowd, appears to degrade women and seemingly seeks to turn them back into mere objects of sex, and/or sexual violence, and/or subjugation by men, most particularly by the so-called "artists" themselves (who write and promote the messages) and by so-called "sports stars and media personalities", who perpetuate it.

I often wonder what it is that will bring this generation back to a more centered, more principled and more stable existence and lifestyle. Today's society makes it seem that most of our young people are experiencing the equivalent of being dropped into the center of a Roman-style orgy of all of the above, in high schools, in society, and on most college campuses and are then simply asked, told, or forced by the circumstances of their individual situations, to just figure it out for themselves. Certainly this doesn't apply to all young people, but indeed, many are forced to grow up in this type of environment, in my opinion.

Now, admittedly, there are as many different young adults, in as many different circumstances, as there are parents who raised them and most, like me and our parents before us, struggle to make sense of it all. And most, like me and our parents before us, use our own, individual frames of reference through which we view and interpret both the world and time we are living in.

I don't know about you, but growing up, I did not have anything close to the environment that children today must deal with. Face it, it was a much more innocent time and even then, not always so innocent. I was pulled in many different directions and eventually, I had to make more than just real-time decisions about what to believe, about how to interpret the world around me and ultimately, about what direction to take in my path through this world, as well as make conscious decisions about what directions not to take and why.

I was fortunate to have grown up in a family who loved me and who did instill values and likewise gave me a strong moral compass. As funny as it may sound (or not sound), on some level, I always seemed to sense or think about which action or path would be nourishing or positive to my human spirit and which would not be, measured against what I had been taught and measured against how I had seen my parents behave, by way of example. And, as I'm sure is true for many, I sometimes consciously chose a path that I knew, inherently, would not be nourishing to my human spirit. As many other kids do, I simply chose, or wanted to experience what lay down that other path sometimes, simply because of no other reason than it drew me and I was curious. Sometimes that path involved drugs, sometimes sex and sometimes other things. But I never strayed far and I never strayed for very long. I was always brought back to center, somehow.

Now, why is it that I was always brought back to center? Part of it is because I was fortunate that I had parents who taught me certain values and principles and who set certain examples and drew clear lines of what is and is not acceptable and kept it simple and clear. They also enforced clear consequences for actions that went against these principles. But another part of it is because much of what I saw portrayed on TV and in movies growing up, reinforced the values that my parents and my teachers taught me. This is unlike today, where the percentages are upside down and a much higher percentage of the values that are reinforced (particularly on TV and in the media) generally tend to be the polar opposites of what I was taught and what my wife and I tried hard to teach our children growing up.

Now, as a parent, I always hope and pray that my children take the paths that will be nourishing to their human spirit and which embrace the values that my wife and I and others have tried to teach them. We hope that these will bring them a sense of spirituality, self-worth, validation, moral perspective and certainty, and through this, **happiness**. I always hope that, ultimately, they will make a positive contribution to our society, our country and most importantly to their respective, immediate families and in-particular, to the lives of their children, when they eventually have children (should they do so).

This said, it is also clear that they will, from time-to-time, as we all did, make decisions that are not consistent with good judgment and the values that they were taught and raised with and that are not nourishing to their human spirit. If and when they venture down these paths (which I hope are few to none), I find myself thinking about what it is that will bring them back and center them. I believe that the answer to that question relates directly to the values that they have been taught and raised with and the examples they have seen and experienced in their home.

If this is so, then I think we all have some questions to ask ourselves, whether Mr. Bill Maher agrees or not. Does our conduct as parents impact our children? If so, does our children's conduct impact society? If so, does society's conduct reflect the conduct of parents and children of that society? It's your answers to these questions and your decisions based upon these answers, which will be critically important to what type of society we have today, and moving forward...

So what is American society's responsibility, relative to the impact it has in raising our young...and who today really is big brother?

I can already hear the unabashed, money-grubbing directors, producers and other purveyors of perversity, violence, filth and smut in our TV shows, movies and internet programming, laughing uproariously and going through the normal motions of taking out their pitchforks and torches, as well as their label-makers, to both defend their wallets and pocketbooks, which bulge from the booty of their clearly popular junk, as well as to label people like me as conservative, religious-type-reactionaries, who want to control people's thoughts, words and behavior. In other words, people who think like I do now, they would accuse of being akin to Orwell's "Big Brother", or even worse, if a majority of congress reflected my perspectives.

Well, I've got a news-flash for you...and what might be a scary twist for some, which I ask you to consider...

I maintain that society has passed the so-called "tipping-point" and is now upside down. I maintain that Big Brother is now the Media Industrial Complex and the media elite. They are the ones who are now in day-to-day control of what we see and what we hear, and they would like desperately to be in control of what we think, because what we think has a direct impact on power and money ($$$). They now determine the rules of "Political Correctness" in our society today and thereby determine, by their own standards, who is "Politically Incorrect" and who is "Politically Correct".

I maintain that, to a great degree, <u>they</u> are determining the political subject matter and conversation, and thereby the political agenda in society today. They are watching our behavior and chastising <u>us</u>, should we dare get out of line and have the audacity to bring up values and standards of behavior and conduct, and actually challenge or criticize their status-quo of "anything goes". Take it a step-up and maybe it's important to begin to look at who controls the media...

Now, I believe that the vast majority of Americans from the middle (middle-class, middle-income, middle-America); we, the unheard, unwashed masses out there, have all noticed that anyone like us, who dares to speak out on these issues and point out our concerns about the Media Industrial Complex and media elite (who in my opinion are in defacto control of the content of TV, movies, news, et al.), well, we're labeled as either being stupid, red-necks, uneducated, right-wingers, or Tea-Party extremists, or some combination of the above. Yet most of us are from the middle and we consist of a mix of Democrats, Republicans and Independents of every race, gender and sexual orientation.

We're also accused of being religious freaks or fanatics, whether we embrace formal religion, or not. There is a focused and well-orchestrated purpose to this of course. The purpose is to refer to us by any term that will compartmentalize us, label us, and allow the Media Industrial Complex and media elite to marginalize us, dismiss us and sweep us under the carpet as if we're irrelevant and don't have a right to be heard, because if we make our voice heard, it threatens their influence and control over us.

This is a standard, common, everyday tactic of the Media Industrial complex and media elite and unfortunately, the only ones who are beginning to point this out and fight against it, are networks like Fox News, who are being steadily filled-up with their own extremists and screamers and, who frankly, I have grown tired of even attempting to listen to, most times. They are slowly becoming the opposite, mirror image (and just as dangerous) of that which they say they decry and fight. Now, I wouldn't necessarily mind this if they were honest about what they are doing, except that all are being disingenuous and phony about it, claiming one and all (whether Fox or MSNBC, or CBS or ABC, etc.), to be reporting the news, or to be both "fair and balanced", or a similar version of the same phrase. Frankly, I can't find one media outlet that is truly reporting the news, much less one that is fair and balanced about it.

A HARD LOOK IN THE MIRROR

The TV and cable networks and Hollywood are simply not much better than prostitutes today. They prostitute their values, their sense of right and wrong, their very clear understanding of what this is all contributing to in the development and undermining of our young people and society-in-general and they are either turning a blind-eye, or holding up the battle flag of righteous indignation and freedom of expression, which is the ultimate indignant argument that "arteests" use to keep the cash flowing in, despite knowing better. No, it's not a misspelling. These are not "artists" in the true sense of the word. Although, I'm sure there's no shortage of self-flattery and pomposity, claiming that this is exactly what they are, fanning the bonfire of their own vanities (to borrow a phrase), like Mr. Maher and his ilk, while they never lose sight of the most important priority...which is to keep the cash machine running no matter what.

Now, what about our young, our society, and the effect it's having upon them? The "arteests" simply take the position, "DAMN THE TORPEDOES...FULL SPEED AHEAD". God forbid anything should interfere with these hypocrites and their ever-important flow of cash.

Do you think they ever say, "Hey, maybe we should examine our values, you know? Maybe we ought to think about what effect some of this garbage we're putting out is having on our children and our society?" Oh hell no, why do that? They have their kids in the best private schools, as if that will completely shelter them from the world they and we are creating for these kids. Do you really think your children will be sheltered, oh Gods of the Media Industrial Complex and media elite, from the mores, the society, and the world you are creating for them (and we are allowing you to create)? Here, let me give you all a glimpse of yourselves for reflection:

PATRICK F. WALSH

The Media Industrial Complex & Hollywood – "Keep the money flowing ladies and gentlemen & damn the torpedoes... and damn the consequences to our children..."

Sorry to break the news to you all, but the answer is that you are short-sighted and narrow-minded on a scale that is both epic and tragic and it appears that you are working hard to take everyone down with you, intentionally or unintentionally. And guess what...this is one ship, these United States of America, and we are all brothers and sisters together on this ship. And if you take this ship of society down...we all go down with you and your world and your kid's world will go with it, no matter how much money you make...and no temporary, expensive life preserver will change that.

Where is the so-called high-principled, utopian society that our college students of the 60's were protesting and demonstrating to achieve? I'll tell you where it is. The sad truth is that they sold-out in a lot of different areas. The fact is that it was the generation before them that won World War II and sacrificed so very much. It was the generation immediately before them that started the Civil Rights movement in our armed forces,

114

in our society and in congress (e.g. Harry S. Truman, Martin Luther King Jr., Lyndon Johnson, and John F. Kennedy). The children of the 60's certainly jumped on-board and it's to their credit that they did. But it was the generation before them that realized the error and injustice of our ways as a people, with respect to civil rights and with the leadership and sacrifice of Dr. Martin Luther King Jr. They worked to change it. They seemed to examine their collective consciences and eventually had a much healthier message to deliver to our young (through the media in-general), than the generation that is in power today (within the media and behind the media).

The sad part of all of this is that you in the Media Industrial Complex and media elite today are contributing to taking down the most vulnerable members of our society; our children. And you do so callously, for ratings, money and self-preservation and you justify it by using the very principles of freedom upon which this country was founded. However, freedom can also be perverted by those intent on doing the perverting. The reasons may be many, or few; complex or simple... maybe as simple as money and ratings...and the rest is a by-product of your own version of self-preservation in the style and at the level you have become accustomed to.

No one can force you to do the right things. But should anyone have to? Are you children yourselves, after all, or are you adult Americans with children of your own and a sense of moral fortitude and determination and commitment to our country, our people, our heritage, and most importantly, to our future?

Sometimes, it is as simple and as complicated as reflecting upon your actions and cleaning up your act and just **doing the right thing, for the right reasons!**

PATRICK F. WALSH

SO WHAT FOUNDATION CAN OUR KIDS BUILD UPON AND RETURN TO?

As parents, have we all established a foundation for our families? Have we brought our children up telling them to "do what I say and not what I do"? The most powerful foundation is established by children's parents, in the home. It is reinforced by the people they encounter in the school system, their teachers, primarily. As I mentioned in an earlier chapter, it is not the teacher's job to parent a child, or to be expected to be a baby-sitter or stand-in parent. And their foundation is also reinforced by the programs they watch on TV, the movies they see at the theatre and the way they see the people in their government conduct business. They look for and need consistency in the values that are taught to them by their parents, reinforced by their teachers, and hopefully, some day, exemplified in their federal, state and local representatives. I know...the latter is probably the biggest of pipe-dreams. But it sure would be nice.

It only takes a decision. Sound naïve and oversimplified? Maybe. But if there is one conclusion that I have come to in this life, it is that the end-result of what we reap in this life is based upon the results of our choices and our decisions and there are always choices and always decisions. Even in the most narrow of circumstances, believe me, there is always a choice to be made and always a decision involved.

I'll get into this subject more in a subsequent chapter, regarding my opinions about choices and decisions, but I assure you this, we will not elect people of principle and character and we will not turn the tide in the volume of garbage coming out of the Media Industrial Complex and the media elite, unless we walk-the-walk and talk-the-talk, individually, in our own homes, as Americans of every race, gender and preference.

A HARD LOOK IN THE MIRROR

Whether you are a CEO, or a board member of a Hollywood studio or network, or whether you are sweeping the hallways of a school or office building in Smalltown, USA, it starts with us. Take the time, participate, engage, talk to your children, shut off the TV and give your loved-ones the undivided attention and conversation they need in order to know who you are, what you believe and why you believe it and walk-the-walk and talk-the-talk and set the example that our children will reflect upon and ultimately return to, when they stray down that road that you'd rather they not. Because they will, at one time or another, just like you did and I did. They are human, after all.

You must be their foundation as a parent and you must conduct yourself as one, in your relationship with them, as well as in your work and in your life, period. Be courageous and draw the lines and the boundaries, and control what they watch and proudly let them know why and that your no. 1 role is to be their parent, not their best friend, and to take positions and make decisions, based upon their best interest in developing them as responsible, good people and good citizens. Be proud of that role and that stance. It is the most important role we fulfill in our lives. We must all be their foundation. If we do this in our home life, in our work life...in our LIFE, our problems will eventually resolve themselves, over time. Some things can't be legislated...

Will they still rebel? Yes, of course! Will they still stray? In most cases, probably, yes. The important thing is to show them the right standards as best you can and hold-fast to these standards that will ultimately guide them. Because as they stray down some of those wrong roads and find themselves empty inside, or lost in some ways, they will ultimately reflect back upon your example and they will come to know and understand and accept that it was the right example, or at least a version of the right example (we're not perfect as parents, after all). And a funny thing will happen in most cases, I think. They will return to that example and use it as a guide and as a roadmap to return to the right path and they will ultimately thank you for it; if not in words, then surely in actions and you may just have to accept that your thanks will come in the form of seeing them return to a road or path that is a reasonably good one.

THE MOST IMPORTANT LESSONS ARE STILL TAUGHT AT HOME!

CHAPTER 9

EDUCATION AND OUR MIDDLE CLASS - THE STRENGTH OF OUR NATION DEPENDS UPON THE VALUE WE PLACE ON OUR CHILDREN'S EDUCATION

I was educated in the public school system through High School and attended a public University, afterward. I look back upon the experience and feel very fortunate to have grown up in a time when our educational system, for the most part, actually exceeded expectations and in my view, worked as designed. If you applied yourself, you could get a very good education. It's a significant part of what made this country great, both before and after World War II.

I feel fortunate to have had teachers who were hard-working, educated and seemed to love, or at least like what they were doing. In addition, parents then seemed to truly appreciate the work that teachers did and valued their role and contribution in educating our children and helping them to become good and patriotic citizens. There was trust there, flowing back and forth between parents, teachers and children, and in looking back, there was a true appreciation for the role that teachers played in our children's lives and in our country's social infrastructure. It was, and is one of the most important jobs in our society and influences so many important areas of our way of life and development as a society, that it cannot be over-estimated. Our teachers are a major element of the lifeblood of our society. Anyone growing up, who has had a truly great teacher and a truly poor teacher, understands what I am talking about.

Yet, in our society today, we treat our public school teachers with only a slightly higher level of attention and degree of importance as bag-clerks in a grocery store. We look at them as more of a public utility, rather than people who are truly valued and hold a position of great trust and who spend more time with our children during the day than we do. Our teachers have as much or more time to influence our children during the course of a week than parents do. The work that teachers perform helps to determine the type of society we will continue to have, as well as the quality of the education and opportunities our children will receive.

Therefore, how well they teach and how passionate they are about their work is critical. Much of the foregoing depends upon how valued we, as a society, make them feel in doing their job, amongst other things. Our teachers and educational system must be a critical priority for us as parents and as Americans. What are the qualifications that our teachers should bring to the table? What interest do we take in the curriculum they teach? How well do we support their efforts, as parents, to do their job? How well and how often do we communicate with our teachers, on more than just a superficial level? How important do we make them feel about the incredibly important role they fill and job they do? What should their compensation levels be for the qualifications and the demonstrated performance we should be demanding of our teachers and our educational system? Do they have the basic resources they require to do the job we want and expect them to do?

Forget about the answers for the moment. Let's face it, as parents, we haven't even been asking the right questions for way too long. I'm also fairly certain that some of the teachers' unions might maintain that we have no right to ask a few of the questions I've posed, which is another issue which must be examined.

It's these last two points, perhaps, which may be the biggest part of our problem. They suggest that, as parents, many of us just don't show enough interest, much less take some ownership of our educational system, to the degree that we don't know the right questions we should be asking and further, that we've handed over our influence and right to know, relative to educational content and oversight, almost exclusively to the teachers unions and administrators.

Yet, since it is our taxpayer money that is being spent and our children who are being taught, how can we:

A) Not take ownership as parents?
B) Not exercise our right to contribute input into the educational standards and curriculum?
C) Not exercise our right to demand accountability and performance?

What's wrong with this picture?

Unfortunately, when it comes to the public school system, as parents and as a society (excluding the teachers for now), I give us all a collective "F" on our report card. We parents and our politicians and school boards are failing miserably. If there is anyone other than a politician or school board member who would dispute that, I'm not aware of whom they are. I think I've found at least one subject that a vast majority of Americans can agree on.

If you want some hard data to see how our students are doing, note that the OECD Programme for International Student Assessment (PISA) report, which compares the knowledge and skills of 15-year-olds in 65 countries around the world, ranked the United States a below-average 36th out of 65 OECD countries for mathematics, 24th for science and 28th for reading skills.

[Source: PISA OECD Report 2012]

Now, before I start talking too much about the teachers and the unions, which seem to dominate the landscape, I'll first make a few observations about us, the parents, as well as the politicians **we elected** to administer our educational system.

Let's talk first about a state I know a little about, because I live here. A few years after I moved to Florida, someone in state government came up with the bright idea to have a state-run Lottery! And guess what? It was sold to us, the citizens, as The Education Lottery! Just what the doctor ordered, right? It was supposed to voluntarily generate hundreds of millions of dollars *for the education of our children*! Sounds pretty good, right? Heck yes! What could possibly be wrong with that? We want a better education for our kids...right? What parent would answer "no" to that question?

So we approved the Florida Lottery and sure enough, it began generating a windfall of money. Problems solved, right? It got so good that the politicians wanted more and they collectively said amongst themselves "Heck, if we have the drawing twice a week instead of once a week, it could generate up to twice as much cash for us to get our grubby hands on! "Yeehaw" (Cracker politician expression for "heck yes")! And "Si, si, absolutamente... como no?" (Latino-Banana Republic political expression for "Heck yes")!

So the always greedy Crackers and Banana Republicans agreed and said, "Heck yes, here's something we can agree on. Let's do it!" And so they did; and it did generate even more cash.

A HARD LOOK IN THE MIRROR

And since that eventful day, it has been a resounding success...**FOR THE POLITICIANS**.

There's only one problem. The unified, corrupt, Gringo-Cracker-Latino political block that came together in this magnanimous decision, did little more than give the public, the parents, and the children of Florida a unified shafting. **They perpetrated a unique flimflam on every Florida voter. They essentially stole from our children, you see, when you consider the original intent of the Florida Lottery and how it was sold and packaged to the voters.**

What did they do that was so wrong, you ask? Probably the same thing that politicians in other states have done, who used the same deceptive selling strategy with their constituents. They played a multi-billion dollar shell-game with the citizens, and worse, with the children of Florida. Oh, they put the lottery money into education all right. What they didn't tell us was that they took the money that was already being spent on education **prior** to the Lottery and then diverted it to other uses and projects, while substituting the lottery proceeds in what amounts to a zero-sum shell-game (in principle).

They made us think that spending on education would be augmented by this lottery windfall and instead, they pulled money out of the education system with one hand and replaced it with the lottery money with the other. This was done, of course, so that they could put that money to other good uses for the citizens of Florida...you know, like indirectly funding several of the scandals we have seen in our own U.S. version of the Banana Republic, from construction projects and road-building projects that have had relatives of politicos jailed for paying or receiving kickbacks under-the-table, to a huge control tower built in a major international airport in Florida, that had to be partially re-built because you couldn't see the runways from the control tower and for which, again, relatives of politicos were jailed amid scandalous headlines. The politicians are certainly consistent in one thing...they just continue to fail us.

Ok, so much for the politicos. Now, how about us as parents? Clearly, we have the responsibility to be more than just caretakers of our kids, right? We must be PARENTS and advocates and examples to our kids, bringing them up with moral values amidst all of the smut, corruption and drug use in our society. Unfortunately, many of us parents seem to have gotten confused. We seem to have forgotten that our parents raised us in a somewhat different manner and were more interested in being, oh; I don't know...OUR PARENTS, MAYBE?

When I look at some parents today, by contrast, it seems clear to me that in many cases their priorities are reversed. Their interest appears to lie in trying to be their children's best friend, first and foremost in many cases, and being a parent, second, which I don't understand. I know that when I was growing up, parents realized that their primary role was to be our parents, teaching us self-control and limits, morals and values, and teaching us how to treat others with dignity and respect, as well as helping us to know right from wrong and to be certain we received a proper education. They also made certain that when we strayed, they enforced these well-taught principles with consequences, from a smack on the keester, to being restricted to one's room, to having privileges taken away, to writing 100 times "I will not stick my sister's hair in her mashed potatoes at dinnertime".

These responsibilities (among others) and how we carry them out as parents, combined with how involved we are in our children's lives, has a direct correlation to the quality of the education they receive. I will make the connection, shortly.

A HARD LOOK IN THE MIRROR

Unlike the simple concerns of the past, today we're worrying about kids bringing shivs, knives, razors, or automatic weapons into public schools [violence on TV doesn't affect kids, eh?]. Sounds like concerns more appropriate for a federal prison, than our public schools, doesn't it? Today, kids are getting pregnant, getting infected with STD's and using drugs at an alarming rate and at an ever-younger age. Whose fault is it? **"Well, society's of course"**, you may say. Well, my brother and sister American parents of every race, gender, ethnicity and preference, I have a shocking revelation to deliver...**WE'RE SOCIETY**!

Now, taking out and using our old "We're Americans First Filter" and before we look at the school system and our teachers, we have to first look ourselves in the mirror as parents and as brother and sister Americans and admit we have a very serious problem and we're making very serious mistakes and these mistakes are hurting the people we most love, our children, and threatening the future economic and structural security of our nation. We're making our kids grow up much too fast, in a very fast society and we don't seem to care much that we're robbing them of their childhood, not to mention their innocence, at a very early age!

I hear us already...after all, we've got jobs to hold down, reality shows and ESPN to watch, and the next new gadget to buy or website to visit. Think this doesn't affect the quality of education? Read on, please.

Remember, our kids are our future and represent the future of our country. We've got to buckle-down and re-align our priorities as individuals, as families, and as parents and citizens. We've got stop trying to be our kid's best friends, or worse, being uninvolved and distracted, and go back to being their adult parents; focusing on them, enforcing limits and protecting them from the money-grubbing and valueless hordes of movie execs, network execs, drug-dealers and sexual predators in our society.

We need to demand more accountability and action from our politicians. We need to be responsible, devoted and focused parents to our children. We can't be afraid of tough-love or conflict within our households, in standing up to protect our kids and instill values. We must put them first, not our jobs and not ourselves.

We must monitor their TV watching habits and their internet activity when young. Don't order the cable TV channels into your home that peddle smut. Put a filter on your internet access. Monitor their behavior in and out of school and take responsibility for it. Shut off the TV and review their school assignments and enforce study habits. Put aside money to get them extra help when they fall behind (if we can't help them with the study material ourselves). Do without the extras or the perks, or live in a smaller home and make-do with a smaller car, if necessary, to get them the extra tutoring or help that will keep them up-to-speed in their school work and keep their confidence and self-esteem high, when it comes to their studies. Put your money and your time where your mouth is, if you're telling them that education is important. Put them first, not yourself.

CREATIVE, NON-VIOLENT ENFORCEMENT OF STANDARDS – BE THE PARENT

You know, as my kids were growing up, they started challenging the status quo, as all kids do. Once they were beyond 5 or 6 years old, I didn't feel comfortable with giving them a swat on the behind. The old line of "you have to do it because I say so", well, that only works up to a point. So I thought to myself...what form of punishment did I most despise growing up, which was not demeaning, which was not physical and that actually improved something?

Well, in my day, when you did something wrong in school, the teacher would make you write 100 times on paper, "I will not put tacks on

126

Johnny's seat again, for the rest of my natural life." For me, that was the worst. It was tedious, boring, made your hand and fingers cramp-up and made you miss recess time outside with your friends, or made you miss watching your favorite show on TV. I also realized that it improved penmanship. So I tried it with my kids. Guess what? It worked like a charm. They absolutely despised it, just like I did. But they did it, of course, and they weren't allowed out until it was completed. It wasn't demeaning, it wasn't physical and it improved their handwriting and it was effective in changing their behavior. Because they knew I would follow through, even the threat of it became very effective. So, that's just a suggestion for other parents out there.

OK, ENFORCEMENT OF WHAT STANDARDS AND WHAT'S THE CONNECTION TO EDUCATION?

Back to the point; how does all of this relate to education? Well, if we don't send well-behaved, well-disciplined, respectful children (who can demonstrate reasonable self-control) to our teachers, then what do we really expect our teachers to accomplish with our children? If someone gives you a broken-down 1972 Chevy and tells you to work with it so it performs to the level a 2014 Mercedes Benz...well, how successful will you be in doing that? Forget it, right? You must be joking, yes?

Now, using the "We're Americans First Filter", each of us, as brother and sister Americans, have an obligation to each other and to our teachers, to send our teachers children who are well-behaved, respectful and disciplined. That is our most basic job responsibility as parents, relative to our teachers and public schools. So, if we're not doing our job, then how can we possibly expect our teachers to do theirs? Answer: "We can't". They can't do a job that is ours to do and they can't possibly succeed at their job if we don't succeed at ours.

Now, I hesitate to use the expression that I.T. professionals overuse so much, particularly since we're talking about human beings who happen to be our children. But for impact-value alone, maybe it's excusable for me to use it, just this once, to make an impression and a point: "Garbage-In/Garbage-Out..."

Are you angry? Are you appalled? Did I get your attention? Good, that was the intent. The message is for us Parents (yes, with a capital "P"), to "clean up our act", first. Now, this may not be easy and may require some re-prioritizing in our lives. It will require that we put our children's environment, stability and mental state, first. By mental state, I mean providing them first and foremost with a primary parent's time, so that this parent may provide a structured, orderly, secure environment, focusing on love, affection, God, morals, health, hygiene, mental stimulation and challenge, schooling and exercise and to provide this in a structured routine, daily, weekly, monthly, consistently. Kids need and thrive on the right structure and it's an essential part of them feeling loved and secure in their environment and in developing a confident, well-grounded human being (by the way, in the interests of full disclosure, my wife taught me all of this!).

These structured routines build a child's sense of security and self-esteem. Before they ever reach school-age, it means assuring that they get proper sleep required for proper development and that they rise at a consistent time, eat meals at consistent times (that are nutritious and wholesome) and those daily routines of reading to our children and seeing that they get exercise and observe proper hygiene rules, takes place. It means educating ourselves as parents to understand what it takes to raise a well-rounded child.

It means teaching them the difference between right and wrong and teaching them morals and enforcing the correct behavior. It means teaching them these things in a disciplined way and drawing lines of acceptable and non-acceptable behavior and enforcing those lines; not as their friend, but as their parent; which is a sacred role. Do you think these things taught at home don't have an impact on the overall quality of education they receive? Read on, please.

It means taking an interest in teaching them rules of conduct and when they enter pre-school and elementary school, taking an interest in what they are learning and whether or not they are both understanding and learning it. It also means helping them so that they can stay focused and don't fall behind. So if you don't have the time, knowledge, or the temperament to help them, then find a few dollars by cutting expenses, or earn some extra dollars to get them that help. Because the better prepared they feel and the more you as a parent can get them ahead of the game, the higher their self-esteem and confidence and the greater their appreciation and love for learning and education.

HOW THE HECK CAN I DO MORE, I DON'T HAVE THE RESOURCES OR TIME?

How can I do this, some of us may ask? I don't make enough money and we need both parents working, you say? Well, it may require that we sacrifice and settle for less of life's necessities, conveniences and pleasures. No way around that. It may require that we do what's necessary to keep our marriages and our homes together, for the children's good, whether your wife or husband drives you crazy, or not. It may require that we get off of our collective behinds from in front of the TV set, or leave our work earlier, to know and be interested in what our children are doing and get them involved in sports, the arts and other after-school activities and actually attend those events.

It may require that we take a "Back to the Future" approach and have a parent in the home full-time; whenever possible (this would be the ideal approach). Some may still say this last one is not economically feasible. Well, you know what? My wife and I moved out of a house and downsized. I drove a car that was 8 years old and had over a hundred thousand miles on it and we got by on less, so that she could be full-time with our kids and you know what? Within one month we could see an astounding, positive difference in our kids. I take my hat off to my wife for this decision and for being there for our kids. Looking back, it was the best thing we could have done for our family and for them. It made all the difference in how our kids are turning out.

So, let's look at ourselves as parents first, which is our primary role, before we look at the teachers and school system. This is the first and most important half of the equation (we'll tackle the other half in a moment). Let's make certain we assume ownership and control over our children and stop trying to be their best friend at the expense of being their father and mother and I assure you, your kids will think better of you for it. They need guidance and limits and they don't need to grow up so fast. They need to have a childhood and they need to be able to experience their own, personal "age of innocence", before they enter into an unforgiving world.

In today's media-driven society, only you/we, their parents can protect them and it requires more vigilance and effort than ever before, because we don't live in the America of our fathers and mothers. While I'm just a middle-class, middle-America guy, I realize this and I think it's clear to most parents out there.

At the end of the day, if we're not prepared to make the changes and sacrifices necessary to be good parents and fulfill our half of the responsibilities in our children's development (before we go pointing fingers at the teachers and the public school system), then I suggest that we instead use a little of the available science out there and reading material and don't impregnate a woman in the first place; and women, don't get pregnant in the first place. Brother and sister Americans, we must take at least this much personal responsibility.

OK, BUT WHAT ABOUT OUR POLITICIANS, OUR SCHOOL SYSTEM AND OUR TEACHERS?

Now, what about our politicians, our schools systems and our teachers, you ask? Well, there are still many good-eggs out there. But we've allowed our system of education to decay. Our kids score poorly compared to other industrialized countries and our public schools have turned into glorified day-care centers. In many cases our schools are being sent problem-children (our problem children) and they are staffed with some teachers who are more concerned with their power base, their benefits and their Union, than they are about truly teaching our children and getting quality, meaningful results. So, what do we need to do?

In my personal view, we have to attack these issues on multiple fronts. I may be a middle-class, middle-income citizen, but having been in business for many years, I have been responsible, at times, for running regional organizations of up to about 600 or more people for some large global companies and budgets of over $100 million with multiple facilities. Therefore, I can tell you that, from my perspective, we have to take a different approach and look at the whole system more in-line with running a business; **the business of education**.

There is nothing wrong, in my opinion, with applying certain business principles to education. A business approach forces one to identify short, medium, and long-term goals and objectives. It causes us to analyze and identify those issues and problems that are causing us to fail in meeting those goals and objectives. It forces us to identify the root-causes and the corrective actions necessary to fix the problems and to identify precisely how we go about implementing those corrective actions. It requires that we monitor those corrective actions to assure they are working and that we have both identified and addressed the correct root-cause(s) and the effective corrective actions, or failing that, to go back and re-analyze.

It also requires that we hold the management responsible for achieving turn-around results and for making the changes in personnel, process and policy, required to do that. To illustrate what I'm talking about, let me provide some examples:

1. **Root-Cause #1**: Are we sending the schools and our teachers well-behaved, well-disciplined, respectful children who are prepared to learn? In many cases no.

   Corrective Action #1: I have addressed part of the corrective action, above, in my comments about our responsibilities as parents. The second part of the corrective action is to empower administrators to send children who are not well-behaved, well-disciplined and respectful, home to their parents, until they are.

   What are the parents supposed to do? I don't know and quite frankly I don't care. It's not my concern. It's their concern and they need to take ownership and they need to figure it out. We can't keep dumping problem-kids on our teachers and the school system. It's a school system, not a day-care system. These kids that have the behavior and attitude problems are hurting the kids that want to learn and are keeping the teachers and administrators from being able to do their jobs in a fair, responsible and efficient manner. This is a parent-problem, not a school or teacher problem.

2. **Root-Cause #2** - Quality of our Public School Teachers and their Management: Let the outcry from our teachers and their unions,

begin...I'm sure that if any teachers'-union type reads this, I'll be vilified for it. Sorry, but someone has to be willing to tell the Emperor he's wearing no clothes.

In business, assuming one has a viable product or service, success can be based, to a great extent, upon a company's ability to attract and hire the best people, and for the management of that company to select and surround itself with the best possible leadership talent. Like baseball, football or business, all other things being equal, it is the talent that you are able to attract and hire that will be the primary difference-maker between success and failure of a business.

How that talent is led, developed, managed, coached and deployed, are the other critical factors in the equation. In our school systems today, we are clearly failing in our competition with the rest of the industrialized world (for the most part). I cite the previous performance report mentioned. We are not focused clearly enough on the quality of our leadership in our schools, their management, or on the teachers we are recruiting. We are not focused enough on the relevance of the curriculum they teach, or the processes they employ in teaching it.

We are not correctly targeting and mandating the right objectives and goal-oriented outcomes. We are absolutely setting the bar too low in these areas, and we are demonstrating this by paying our teachers...sorry to say...dirt in many cases and by not creating a desirable, rewarding, and competitive environment in which teachers may practice their craft as valued professionals and be paid competitive wages with the private sector, which by the way, is what successful businesses do. That's just the way it is!

Corrective Action #2: - Using our "We're Americans First Filter" (yes, that pesky thing), we see that we have to make a few fundamental, value-based decisions. How much do we value our kids and how serious are we about preserving the middle class (and access to move into the middle class for those less fortunate)?

We must decide this because access to the middle class relies upon the availability of quality public education for upward mobility! We must also decide how much we value our leadership position in the world, because if you don't think this relies on access to quality public education as well, then think again. Now, if we value these things, and I for one do, then are we willing to **efficiently and effectively** put our money where our mouth is?

If the answer is yes, then we have to do at least four things, in addition to other measures I've mentioned (and some I haven't yet covered):

First, we have to assure that curriculums are revamped, including a heavy dose of True American History, so our children know who they are and from whence they came (as Americans), and the rich heritage they share, whether they just arrived in the U.S. yesterday, or whether their roots go back generations.

Second: We have to re-institute the classics and begin to teach children that culture and a well-rounded education leads to a well-rounded person and a well-rounded adult, who can engage in meaningful reflection, contribute to society and to the world-at-large in an articulate, well-balanced, well-rounded manner that is value-based.

A HARD LOOK IN THE MIRROR

Third: We have to set much higher standards and implement stricter quantitative and qualitative testing for entry into the teaching profession. We must also incorporate personality testing and analysis requirements into the mix, for someone to become a teacher in our society (personality analysis is commonly done in private industry today).

We must do this in order to reasonably assure that they have the knowledge, discipline, and personality makeup to be a successful teacher and thereby give the role and the profession the recognition and the value it deserves (and should have), and to assure that we are hiring well-rounded, well-educated, capable individuals, so as to set our teachers up for success, in order to teach the treasure that is our children and is the future of our society and our country.

Fourth: We must significantly increase the pay-scales for this honorable and important profession, across the board. As in business, if you hire more qualified people and set higher entry standards than other, similar companies and want to be a leader in your industry and create a value-based organization, then you'd better be prepared to pay more for the better-educated, more well-rounded and more highly motivated talent; and make no mistake about it, generally speaking, those who have put in the hard work and deliver the better results, are, the majority of the time, the more highly motivated individuals.

You can't set higher standards without higher compensation levels. You simply won't attract the talent. One without the other doesn't work.

Furthermore, it's important to consider that teaching our nation's children might be a highly desirable job for many people. It can be a noble and rewarding profession. One reason that the job doesn't attract the best and the brightest in most cases, is because few of the best and brightest are willing to make the sacrifices to go into the environment of today's public school system, which does not value teachers and what they are trying to accomplish, particularly for the amount of money they would make. Both areas, amongst others I've mentioned, must be addressed, decisively.

One word of caution: should anyone in government be thinking that you can raise the standards without raising the compensation and without paying the most qualified people more money, then you've missed the point and are doomed to failure, not to mention the fact that you are living in a world of fantasy.

Root-Cause #3 - Lack of local, parental involvement with our schools, school boards and elections: We drop our kids at school, go to work, come home, turn on the TV, or read social media, or the newspaper, and the schools run themselves.

Let me ask a question...Does any business put the general employees in charge of determining business strategy, tactics, long-term goals and objectives and hiring? So, if we as parents have the control...and make no mistake about it, we do, and many don't realize it, then why are we not asserting ourselves and our control? We are, after all, the board of directors (the last time I checked) and the school board and teachers ultimately report to us. If we are not active in consistently being aware of our children's curriculum and if we are not meeting with their teachers, regularly, and assuring that our kids do their homework correctly every night and understand it, and if we are not participating in school board elections and attending PTA meetings, then it's a fair bet we're not nearly as involved as we should be with our role as the board of directors of the school system. Let's face it, at the end of the day IT'S ON US! The quality of our children's education will be only as good as the level of our involvement and our oversight.

Corrective Action #3 – Put down the remote, get offline, put down your iphone, put down the sports section and find out how your school system really runs. Learn about the school board, its candidates, their views, philosophies, backgrounds and training and get others involved. Ask the principal of your child's school these questions, simply as a matter of educating yourself about the system and then educate like-minded parents. Get involved and attend meetings. You not only have the right, but you have the **obligation** to be a member of the Board of Directors that puts the people in place who make these decisions and who are **supposed to make these decisions in your behalf, for the benefit of your children!**

All in all, we have to be the parents that many of our parents were to us, back in the day. Our teachers and our school systems have to go "Back to the Future", to re-claim one of the jewels in the crown that made this country and our society, great. We need to put ourselves last and our country's children, first! If we're not willing to do that, then we're not willing to continue to be in contention to remain one of the greatest countries in the world. We are straying too far from the core-values and the model educational system that were part of the foundation that built this country.

PATRICK F. WALSH

One more point and please don't react until you've read this in its entirety:

In making significant changes of the type I'm suggesting, it may be necessary for congress to curb the power of public school teachers unions. We cannot have teachers unions setting the agenda, or we will continue with the malaise we have today. Let's face it, teachers unions' agendas (they way they've been run in this day and age) are to lower standards, raise pay, reduce working hours and obtain better benefits. They are not focused on what's best for the children. They are focused on what's best for the teachers, within a very narrow band of self-interest, in my opinion.

In my view, the vocation of teaching is a public trust, not a private enterprise, even though I have introduced elements of private enterprise into the recommendations I've made for change, simply because they are proven to be efficient and get results. We must have the children's interest at heart, first and foremost, as well as the nation's best interest at heart.

Overall, to do what I suggest requires guts, vision, integrity and commitment. If you curb the power of the teachers unions, raise the qualifications and entry requirements to become a teacher, raise the pay and benefits across the board and tie pay raises, bonuses and promotions to performance, outcomes and continuing professional education and install strong management and leadership, then and only then, may we have a winning formula again. Do these things and we'll be elevating the honorable profession and title of teacher to the level of appreciation and admiration it should have, in a society that values learning, values achievement and values its' children and its' educational system.

To get us to where we want to be again as a nation, our educational system needs to be the Crown Jewel of our society and our country. Equality starts with equal access to quality public education and today that's just not the case. It's one of the foundational elements of our country and our society, which is today suffering, as the rich get richer, the poor get poorer, and the middle class shrinks.

My wife and I gave up on the public school system, early on in our children's lives. We saw what had become of what was once the Crown Jewel of our society. It had become nothing more than a polished piece of glass, chipped and broken. We sacrificed mightily, with money we didn't have, to put and keep our kids in private school. We begged, borrowed and borrowed some more. But we got them the quality education we wanted for them.

We, you, all of us as Americans, should never have to sacrifice our present and future financial stability and security to pay for that which should be our birthright as citizens of this great country.

Let's commit to this as a nation and as Americans of every race, gender and preference. Believe me; we'll be proud of ourselves if we vote people into office that will help us to do this and if we also take our own personal, active roles in our neighborhood schools and school boards to see it done.

...and make no mistake, if you take nothing else from these pages, please take this with you. **It is our Values, our Work Ethic and our Courage that have made this a great nation; not our money or our guns. Let's assure we continue to make the right choices, when it comes to our children and their education and what has been their birthright.**

Chapter 10

GOD, RELIGION AND ETHICS, UNDER FIRE IN AMERICA? ...

I've really been looking forward to expressing what I'm sure certain pundits and the media elite would characterize as primitive, neanderthalish, Pollyanna-ish type opinions on this subject...

I look around and have seen people like former Senator John Edwards, The Acorn group, Tiger Woods, Lindsey Lohan, Michael Jackson, Governor Rod Blagojevich, Anna Nicole Smith, Governor Mark Sanford and others who seem to have lost their way in life; that is, who appear to have morally lost their way and who have veered off the course they might normally have followed, had they been using a working moral-compass. Two tragically lost their lives and the others, I hope, are only temporarily lost. Acorn, as you may remember, in its own right, was seemingly a morally-flawed organization. In all of these cases, there seems to be the lack of, or failure of a certain moral-spiritual grounding that might otherwise have kept them on course, either preventing them from losing their way, or from giving in, or from becoming confused; or at least when lost, to have been able to engage in a rapid course correction to put them more quickly, but not necessarily painlessly, back on their way.

PATRICK F. WALSH

LOOK AROUND, WHAT DO YOU SEE?

I look around and see rampant sex and promiscuity celebrated and defended by the media elite, as perceived societal norms today, being both popularly accepted and acceptable, held up to be mimicked, with little regard to seriously examining or even wanting to examine the repercussions, which we and our children are experiencing every day. Few if any media-born adults (a term I will explain) want to even consider examining this in any deeply introspective way, in terms of the effects on our youngest, most defenseless members of our society...our children, who are being forced by the avaricious, irresponsible, and/or downright lazy adults and media in our society, to grow-up way too fast, much faster than I ever did, and to be forced to do so without a choice or say-so in the matter. This, while sexually transmitted diseases are running rampant in our country, with few if any in the media caring about the cost and the tragedy this presents to the health, the spirit, the psyche, or the innocent-essence of these most precious members of our society, who will be the future of our great Democratic-Republic.

Our children are being systematically robbed of anything resembling the type of childhood that was a birthright for many; the birthright that allowed them to be kids for a time, except in the most deprived or depraved of situations.

I see what were once serious news organizations, ignoring the danger and the chaos, spending their time criticizing and marginalizing those who hold strong moral and religious beliefs and who make efforts to hold back the tide, criticizing those who embrace God and who believe, as I do, that this great nation and its Founding Fathers were a creation intended by and inspired by God, as a beacon to the world, which was and is intended to show how a society of men and women can overcome some of their common human weaknesses, imperfections and even temptations to, day-by-day, build a great society and evolve constantly, moving to become a more unified, brotherly, strong and free society, hopefully within the guidelines of divinely inspired moral standards, intended for our good as a people and as a society.

I hear the outcry from parents, surely most parents, not just the ones I know, regarding how difficult it is to raise children in our society today, which gives the appearance of a society both morally and spiritually in decline and in the process of potentially running amok.

Surely the children of our media-born elite, the so called trend-setters, the ever-so-in-crowd, are just as challenged as other children are; meaning that our media-born elite, as parents, are also just as challenged, even if they prefer not to admit it to themselves or others, lest they have to admit certain "inconvenient truths" to themselves, if not to others...

SO WHAT IS THE MEDIA-BORN ELITE AND WHO ARE THEY?

Now, back to the term media-born elite...and get ready for a mouthful. I was trying to come up with a term to describe the self-absorbed, narcissistic, race-baiting, conflict-inspiring, overbearing, fingernail-on-blackboard screeching media elite of our day, who seem intent on drawing attention and ratings to themselves by exhibiting this very behavior described. This seems, in theory, to be the modern-day process to achieve short-to-medium term media stardom and, sadly, also appears to be accepted as a modern-day substitute for brains, logic, intelligent discourse, and a perspective on history.

In this crowd, I throw both liberal and conservative types. The poster-boy and personally most annoying of the liberals, is of course, Bill Maher.

PATRICK F. WALSH

There is no one in today's popular media, liberal or conservative in my opinion, who behaves in a more shallow, callous, or hostile way towards traditional American values than Maher. I must admit to a certain bias in this. Truthfully, this guy just rubs me the wrong way and his inability to offer an in-depth, well thought-out position, while at the same time articulating mostly emotional hot-air, drivel and contempt for traditional values and religion, combined with his lack of understanding of basic economic principles, while holding himself out as some type of modern-day sage, puts him at the very top of my media-born elite list of the most intellectually light-weight contrarians to the vision of the Founding Fathers. But of course, I will defend unto my death, his right to drivel-on...

Now, the poster-boy for the conservative right, the foil to Maher, well, I must give first place to the one of many (as opposed to the one and only), Sean Hannity. Hannity certainly has more intellectual firepower than Maher. Now, I'll be the first to say that maybe I'm not being fair to Hannity, in comparing him to Maher, but this is his own fault. Like Maher, I can't listen to Hannity for any length of time that would allow me to discern further. His immature style and his emotional screeching (like Maher's), has me turning him off within minutes, and sometimes even seconds.

These two remind me of petulant children on a rant, jumping up and down, and anyone who disagrees with either of them just gets an immediate blast of hot-air to try and overpower, bully, interrupt or destabilize the person holding a different opinion. They are the epitome of today's media-born elite. The modern media; mostly short on history, facts, disciplined minds and perspective, and long on hype, emotion and superficiality, have given birth to this type of media man-child; thus the term, media-born elite.

Ok, here's the hard part. It pains me to say that a close second on the right is Bill O'Reilly. My sincere apologies in advance to O'Reilly in one sense, because I actually hold with several of his positions on traditional values and education, at least as I perceive his positions to be, and I respect his guts and actually like the man. There's something traditional and endearing about him, as I referenced in an earlier chapter, above and beyond the rhetoric.

But when it comes to vitriolic, hyperbole-addicted monologue and over-bearing, fingernail-on-the-blackboard bully-boys...well, O'Reilly definitely qualifies, just behind Maher and Hannity. Sometimes I find that I want to reach through the TV screen, grab him by the lapels, shake him like his mother or father might have done (or should have done) and yell: "For heaven's sake, O'Reilly, give somebody the courtesy of allowing them to speak and finish their sentences. Certainly your parents must have taught you the manners of civil conversation and discourse, as well as basic respect for others opinions and their right to speak!"

Other times, when it gets to be just too much and the constant interruption and talking-over others becomes just too oafish, I simply shut it off, out of my own personal annoyance and, oddly, out of some measure of embarrassment for him and his guest. Nothing personal you understand. As I said, I respect him and his guts and, for me, he's a likeable person, when not being a boor.

ARE WE GOING THE WAY OF PAST, FAILED-SOCIETIES AND CULTURES? THE GLUE THAT HOLDS US TOGETHER AS A NATION...

While many of us have asked this question about our country over time, today, we do seem more and more to be going the way of the old Roman Empire and other morally decayed, spiritually bankrupt, live-for-today and anything-goes-type societies. **We of course can now add "economically suicidal" to the description to complete the picture.** Anyone who wants to deny that simply does not want to see reality or think logically. They are being willfully blind.

Let's see, through no choice or fault of their own, our innocent children and young adults of today have been forced to be overexposed to sex, violence, and drug use from a young age. They see it in television, movies, and publications from our friends in Hollywood and on Madison Avenue, as well as in the school systems. Then on top of that, we're setting them up for a debt burden sure to bring about heavy economic consequences. If we keep going like this, they're not going to refer to US as the "greatest generation". They'll instead be referring to us with the seven words you thought you couldn't say on TV (until we got through with the medium, of course).

We are now making condoms available in "enlightened" school systems in the Northeast, from kindergarten, up. How proud we should be of our liberal, worldly perspective now, eh? What a pathetic milestone we've reached and what a sad testament to our society this represents, that this has been deemed necessary for our children? It wasn't necessary in my day...Kindergarten...? Really?

Well, we do have sexually transmitted diseases at some of the highest levels in our history and especially amongst the young, teenage and college-age segment of our society. So one may argue that this is why we are handing out condoms to our kindergarteners. **Hell, it's easier than doing the right thing, I guess...**

If you listen to the Bill Maher crowd, the problems are not a function of our morality as a society (or lack thereof), or our irresponsibility in protecting our young, or in our failure to make or enforce laws to try and clean up society a bit. If you listen to his crowd, it's not a function of the fact that we don't demand more of each other as responsible adults and parents (whether we work in Hollywood, on Madison Avenue, or on Main Street) and likewise require more responsible conduct on the part of the media, so that our next generation *of children,* and the generation after that, is more protected and not robbed of their childhood and their innocence...Heck, it's not about being smart and doing what's in our children's best interest, is it? Oh, hell no! It's not about any of that "responsible adult", "responsible society" stuff! It's about education and condoms! That's the ticket!

Well, if you're going to put our children on a steady diet of filth, porn, violence and drug-themed material from a young age, and apparently revel in that and celebrate what a great free, enlightened and liberal society we have as a result, then I guess there *is* some logic to handing out condoms to kindergartners! Can't argue with that; except insofar as the inherent, blatant, shortsightedness and stupidity that it demonstrates of course...

Oops, that's right, excuse me, I'm not supposed to think, question, or engage my mind...I'm not supposed to notice, or point out the obvious logical conclusion. And by the way, neither are **YOU!** And that's what they count on. Oops, sorry, I forgot again. It's not politically correct. But you know what? That felt kind of good. Let me sneak another one in... **"The Emperor has no clothes on..."**

Is there anyone with a brain and some adult perspective who does not believe that any society that feels that it has to hand out condoms to kindergartners, has a serious problem and has some inherent societal disease going on that is corrupting that society from within? Really, isn't it safe to conclude this, if you are a thinking, functioning, rational adult, who does not have his or her head stuck deep in the ground, or deep into some bodily orifice? Are we in such societal denial and lacking such rational perspective that we can't see the obvious?

But listen to Mr. Maher and some of the other pundits and Hollywood-types, and a fair number of liberal Americans, and they will tell you that handing out condoms to kindergartners is our current version of responsible, adult logic from our current Great Society. By this logic then, it's always better to treat the symptom, not the cause of the illness. Of course, to sane, rational, adult people with a functioning mind, this is nothing but crazy, not to mention rather horrifying.

Well, I suppose if you were going to distribute handguns to kids in class (e.g. give them the societal message that carrying and using handguns is a good and healthy thing for kindergartners), then it would also make logical sense to hand out Kevlar body armor too, right? It doesn't mean it's smart, or in the children's best interest. But it's logical, right?...Right, Mr. Maher and friends?

Oh hell! Just give me a break, ok? This is about the filth and violence in our movies, on our television sets, in our homes, on the internet, and on our streets. This is about Dateline finding no shortage of shameless perverts, audacious enough to go to children's homes to try to molest them.

Now, I'm not so naïve as to think we can make a wish and suddenly the genie goes back in the bottle, but I am saying that if we don't do something, the comparisons to the old Roman Empire and the disintegration of our moral and societal fabric will be more practical fact, than some esoteric discussion. I frankly think we're getting there and moving ever-more-quickly towards it.

Violence...teen violence to be exact? You've seen the news excerpts and videos from YouTube and other sites showing teen-on-teen violence, even among teenage girls. You've seen the weapons being brought into our schools and the need for metal detectors, police on school property, and outsourced security guards. I came from a very average, middle-class family. We didn't have any of that, nor did we need it.

Now, as an adult, in my own county here in South Florida, a young boy was set aflame while sitting on a chair next to a pool. Two of his classmates poured a flammable liquid on him and set him on fire. He was in the hospital for months, fighting for his life. Yet, I'm certain that the liberal media and Mr. Maher and his contemporaries would tell you that these things have nothing whatever to do with the rampant violence on TV and in video games and on the internet, which portray violence simply for violence' sake, not even as the means towards any particular ends, except sales revenue $$$.

They might also tell you that it has nothing whatever to do with the trend in media-society to expunge God and religious and moral teachings from every aspect of our children's lives.

I'm not saying that any other modern society on the planet is in significantly better shape, but I am saying that this has contributed to causing our society, "one nation, under-God, indivisible, with liberty and justice for all", to begin to crack at the seams. The mortar that holds our society together, in my opinion, is our moral values and our commitment to each other as Americans and as Parents (yes, again with the capital "P"), to protect the weakest and most vulnerable in our society. The other elements I have mentioned are also critical to maintaining our place in the world, as well as to continuing our growth and development as a nation. For you see, without these, we cannot not be credible (even amongst ourselves) in believing that we are the greatest nation in the world.

Our founding ideals, our independence, our personal freedoms, our natural resources, our system of government, our commitment to Capitalism, our laws, our history of bringing peoples of all cultures and nations to our shores as Americans; all of these are elements that, in-part, provide the foundation for a potentially great society and people. But the key ingredient which transforms these basic elements into a truly great society, which inspires us to love this nation, to love each other as fellow Americans, to welcome others to our shores, to abolish slavery,

149

and which has allowed us to proudly elect our first black President? **Well, we are, at our heart, a nation that holds moral values and human justice, which are derived from religion, and thereby God, in the very highest regard, and it was and is central to our birth, development, and existence as a nation, and as a government By, For and Of the People. Just ask the Pilgrims...**

Now, many other peoples and nations have viewed us as a nation of glorified Pollyanna's; the simple, unsophisticated, sometimes oafish and unrefined, too-honest-for-our-own-good Americans. The Europeans, Russians and countless others have snickered at us, both behind our backs and to our faces. But they were all, eventually, made to face the folly of their own arrogance. After all, one can't argue with results. In the end, our Pollyanna-ish, unsophisticated, oafish and mostly honest ways, combined with the many other critical factors I have mentioned, contributed to building the greatest nation the world has ever seen (so far).

Now it seems that it's the Chinese who see us in the same light others have. Will they similarly be proven wrong? The question in my mind is can we sustain it? Can we reinforce and maintain the foundation of our moral values? Can we continue to successfully replace the mortar that is cracking, before the structure begins to crumble? All the elements to replace the cracking mortar are still there. They have all been provided and earned by those before us. But the real question is, do we have the moral will, commitment, and desire as a people, to see what we must do and do it? We must also remember that, if the mortar is cracking, as I maintain, then we likewise have the moral obligation to do something about it, because we, as others before us, perpetually owe a debt that will never be fully paid, to God, to our Founding Fathers and to our brother and sister Americans before us, and to those who have laid down their lives, defending the values of our nation and our Great American Experiment. Will we, as a people, be up to the challenge?

A HARD LOOK IN THE MIRROR

CAN WE CHANGE COURSE?

Well, we have all the critical elements required to change course. We still have our freedom, our system of government, and I believe the most critical elements, our collective will as a people and our connection, loyalty, and devotion to each other and to this great country, as Americans of every race and gender!

I believe that in our hearts, we all want the best for our children and our country, including the Bill Maher's and his genre. I think we all realize that there is something seriously wrong with our society and the direction taken by many of our young, with graduation rates in high school dropping and gang violence and the number of kids participating in gangs, rising.

If that's so and if we agree that this is so, then it means we admit we have a problem and that's the first step in solving it. Then the only things we need are strong leaders and a political party and platform that will carry out our will as a people. We can reverse course and send this country back on the right path. Our vote is still the most powerful weapon we wield in any fight to win important battles from within our borders, as long as we are not lazy about it and as long as we take ownership of our shared responsibilities to each other.

We can influence the makeup of our congress and our courts and we can determine our President. It is our decisions about who will hold these positions in all three areas, as well as in our local governments and school boards, which will ultimately decide how significantly and quickly we can change course. We can, as a people, influence the laws governing the protection of our young in school, in the classroom, in the television medium and in the motion picture medium, through regulation of the industry. We can say "no" to the purveyors of filth and the purveyors of extreme violence for violence' sake, when it comes to our children being force-fed a steady diet of same (whether we as parents like it or not). Really, it needs to start with us. We need to exercise moral self-discipline, if we wish to instill it in our young. At the end, we are the examples they will learn from. It starts with us.

We can also protect our young physically, in the schools, as mentioned previously, by allowing administrators to eject those who disrupt the teaching environment, placing the responsibility where it belongs, on us, the parents, to keep our children in-line, behaving as they should and by allowing the legal system to harshly punish those who commit violence in our schools, or who commit sex crimes against our young.

We can influence the agenda of what is taught in our schools, by participating in school-board elections and school board meetings. We simply need to turn the TV off, get off the couch and get on with our responsibilities as Americans in this grand and noble experiment started by our Founding Fathers, which they fully intended for us to take seriously and to own. We can never lose sight of that.

We seem to have voluntarily given up ownership of our country, our cities, our towns, and control of our children's educational agenda, in order to stay glued to our flat-screen TV's and our sports-fixes, our reality-shows and our fantasy leagues. Reversing course in the areas we should is well within our control, should we choose to responsibly exercise that control and should we send the right messages to the politicians. As I stated previously, in my opinion, the first move is to CLEAN HOUSE with the majority of them and implement immediate term limits and require those running for office to state their key positions in writing, and essentially make a contract with their constituency. If we put the correct people in office at the Presidential and Congressional levels and do the same at the gubernatorial and at the lower, local level positions, then we will, by default, get the judiciary we need to carry out our will in the courts, as well.

So the answer is yes, we can address what ails us as a country. As long as the majority of Americans are on the same page as to what we need to do. The main thing is that The American People must clearly understand and accept that WE hold the power in our hands, until such time as WE allow it to be taken away, or WE voluntarily give it away, through laziness and apathy. WE hold the ultimate power in our hands and it is indeed, our vote. But we can't be lazy and apathetic about it. We must be clear about what we want and what we indeed demand. We must not elect those who are not prepared to give us what we want, namely, that which we believe is in the best interests of our young people, our country, and our legacy as Americans. We don't want to end up as the generation that let our country down. We must be clear and we must be together on this, without regard to race, color, gender, or national origin. **This must be a new day.**

CHAPTER 11

IMMIGRATION REFORM AND DOING THE RIGHT THING...

Staying True to Our Foundational American Values, While Keeping the Faith with Ourselves and Those Seeking Freedom

The Year is 1907

Theodore Roosevelt's ideas on Immigrants and being an AMERICAN in 1907.

'In the first place, we should insist that if the immigrant who comes here in good faith becomes an American and assimilates himself to

A HARD LOOK IN THE MIRROR

us, he shall be treated on an exact equality with everyone else, for it is an outrage to discriminate against any such man because of creed, or birthplace, or origin. But this is predicated upon the person's becoming in every facet an American, and nothing but an American... There can be no divided allegiance here. Any man who says he is an American, but something else also, isn't an American at all. We have room for but one flag, the American flag... We have room for but one language here, and that is the English language. And we have room for but one sole loyalty and that is a loyalty to the American people.'

- Theodore Roosevelt 1907

Ok, black or white, man or woman, whatever national origin you may be...let's put our cards on the table, *together.* Let's get into our "We're all Americans First" state of mind and simply talk intelligently to each other, understanding that there are sensitivities involved in this subject, but that we must have an honest conversation with each other.

Take a moment and look again at the photo above and read the words of one of our great President's, who was closely connected to the character, vision and mindset of our 1776 Founding Fathers. He cared deeply about our nation. He cared deeply about **all of our people** of every ethnicity and gender. He cared profoundly about all of our lands and was an avid and passionate conservationist. Indeed, the case can be made that he was the first "Green" President in our Nation's history and a prolific proponent of the National Parks movement, to conserve our treasured natural resources and forests.

Do you resent and find demeaning (as I do), the labels that Politically Correct society and politicians have us bear? Do you resent the hyphenation of our identity as "fill-in-the-blank Americans", as I do? Based upon the words spoken above by the great Theodore Roosevelt, I believe he would have found this modern hyphenation of our identity an "outrage", as he puts it, above.

Do you ever wonder, as I do, why there seems to be a necessity these days in our society to label fellow Americans by assigning prefixes to their status as Americans, which denotes cultural, ethnic, or national origins? Do you ever resent and find fault with this practice, as I do, because you feel that it is a means to try and pry us apart from each other, rather than unify us as Americans; the unity our Founding Fathers and leaders like Theodore Roosevelt intended for us?

"She's African-American...", "He's Latino-American...", She's Asian-American...", "He's Spanish-American...", "He's Arab-American".

Honestly, this makes me ill and I'd imagine it makes a fair number of other Americans ill, particularly those who are the subject of the labels. Now, I'm not of African descent, nor Latino descent, nor Asian descent. I do have Irish and Italian heritage in my family background, as well as German, but I've never thought of myself as Irish-American, Italian-American or German-American. I've never been labeled that, either. And if I was labeled that, I can tell you for certain that I'd resent the hell out of it. Why, you ask? Am I ashamed of my family's heritage? Of course I'm not. I'm proud of it. But I've never thought of myself as anything but an American. Because I embrace our country's roots and its heritage, going all the way back to 1776, and because I believe, as Theodore Roosevelt believed, *"that if the immigrant who comes here in good faith becomes an American and assimilates himself to us, he shall be treated on an exact equality with everyone else, for it is an outrage to discriminate against any such man [or woman] because of creed, or birthplace, or origin. But this is predicated upon the person's becoming in every facet an American, and nothing but an American...There can be no divided allegiance here. Any man [or woman] who says he is an American, but something else also, isn't an American at all."*

A HARD LOOK IN THE MIRROR

This great former President would himself have found this practice to be an "outrage", going against the very principles this country was founded upon. I believe he would have deemed it a form of discrimination to call someone an African-American, a Latino-American, etc., as he describes above. And I would go on to add that any of us who refer to a fellow American by those hyphenated labels, demeans that person's status as an American, and by doing so, suggests he or she is something other than a legitimate, complete American. We are all brother and sister Americans, equal in our status as citizens and no such distinctions should be made, lest we divide ourselves as a people and country. That's my opinion and it doesn't matter to me who wants to disagree. I do indeed believe that "a house divided cannot stand."

Remember, America has always been about all of us being united as a single people. Most of our families before us, immigrated to these shores in hopes of becoming Americans. Certainly we embrace our respective national origins and cultures and that will always be part of our American DNA and we should all love and respect that about each other. It adds so very much to the rich fabric of our society and our very diversity has lent itself to spawning companies and industries within our country.

But we must also be frank with each other and realize that what has made this country what it is and what has made us brother and sister Americans, is that all Americans before us who built this country, eventually, have always let go of the fixation and the mentality that they were something other than Americans, first. They embraced the history, heritage, hopes and dreams of this country and its Founding Fathers, and through good times and bad, we saw each other through some of the darkest challenges this country has faced...and make no mistake about it, what saw us through these darkest of times was our faith; faith in God, faith in the values and principles of our people and country, and our commitment to each other and to the history, heritage, hopes and dreams of this country, as established by our Founding Fathers.

So when I see this unending wave of Political Correctness flow over our country and the labels now affixed to our people as African-Americans, Latino-Americans, Asian-Americans, etc., I can't help but wonder as to its purpose? And when I look to its purpose, I simply see it as a designed method for politicians and the Media Industrial Complex and special interests, to separate us from each other and sow seeds of distrust, so that these can be exploited for the purposes of garnering favor with the respective groups, along political lines, so that constituencies can be built along these lines, for the purposes of setting one group's interests against another's, with the intent of building coalitions of voters who will support the politicians who are exploiting these divisions.

To me, and I hope to you my brother and sister Americans, this is simply wrong and goes against what our Founding Fathers intended for us, as a nation, as a people, and as a society.

Although (due to my heritage) I have never experienced the deep discrimination and painful racism that has been part of our American journey, I would hope that, after all, the logical conclusion of our progress together as a people, would instead result in us all simply being "**<u>Americans</u>**". Further, I never have thought of my black, or Latino, or Asian brother and sister Americans as African-Americans, Latino-Americans, or Asian-Americans. To me, that is counter, in-part, to what our Founding Fathers and citizens fought and died for in 1776 and flies in the face of the words of President Theodore Roosevelt, above.

Rather, I think that part of the culmination of their sacrifice for the American Dream would be the contrary; that we instead see ourselves always as Americans first, last, and always, and never see ourselves as different divisions within that proud identity, established through the noble ideas, laws, and concepts so clearly inspired by God and embraced by our Founding Fathers and purchased with the blood and sacrifice of many of our brother and sister citizens through many wars, including the most noble battles fought by another great American patriot, the honorable Rev. Dr. Martin Luther King Jr. and his committed supporters.

These were true American Patriots, who fought not with guns as their weapons, but with ideas; ideas of equality, justice, honor, and love of country. It was Dr. King and his courageous army of AMERICANS, who in my mind, fought the battle to take our country out of the shameful dark ages of racism and bigotry, not so very long ago, and helped us to again, as a people and country, begin to regain our honor and *together* move our great Nation forward on its continued journey toward perfection; a destination that will never be reached, but which we all hope, will always be continuously pursued.

CONTRARY TO POPULAR BELIEF, AMERICANS ARE NOT BORN, THEY ARE MADE...

President Theodore Roosevelt knew that, in order to have a strong America and a United People, we could *not* have divided allegiances. He insisted that, whatever our respective race, gender, or national origin, that if we wanted to be, or to become Americans, we needed to check our competing allegiances and national origins at the door and truly understand and embrace the ideals, the commitment, and the shared values that being truly American, demands. This means that we need to likewise understand and accept the full and very serious obligations that being an American requires of us all, as citizens. These are the same obligations that have been passed down to us from our Founding Fathers and from our brother and sister citizens since 1776; including the ultimate obligation; to be so committed and to love our country, our heritage, and each other so deeply, that we are prepared and willing to lay down our lives for our country and our people, if called upon to do so, so that our children and our children's children may receive the same heritage and legacy from us and our generation, that we received from those before us, going all the way back to 1776.

To come to these United States in hopes of becoming an American and to be told that you, or your son or daughter may be called upon to go so far as to risk and possibly lay down your life in defense of our country, is a pretty heavy concept to embrace and is not something to be taken lightly. After all, one cannot be an American only when it suits him or her; when it is convenient and beneficial, and then turn ones back when the going gets tough.

To be willing to lay down one's life in defense of our country and to make a serious commitment of the magnitude I have described, makes it imperative that every American, or prospective American, also fully understand the magnitude of what this means and have a complete and thorough understanding of the noble and proud heritage and values that, as Americans, we are asked to embrace, protect, defend, and cherish. For if one does not understand and cherish these things in their heart and soul, then how can they truly be prepared to make the level of commitment to America and to their brother and sister Americans, which is central to our American DNA? Therefore, I maintain that it is absolutely critical and imperative that we insist that all those who wish to become citizens, be required to:

1. Understand as fully and completely as is reasonably possible, the history of this country, from the founding of the Plymouth Colony, through to our Declaration of Independence in 1776, through each of our subsequent wars, to the present day.

2. Understand the foundational ideals we embrace and have fought for as a people and given up our lives for, going all the way back to the seeking of religious freedom by the Pilgrims at Plymouth Colony, to the Declaration of Independence in 1776 (seeking our freedom to pursue life, liberty and happiness), to the adoption of our Constitution and Bill of Rights, to the painful and agonizing journey through slavery and the Civil War, through to women's suffrage and the right to vote for all Americans; as well as the fight for Civil Rights and the incredible leadership and non-violent struggle of Rev. Dr. Martin Luther King Jr. and his devoted supporters.

   It is so very important that prospective Americans understand why the ideals that we hold so dear, make up so much of the fabric of who we are, and the fabric of who they will eventually become and share in as Americans, and which we must together preserve at all costs and be prepared, together, to make the ultimate sacrifice for if called upon to do so, as a legacy and birthright to our children, which are also their children...Americans all.

3. Understand the progressive growth and evolution of this nation, the development of its' values and moral character; again, from the birth of our nation, through our national and human shame (owing to the stain of slavery), to the Civil War that freed our African-American brothers and sisters so that they could continue the fight for civil rights and true freedom, which ultimately led to the election of our first African-American President, Barack Obama (excuse the ethnic prefix here, but it served an important historical reference purpose).

4. Understand the plight of the immigrants who first came to these shores and were responsible for the "great melting pot" that

ultimately demonstrated the power of freedom, the value of diversity, and the great vision of this noble experiment, which began in 1776.

5. Understand the commitment and sacrifice demonstrated through two World Wars, the Korean and Vietnam Wars, and the Gulf Wars, and the significance of this commitment of America and America's citizen-soldiers.

6. Understand the powerful words of Theodore Roosevelt, above, where those who came to these shores, poor and forlorn, bringing with them little more than hope and faith, *did* check their national origins at the door, remained proud of their roots and proud of the richness of their respective heritage's and cultural origins, but who became Americans completely, embraced this country as their own, and pledged and gave freely their allegiance to this nation and to their brother and sister Americans, and called themselves Americans, first. It is important they understand that huge numbers of these Americans ultimately gave their lives and their children's lives to this country in the fighting of the two World Wars, the Korean and Vietnam Wars, and the Gulf Wars, reaffirming our American brother and sisterhood and our commitment to each other's freedom.

7. Speak and understand the English language to the degree that those committed to becoming Americans can study our history, be certain that they understand the richness and meaning of it, the obligations and the benefits involved in becoming an American, and that this is what they truly want, given the deep obligations and commitments involved.

In this way, they also enable themselves to be able to function effectively in our society, by knowing our language, culture, and rich history, and thereby feel pride in themselves and in what they have both achieved and become, as brother and sister Americans. No one should shy away from this hard work, neither prospective Americans, or our politicians in making this happen. This is so that, with their eyes wide open, prospective Americans will have worked to understand this rich and noble experiment, country, and people, and thereby will take pride in their decision to become Americans, and in the hard work they put-in to achieve their goal.

They will be able to become Americans first, and will understand Theodore Roosevelt's words that they are now Americans, undivided and unclouded in their loyalty and in their patriotism, their love of country, and in their shared appreciation of (and commitment to) the ideals of our Founding Fathers.

They will appreciate and understand their/our obligation to preserve, cherish, and pass on this legacy to their children and our children, fully intact, whatever sacrifice and commitment may be required of us, as a unified people.

BASIC TO *BECOMING AN AMERICAN*: THE PROCESS MUST EMBRACE ABSOLUTE FAIRNESS AND ADHERENCE TO THE LAWS...

You may notice that I am using the words *"Becoming an American"*. This is because I believe that the words "Becoming an American *Citizen*" creates the wrong mindset and sends the wrong message. The latter implies a lawyerly concept of meeting the criteria to become a "citizen", but not necessarily checking ones national origin at the door and "Becoming an *American*". It may seem a small distinction, but in my mind, the difference is **everything**. If someone wants to become an American, then they are forsaking their former allegiances and national identity (not their ethnicity, which they should rightly be proud of) and putting all their chips in the center of the table, "going all-in". They are becoming Americans, with all the rights, privileges and obligations that this entails, as I've described, above.

First, for the reasons I've mentioned, our elected government officials and We the American People, must recognize both the absolute need *and the absolute obligation* to establish a strong foundation of understanding and knowledge in those who come to our shores with the dream and the aim to become Americans. It is their obligation to study and learn, and our obligation to make teaching and study materials available about precisely what it means to *be an American*.

Second, we need to agree that, if we don't adopt and accept President Theodore Roosevelt's most basic precepts and tenets, outlined above, we will never be able to preserve the true American Dream, as it will become diluted and its meaning eventually lost.

WHAT IS THE AMERICAN DREAM?

Despite what some Americans or prospective Americans may believe today, the American Dream is not buying a house and a car, and having a job, and necessarily living better than our fathers did. No one will find that in the Declaration of Independence, the Constitution, or the Bill of Rights.

It is instead, understanding our shared commitment to each other as Americans, to remain free and to preserve our liberties together, as a single people. It is a commitment to preserve the vision and shared

A HARD LOOK IN THE MIRROR

dream of our Founding Fathers and what that bond of Loyalty, Love and Trust truly means, in shared commitment, sacrifice, and when called upon, blood. It means being willing to give this commitment to each other and keep it, for the good of our people, and our children, and their children, no matter what. It means being committed in these ways to our individual and national Freedom, to our way of life, to our culture, and to our way of government.

I believe that our unbending, unyielding, unchanging American commitment to each other, to preserve our freedoms, our liberty, and our way of life, to defend the principles of our Declaration of Independence, our Constitution and our Bill of Rights, for the purposes of making the achievement of our dreams and goals possible, for those willing to put forth the hard work, effort, and commitment required to do so, is the essence of The American Dream.

It's not about being handed a loan by Barney Frank for a house one cannot afford, or coming to this country to live at the expense and hard work of others, or to have a car, and a house with air conditioning and Cable TV and Sportscenter. It is about wanting Freedom, and committing ones very life to whatever it takes to preserve, protect, defend, and maintain that freedom. It is about preserving the opportunity to live and to achieve in a free society, and to work and live with likeminded brothers and sisters, willing to share burden of commitment to that freedom, together pledging themselves and their lives if necessary, to each other.

I say this because I agree, in part, with James Truslow Adams, who first made reference to "The American Dream", in his book of the same name in 1931, where he states that, *"life should be better and richer and fuller for everyone, with opportunity for each according to ability or achievement, regardless of social class or circumstances of birth."*

But to achieve and preserve what Adams describes in the last passage, one must be fully committed to what I have described in the former passages. This is what The American Dream is all about.

I would go a step further and say that **not** to require that those seeking to become Americans go through a rigorous process of study, acclimation, and testing of their knowledge of our history and culture, as well as a testing of their proficiency with our language, is to deprive them of the richness of the opportunity that they seek, and the goal to which they aspire. Because if they truly wish to become Americans, then we have an obligation to them, to ourselves, to our country, and to our Founding Fathers, to provide a correct path for them, so that they can understand, at the deepest and most meaningful levels, what becoming an American truly means, and the obligations this entails. It can only be good for everyone involved, particularly the person who wishes to become an American (not just an American citizen) and for our society as a whole.

WE SHOULD BE OF A SINGLE MIND ON THESE ISSUES OF IMMIGRATION REFORM AND WHAT'S BEST FOR US AS A PEOPLE, AS AMERICANS; IT SHOULDN'T BE THAT HARD TO AGREE...

Going back to my previous thoughts about Politicians and about the Political Correctness mentality created by them (and by much of the media & press), which I believe they perpetuate in order to sow division between us as Americans, I would like for us to think for a moment, logically, as AMERICANS, and not as African-Americans, Latino-Americans, Asian-Americans, etc. While I understand that many may have family members overseas, whom they may wish to bring to America to become citizens, let us agree, as Americans of every race and gender, that we have an obligation to put our country and our fellow Americans

A HARD LOOK IN THE MIRROR

first, as well as an obligation to address our mutual concerns for the well-being of our economy and our security, most especially.

I hope we can all agree, not as "hyphenated-Americans", but simply as Americans, that we must proceed in a manner that is best for us, as a single people and as a country.

Our health and social services are being overburdened and are collapsing under financial strain. Our educational system is also a shell of what it once was back in the 50's, 60's and 70's, in terms of quality of teachers, quality of education, and classroom size. In global testing of our young, we now score last among industrialized nations. Our legal and penal system is busting at the seams with approximately 30% of the prison population occupying our prisons, consisting of illegal immigrants, requiring our financial support to house and feed them while in our custody, along with the inherent dangers to our citizens, represented by allowing criminals into our country.

We must put a stop to the problems, if we are going to continue to be a great country and a beacon to the world. We cannot let ethnic, or even family loyalties become such a blinding preoccupation or obsession, that it blinds some Americans to their obligations to America as a whole, dragging the nation down into socio-economic chaos and disaster.

Americans who think of placing their overseas relatives or friends first, as difficult as it may sound, must instead keep the faith with America and with their brother and sister Americans and must do what is right for this country, which is their country. They must recognize that they must subjugate their own, personal priorities to the good of this, ***their nation***, when those personal priorities are in conflict with our nation's best interests. All must follow the immigration rules, *for the good of all!*

There's just no easy way to say that, but it must be said and it must be recognized and accepted by *all Americans*, by WE THE PEOPLE.

Certainly, if we step back and take the emotion out of the equation (as much as possible), we must agree together that we can only sustain a certain amount of orderly, controlled immigration annually, particularly if we're going to require the proper education and testing of prospective citizens, educating them in our history, culture and language. We must have policies and priorities that speak to this for the good of our country and our people, as well as for the stability our social services, our educational system and our legal and law enforcement infrastructure. These institutions and services, which make up an important part of our infrastructure, must not be overburdened to the extent that Americans, as a whole, suffer. It is not right and it is not fair, and those Americans who expect that America and its citizens should welcome uncontrolled immigration, whatever the cost, well, they are being the most selfish of all Americans and are not, in my estimation, Americans who understand what the American Dream, our country, our heritage, ***and their obligations as Americans*** is all about and if they do understand, then they are not committed to it, or to America.

SO, WHAT SHOULD THE PROCESS OF LEGALLY BECOMING AN AMERICAN INVOLVE AND HOW SHOULD WE HANDLE THOSE PEOPLE WHO ARE HERE ILLEGALLY, AND WHAT SHOULD WE DO ABOUT OUR BORDERS?

So, given this foundation, how should we proceed with the question of the process of immigration reform and becoming an American?

1. I think that most Americans will agree that, to start with, there needs to be complete fairness and consistency in the criteria,

standards and process for granting people admission to this country and for becoming Americans, without regard to gender, faith, race, or national origin.

2. I think that most Americans will agree that people who are here legally and who have followed the laws of the land in applying for citizenship must be given priority and preference over those who are not here legally and who have not followed the laws of the land for becoming citizens.

3. I think that, given the fact that approximately one-third of our prison population is made up of illegal aliens, that these folks should be sent back to their countries, following the serving of their full sentences here, and that those countries that they are citizens of and from whence they came, should bear the full cost of care for the years they were incarcerated here, as well as the full cost of their repatriation to their home countries. If those Countries do not want to agree to do this, then those countries should be barred from trading with the United States (provided it does not deprive us of important strategic resources) and we should close off our markets to them. This should provide sufficient incentive for them to control their borders and to likewise punish those who violate the mutual laws and treaties we have between us, governing emigration/immigration. After all, as citizens of those countries, don't they have an obligation to obey the laws and treaties established between their own respective countries and ours?

This also would mean that, if foreign citizens are in our penal system for violating our laws, then once returned to their home countries, they will likely face additional jail time there for violating emigration/immigration laws and treaties between our countries, particularly in the face of the home country having to reimburse the U.S. and its respective states, for the costs of the person's incarceration here. If they face jail-time here and face jail-time in their own countries, once returned there, the deterrence will be effective.

4. For the reasons I have outlined, I believe that quotas should be established and observed, for the good of the United States first and foremost, to assure that we can efficiently and effectively assimilate the appropriate number of New Americans each year that WE THE PEOPLE deem appropriate, so that we can maintain order, balance, and influx of new blood, ideas, vigor and vitality into our National Melting Pot, which has, as in the past, always been the strength and lifeblood of our nation.

    This is in keeping with our truly American ideals and heritage of giving hope to the hopeless and the oppressed. If we do not control our borders and establish some control and order over the process though, we risk becoming a nation immersed in chaos and we are well on the way to chaos already, as we can all plainly see. If this happens, we will certainly end up betraying our responsibilities to our Founding Fathers, to our nation, to our children and to their children. So we must put people into office who share these concerns and are prepared to address these issues and follow the WILL OF THE PEOPLE (for a change).

5. For the reasons I have outlined, and in order to assure that we achieve the all-important "Melting-Pot Effect" that made this nation strong, we must implement stringent requirements for education and testing of those wishing to become Americans, to assure that they understand the commitment they are making, the rich heritage they are becoming a part of, and the ideals and responsibilities that go with it. They must become true

A HARD LOOK IN THE MIRROR

Americans in their heart-of-hearts and one cannot possibly do this without studying and understanding, in a fundamentally strong way, the history of our nation.

It is also critical that they have a basic command of the English language, so that they can have a greater probability of successful assimilation into our society and probability of success in their chosen occupation, so as to provide for themselves economically and contribute their fair share to the economy, the national defense, and the running of our government.

6. I believe that we also cannot bury our heads in the sand. I believe it has been sufficiently demonstrated that some number of guest workers should be legally allowed to enter the country each year, in a controlled way. The case has been made that it is a fundamental necessity of our economy, and if we are to control our borders, we must have a mechanism to allow for this process. So we should proceed with implementing a very controlled and expeditious process, involving the issuance of such permissions, along with I.D. cards that will provide for appropriate protections for ourselves and these guest workers. This must be limited and expiration dates established for each guest worker and a very careful program constructed to support this process.

7. For those here illegally, who wanted to share in what they perceive to be the American Dream, but who made a conscious decision to violate our laws, their own country's laws and our borders, and who gave little thought or care to the impact it would have on us as a country and as a society, well, it is my opinion that those people should be carefully screened and reviewed in each case. Then, once reviewed, they must either be repatriated back to their own countries, or if they are holding down steady jobs,

have been paying taxes, and have a consistent history of obeying the rest of our laws, then provided with a path to citizenship, being placed at the very end of the line, behind those who have followed our laws and applied for citizenship legally.

If on the other hand, they are found to have violated our laws, not paid taxes and instead strained our economy by utilizing our social services without contributing to the tax base, then they must be returned to their home countries, without delay, and not considered further for citizenship.

8. With the aforementioned steps implemented; the guest worker program and the policy established for handling current cases, there then remains no excuses whatsoever for not holding employers/businesses 100% fully responsible for upholding our laws and not hiring illegal aliens. We should then have very stringent, even draconian laws for punishing U.S. businesses that violate the laws by carelessly or intentionally hiring illegal aliens, to the degree of being able to punish business owners both criminally, as well as civilly.

9. We should put all resources required into sealing our borders to the greatest degree possible and once accomplished, this will complete the program, covering all of our bases.

10. Oh yes, how do we seal our borders, you ask? Good question. Well, I believe that there are military and security experts who, if allowed to work on an effective plan, without interference from the politicians we currently have in office, would come up with an effective combination of physical and electronic barriers that would balance efficiency, effectiveness, cost and results in a proper and professional way. We have some of the best military,

technical and strategic minds in the world in this country, who if tasked to do this for the security of our nation, in order to protect us from terrorists, drug smugglers and illegal aliens, would be able to do a very effective job, if given a clear mandate and resources. The politics have to be taken out of the equation of course, and if the former steps are put in place (along with this step), it shouldn't be all that hard. This requires that most of the current band of boobs in office, both Democrat and Republican, be given the boot of course.

Ok, now that we've addressed the emotional side of this, there are a lot of other factors that I believe are just as important. For example:

1. In order not to bankrupt the country, how many people should we let in annually and what should be the criteria for being granted legal entry and legal status in this country?

2. How many guest workers should we allow into the country to fill those jobs that we are told Americans don't want to take and how long should they be allowed to stay?

3. We must very quickly move to properly and professionally secure our borders, in order to protect ourselves against terrorism and the disastrous economic effects that illegal immigration has had on our country. After all, just one non-nuclear dirty-bomb [a bomb consisting of conventional explosives, combined with radioactive material (not nuclear, not fissionable)], brought across the border could create havoc for a city. If you don't think about such things as being possible, then you are either naïve or, sorry to say, so irreversibly stupid that you should be exchanged for a more intelligent and deserving immigrant applying for admission and citizenship to this country.

The bottom-line here is that, as a middle-class, average-educated American with business experience, I'm able to at least articulate the issues on this subject and put forward some material and fair-minded ideas about how to handle the problem.

Meanwhile, we've got a band of highly educated nimrods in Washington, who are more concerned with playing political football with our future, than in solving our nation's problems. Hell, none of the current vacuous, empty-suits there seem willing to make a single, value-based decision. They are so far removed from the mindset and ideologies of our Founding Fathers and 1776, that it makes me almost ashamed to be an American. But I am not ashamed to be an American. Indeed, it is they who should be ashamed to call themselves Senators and Congressional Representatives, behaving as they do and spending other people's money as if it were their own, having no sense of stewardship or accountability to the American People. To even suggest that any significant number of this band of boobs has any sense of obligation to the ideals of our Founding Fathers, is just absurd, I'm sorry to say.

Now, there is a very, very small handful that still represents us well. But unfortunately, they exist in a sea of incompetents and charlatans, who just don't deserve the trust and faith of the American people. From selling vacated congressional seats for political favors (Chicago), to bailing out financial institutions that should never have been bailed-out, to the Barney Frank scandals of Fannie Mae and Freddie Mac.

Then there is always the absolutely scandalous hypocrisy of Eric Holder and the Obama Administration, filing a lawsuit against the people of Arizona for trying to do what they can to stem the violence, chaos and mayhem at their border. The Arizona law, while admittedly a bit odious, was/is in harmony with existing federal law. Nevertheless, the Administration decided to file lawsuits, rather than securing the border.

A HARD LOOK IN THE MIRROR

Had the Administration secured the border, Arizona would never have had to resort to such desperate measures. Indeed, as Americans, we should be putting pressure on the Administration to secure the borders, so that Arizonans and other border-state citizens would feel such laws unnecessary. I know I'm not the only one who prefers to think logically, as opposed to politically and emotionally.

I, like many Americans, find the prospect of racial profiling to be distasteful and in direct contradiction to the ideals and vision of our Founding Fathers. But I also find the lack of accountability of the Obama Administration, and before him the Bush Administration, to be equally distasteful, as well as grossly irresponsible. So the Administration should make a deal with the border-states. We'll get your borders secured within 6 months. Once we do, you'll need no such "special laws". Deal? Good, then, do your job Mr. President and Congress…simple.

I'm sorry for us all, my brother and sister Americans. I've provided my thoughts on how to begin to address the immigration issues. But from the political side, in order to get things moving forward and get some results, the only remedy I can think of to address the situation is to throw most all the current bums out of office; the whole bunch of them. The core is rotten. That said, WE, the American People are not. We are the only ones who, together and in a balanced and sensible way, can fix this. We need to rely on each other and the vision and foundation of our Founding Fathers, not the extremists on the right or the left and not the media extremists on the right or the left. We need to throw them all out of office, both through the vote and through our choice of television viewing, radio listening and reading material.

Do you think we can do it? To borrow a line from our President…

"YES WE CAN!"

CHAPTER 12

WINNING STRATEGIES OF WAR; GETTING OUR CITIZEN- SOLDIERS OUT OF AFGHANISTAN & IRAQ, AND SETTING A SANE, MORAL & FINANCIAL COURSE

Clearly, I profess to be no expert on international crises, nor am I a foreign policy expert. I am just a businessman and a middle-class guy from suburbia, who is very worried about the decisions and strategies we are pursuing, as they relate to how we are employing our armed forces today, why we are employing them in the manner we are, and towards what end; thereby risking the lives of our citizen-soldiers in a manner which doesn't make good sense to this American, and probably to a lot of other Americans. I am also very concerned about how we are spending our money, money that today we simply don't have and are thereby, again, using our national credit card to finance and sending the bill to our citizens, our children and our children's children.

FIRST, WHAT IS THE PURPOSE OF OUR MILITARY AND WHAT SHOULD WE ASK OF OUR CITIZEN-SOLDIERS?

A HARD LOOK IN THE MIRROR

WALSH'S SEVEN DEADLY SINS...

First, I am probably amongst the minority in my thinking about the purpose of our military, how it should be employed and for what reasons, but here goes:

1. I believe that our military should be used to defend our country, our people and our way of life against those who threaten armed violence against us.

2. I further believe that our military should be used to defend our closest allies, with whom we have made mutual pacts, or agreements for mutual defense (as opposed to mutual offense, an important distinction), provided the causes are defined and just.

3. I believe that our citizen-soldiers should be asked to defend our lives, our liberty, and our way of life. Our way of life includes our Capitalist system and those who threaten it, because those who directly threaten our Capitalist system, threaten our economic survival, and thereby our freedom, our "Pursuit of Happiness", and our way of life.

4. These threats can be on our borders, or on the borders of nations with whom we have made such aforementioned mutual **defense** pacts, or on the borders of those who materially act and interfere with our freedoms, as previously defined.

5. Economic warfare can also constitute a clear and present danger to our country. Should the threat of armed violence against our nation be made, or should a nation with whom we trade

and upon which our economy depends for significant viability have their freedom threatened (assuming a legitimately elected government is in place and not a despot or dictator), or should a strategic U.S. trading partner be materially threatened with armed violence, then regardless of whether or not a mutual defense pact exists, America has every right to defend our strategic economic interests, for the well-being of our people and our national economy (e.g. Iraq invading Kuwait and seriously threatening the security of Saudi Arabia, both critical, strategic trading partners).

6. Our military should also be asked to defend our borders, if necessary, when drugs or illegal immigration threaten the security and stability of our nation, economically or socially (e.g. crime, violence).

7. Our citizen-soldiers should be asked to defend us against terrorism, where a clear and present danger is identifiable and locatable.

To me, these are seven deadly sins that other nations or groups can commit against us as a people and a nation. Beyond this, generally speaking, I don't believe we should be asking our citizen-soldiers to go into harm's way to risk their lives. One may point out that the above seven leave a lot of room for interpretation and one would be absolutely correct in saying so. One might argue that, without more specificity, the above seven would not cause any change whatsoever in our current and recent overseas adventures, which some (like me) would describe as ill-conceived extravaganzas, which have cost so many of our citizen-soldiers their health, or their very lives, and have cost so many families the presence of their most precious loved ones, altogether.

A HARD LOOK IN THE MIRROR

These have made for fatherless and motherless children, thousands of widows and widowers, and thousands of grandparents, brothers, sisters, mothers and fathers suddenly losing their most precious family members. This is much more than a statistic on the evening news, which by the way, we rarely see any more (except on PBS) and maybe should see much more of. These are our American brothers and sisters, who trust *us* not to send *them* off to war, by letting *our* president and *our* representatives, put *their* lives in jeopardy, unless it is to defend us against the most serious threats to our security, our freedom, and our way of life.

We can't simply point the finger at our politicians, if we don't like what's going on. **We must point the finger at ourselves!** Our representatives are there because we put them in Washington. We The People can't claim absolution or deny our own responsibility, if we don't like the outcome.

Listen brother and sister Americans, we own the restaurant and we hired the cooks in the kitchen, so we'd better take ownership of the outcome of the meals they cook-up and take full responsibility for them if we don't much like the results, rather than claiming impotence or ignorance as voters, as if we are so much cattle. Nor do we have the luxury of saying that we were bamboozled. We have a greater responsibility than that...namely, <u>to be informed before we vote</u>!

I think our Founding Fathers placed more faith in our sense of responsibility, ownership and wisdom, than we choose to accept today. That's right, I said **choose** to accept, because make no mistake about it, taking ownership, or behaving apathetically are **choices** we make. Playing dumb, or claiming we are being taken advantage of is a cowardly, empty excuse, which our Founding Fathers might find shameful, given the sacrifices they made and having put **everything** on the line to achieve their great accomplishment, that we might live in freedom and have the **privilege** of making the choices we have today.

So, allow me then to be more specific and eliminate some of the gray areas and to reflect on the wars we are conducting today and share with you my thoughts, as an average American, regarding these wars and our decisions to put our brother and sister citizen-soldiers in harm's way.

WHAT SHOULD WE <u>NOT</u> USE OUR MILITARY FOR? WHAT SHOULD WE <u>NOT</u> ASK OUR CITIZEN-SOLDIERS TO DO?

1. **<u>Nation Building</u>?** We should not ask our military to be nation-builders. Our military should be used to fight wars, to achieve a set of military objectives, not social objectives. Social objectives are for the politicians to deal with and work on. Those military objectives should be clearly defined and outlined before we go and put our citizen-soldiers in harm's way and the reasons for war should be identified and explained to the American people, in the light of day (which includes our citizen-soldiers). Once achieved, our military should be withdrawn, as soon as is reasonably possible. In this way, we treat our citizen-soldiers as we would want to be treated ourselves, which is only right and just, considering we are asking them (and their families and loved ones) to risk everything they have; their very lives for us.

2. **<u>Iraq</u>?** We should ask our military to defeat enemy regimes that truly threaten us and let the people of the nation in question determine themselves what they wish to install in its place, if indeed our battle is with the regime and not the people, as was the case with Iraq. If they install the wrong regime, or should remnants of

the previous regime regain power, so be it. Employ diplomacy to see to it that the same mistakes are not made again, since usually, there are a fair amount of errors made on both sides that lead to such conflicts. If diplomacy doesn't work, then we may have been foolish to go in there in the first place (keeping in mind that in some instances, based upon circumstances, we may have to go in, regardless of the prospects for post-war stabilization).

In other words, if the post-war regime is foolish enough to again commit the same mistakes of their predecessors, or allow those same mistakes to be made and not fight to establish meaningful change, and instead have their political entities/representatives simply vie for power and re-enter a cycle of political corruption, only to see the new government again fall into the same destructive pattern, or if the professional diplomatic efforts of our State Dept. are not sufficient to avoid future crises with the same regime, then they may again have to be paid a second, limited visit by the U.S. Military, courtesy of us, the taxpayers (provided the aforementioned criteria I laid out is met).

Normally, I must believe this will not be the case. Having witnessed the destruction of the previous regime, in the case of Saddam Hussein, I must believe that it would be unlikely that any succeeding regime would wish to come to a similar end and there is no reason for them to think that they would not, given that we have already demonstrated what we are prepared to do and how effectively we can do it, when we decide to. Therefore, there is a level of built-in common sense that should be a mainstay with representatives of any succeeding regime. This said, unless my aforementioned criteria is met, I would not go back into Iraq again, and certainly not to nation-build, for the aforementioned reasons.

I must also be frank in saying that I don't seriously believe that Saddam Hussein, monster that he was, was threatening, or was going to be threatening the U.S. again, after his first go-around with us in the first Gulf War in 1990. There were no weapons of mass destruction, as it turns out (and I think we knew it), and there has been little evidence that Iraq was running terrorist training camps within their borders at the time of our invasion of Iraq in 2003.

In my own, personal opinion, the first President Bush (George Herbert Walker Bush/Gulf War 1) was correct and astute, as always, in his assessment of the situation following the first Gulf War involving the invasion of Kuwait. He had us leaving Iraq after the objective was achieved and he maintained that Saddam Hussein was essentially left powerless amongst the nations that surrounded him, making him more, not less easy to control. A castrated dog would have had a greater chance to procreate, than Saddam Hussein would have had to seriously threaten us again, or anyone else again for that matter, and I believe he certainly learned a valuable lesson during the first Gulf War. This is just one man's opinion.

Further, the experiment in Iraq is not over. While many declared victory of a sort in the nation-building efforts (because we were not seeing a high, daily death toll there of U.S. Soldiers, there was perceived stability), I believe that the moment we do completely leave, we will likely see the same deterioration of organized, democratic government there that we would have seen had we left after one year.

It is my strong and considered opinion (for whatever that may be worth) that a country whose people do not fight for their own freedom themselves, shedding their own blood and paying dearly for that freedom and its' re-affirmation, as Americans did in 1776, the Civil War, and World Wars I and II, well, those people cannot then achieve organized, stable nationhood. By having their freedom paid for by us, with the lives and blood of American citizen-soldiers, without putting forward their own commitment and experiencing their own loss and personal sacrifice, shedding their own blood for their own freedom, then any failure of the post-war process of installing a stable, successful government, becomes too easy for them to contemplate and accept. If that is so, then the odds are very high that civil war will break out after we leave, or that a similar, corrupt dictator will at some point emerge again in the ensuing chaos.

When a peoples express their own desire for freedom and back that up by fighting their own battles and shedding their own blood for the final victory and experience the sweet, yet painful taste of freedom, then it is clear that a high price has been paid by that peoples for an invaluable education in what freedom really means, and a deep and abiding meaning and appreciation for its cost has been gained and earned, through the most humanly expensive education there is on this earth. This expensive education, paid for in their own people's blood, sacrifice, and treasure, would make certain that failure is not an option in successfully forming a government that will endeavor to make freedom a permanent reality for those who sacrificed so much for it. Those people would naturally take very serious ownership of that freedom and the grave responsibility that goes with it, knowing first-hand the costs they paid to achieve it. They would also be prepared to pay the costs required to maintain it, rather than have to repeat the experience.

It is my belief that for those who do not fight for their own freedom and instead allow others do it for them and then have nationhood and a government of our conception and design imposed upon them, expecting to see it succeed, well, that government just will not work; not because of the form or structure of that government, but because the people for whom it is designed cannot possibly grasp the depth and meaning of the price paid for it by others, not themselves, and therefore do not have the indispensible and meaningful, personal human stake in seeing that government succeed at almost any cost, placing its success and the country's success, above their own, individual or group self-interests.

I dearly and sincerely hope that I am wrong in this for the sake of the families of all of our citizen-soldiers who lost their lives in Iraq and for all the pain and suffering that they and their families have endured in this cause.

We have been there now for over ten years and a successful outcome is still in question and will be in question for years after we leave. I just do not believe in nation-building as a legitimate, moral objective for our military. The lives of our servicemen and women are too dear and too important for this and should not be put in harm's way for it. They didn't sign-on for nation-building, I think, and the cost in lives and the number of years it takes to even have a small chance at some minor success is just too high. In my view, we should have been out of Iraq by 2005 at the latest and I am still very dubious about our reasons for even having gone into Iraq in the first place.

3. **Afghanistan?** I believe from the foregoing, you already know my answer. If there was direct or indirect involvement in 911 by the Taliban, then in my opinion we were justified in going in,

provided we had a well-defined, limited objective, even if the objective was to simply commit our citizen-soldiers to going in and destroying as many of the Taliban terrorists and as much of the political regime as they could identify and lay their hands on and likewise destroy as many of the Taliban terrorist training camps as they could possibly find. Then locate strategic points of potential, future U.S. insurgency strikes to be executed by the U.S. Military Special Forces groups within the various branches of service and get the majority of our forces the hell out of Afghanistan.

In other words, go in, give them the bloodiest nose we possibly could deliver (in a targeted way against the Taliban leadership), identify areas from which our Special Forces could operate in the future, and then do to the Taliban what we did to the Russians... arm the hell out of the groups that did-not/do-not particularly like the Taliban form of government, who genuinely want a free society, and indoctrinate those groups in the ideals of freedom, self-determination and democracy, and keep the Taliban much too busy with those groups and the arms we provide them with to be able to bother us. Let the Afghan people fight their own battles. I assure you, once they achieve hard-fought, true freedom, they will be stable thereafter, for they'd know the price they paid for it. Or alternatively, just get the hell out of Dodge after delivering the aforementioned blow, period. We are not going to change thousands of years of imbedded culture, just because we want to.

4. **The United States and our Citizen-Soldiers: The World's Policemen?**

I think not. Where, after all, has it gotten us? Where has it actually been successful? Let's take some time and briefly examine that together, as Americans:

A. **Korea?** Ummmm...we lost over 36,000 citizen-soldiers lives and we're still there. We're still spending billions there, although I'm sure South Korea is buying a lot of defense weaponry. Maybe that's why we're still there. Remember President Eisenhower's words to "beware the military- industrial complex". When will the Korean government completely take over their own defense, so that we can leave? Maybe never at this rate. The hostilities stopped back in 1953, except for some recent skirmishes. We're still there and still spending money. Heck, it's only been 60+ years. Will Iraq be the same? Will Afghanistan?

Last time I checked, South Korea had a very healthy, vibrant and dynamic economy (their electronics, cars and hi-tech industry competence rivals ours). They have a healthy democracy and yet our soldiers and our tax-dollars are still there. What is the objective? What are the conditions for declaring victory and getting the hell out of there? If we can't get out of Korea under those circumstances, **then how *can* we get out and when**?

Yes, I know that they occupy a very important position geographically and strategically in that part of the world and that they are a strong ally. But really, they are quite a strong, independent, intelligent and vibrant enough people to take over themselves. Let them spend some of that economic prosperity and GNP they earn. We can still sell arms to them and can always support them if there's any legitimate, serious trouble brewing. Their economy is healthier than ours today. What are we doing with our citizen-soldiers and our money there? Someone, please educate me! I'm a poor middle-class businessman. I must be missing something big here.

Oh, maybe it's the military-industrial complex thing; you know, defense dollars, defense spending and a lot of companies getting rich? Hmmm, you know, it's kinda there in Iraq and Afghanistan, too...gee whiz...(think Halliburton and others) and will probably be there for years and years to come...if we don't change our strategies and put our foot down as Americans...What a strange coincidence, huh?

B. **Vietnam**? Ummm...Nope, that didn't work. I'll have to try again. We propped up a failed government. We tied the hands of our military, so that we would not bring other powers into the war against us (or so we are told), and we succeeded in losing the lives of over 58,000 citizen-soldiers, who unlike today, mostly did **not** volunteer for service. Oh, and we lost the war, primarily due to our policies, not due to the failure of our citizen-soldiers. We essentially wasted the lives of 58,000 of our youngest and brightest to try and influence events, prop-up a corrupt and unpopular regime and again, *to try and nation-build*.

In the end, through the killing fields and more, they have begun a slow evolution, which I believe will result in a more free and pluralistic system. They are still a one-party, communist state, but they also have one of Southeast Asia's fastest growing economies. They have done it on their own, through a painfully slow, yet in my opinion, fairly simple evolution. I personally believe that Capitalism is a genie that, once freed, even on a limited basis, cannot be put back in the bottle very easily. Vietnam is now a trading partner and by all appearances, more of a friend today. They seem to be on a similar economic evolution to China, just from my own, middle-class, everyman sort of perspective. I would, however, pose the question, and even the argument, that all of this could have been accomplished by simply leaving the situation alone and not wasting over 58,000 American lives, pointlessly.

Now, one thing is very important. I am in no way pronouncing judgment on the past administrations. I'm commenting here with 20/20 hindsight, which is not always fair. But I do believe it's important to reflect upon it, so that we can learn from it and take this into account in any future situations like Vietnam, so that we don't waste more American lives in such scenarios. If we don't come out of situations like Vietnam, with at least some sobering sense of perspective and lessons learned, then we truly did waste all of those precious American lives.

SO IF WE DON'T GO IN FOR NATION-BUILDING (WHICH HAS FAILED IN THE PAST), THEN LET'S LOOK AT THE ALTERNATIVES AND SEE WHERE OUR STRATEGY OF GOING IN AND DEALING WITH CRISES, SITUATIONALLY, OR IN A LIMITED MANNER, HAS GOTTEN US? HAS IT WORKED?

WITH A LIMITED, DEFINED OBJECTIVE, HAVE WE HAD BETTER RESULTS?

A. **Libya [Early to mid-1980's]:** Back in the 1980's, Libyan strong man Muammar Gaddafi ordered fighter planes to attack U.S. forces in the air over the Gulf of Sidra and sponsored acts of terror against the United States through the mid-1980's. President Ronald Reagan, in 1981, during the Gulf of Sidra incident, ordered the Libyan fighters shot down, which was successfully accomplished. As Gaddafi continued his saber-rattling in the mid-80's, re-emphasizing the now infamous **"Line of Death"** that he had drawn on the map across international waters in the Gulf of Sidra, as well as his continuing sponsorship of terror attacks against U.S. citizens and soldiers (e.g. West Berlin discothèque bombing in which two American servicemen were killed), the U.S. sent warships in to challenge Gaddafi's threats and to send a message about terrorist attacks against Americans, while maintaining our right of passage in those international waters, despite Gaddafi's declaration.

Gaddafi, thereupon, began firing upon U.S. surface ships and their aircraft, from land and from Libyan gunboats. President Reagan ordered the gunboats to be sunk and ordered a joint Air Force/ Navy bombing raid on key offensive targets in Libya, including, as it happens, Gaddafi's bedroom. I suppose that since Gaddafi was issuing the orders, his bedroom automatically became a key, offensive target (gotta marvel at President Reagan's reasoning).

The raids were successful. Sadly, one of Gaddafi's family members was killed in the raid (a stepdaughter, unfortunately), which was designed to kill Gaddafi himself. Two of his sons were also reported injured. The message to Gaddafi was effectively delivered and was apparently clearly received, as this resulted in many years of mostly peace, with Gaddafi and Libya being quiet as church mice, at least until recently, when his own people decided, like President Reagan, that they'd had quite enough of Gaddafi, as well.

Further, to our knowledge, it also resulted in a cessation of Gaddafi's sponsoring of terrorism against the U.S. from that country, which was a regular hobby of his, prior to President Reagan bombing his bedroom. We did not have to enter into a long, protracted ground war, nor did we have to remove Gaddafi and engage in nation-building in this case. I would deem the strategy and the results in this case, successful.

Chalk one up for limited, strategic engagement…(that's 1)

B. **Grenada [October 1983-December 1983]:** In 1983, President Ronald Reagan began warning the international community of the U.S. concerns over the militarization taking place in Grenada. The government of Grenada had been in turmoil for years, having experienced two successful coups, including the arrest and murder of so-called Prime Minister, Maurice Bishop, who had attained his position by overthrowing by force, the previous Prime Minister. There is no argument that the Eastern Bloc nations had military personnel and advisors in Grenada from the Soviet Union, North Korea, East Germany and Bulgaria, as well as from Cuba and Libya. Reagan felt that the airport being constructed, with a 9000 ft. runway, oil storage tanks and other features, was not, in-fact, a purely commercial airport, but was intended to become a Cuban-Soviet military base.

Reagan simply would not have it and likewise cited the need to protect U.S. citizens on the island. So he thought about it a bit more. After thinking about it a bit more, he apparently decided that further diplomacy and attempts at reasonable persuasion were not going to be effective. So as not to be misunderstood about the seriousness of U.S. security concerns, he decided to send a slightly more forceful message...He invaded.

A significant battle ensued and the end-result was that the Eastern Block soldiers and "advisors" were either captured or killed, and were permanently ejected from Grenada and were admonished by President Reagan not to return anytime soon, lest they wish to join their departed brethren in the afterlife. The U.S. Citizens were secured and protected and a government relatively friendly to the U.S. ensued. It is an event that is celebrated each year in Grenada, today. I would therefore deem the strategy and results in this limited action to have been successful and no significant investment of U.S. troops was necessary following the action.

Chalk another one up for limited, strategic engagement... (that's 2)

C. **Panama [December 1989-January 1990]:** In December 1989, President George Herbert Walker Bush ordered the U.S. invasion of Panama. The reasons cited for the invasion were various. President Bush stated that Panamanian dictator and strong-man, Manuel Noriega, had declared that a state of war existed between the U.S. and Panama. Bush also stated that it was his responsibility to safeguard the lives of approximately 35,000 U.S. citizens in Panama, as well as to intervene in the drug trafficking taking place, which was detrimental to both countries, as well as to safeguard the U.S.-owned Panama Canal (critical to U.S. economic and global trade interests) and the integrity of the Torrijos-Carter treaties (the canal was not turned over to Panama until 1999).

The invasion was carried out, Noriega was captured, the objectives were met and the troops withdrawn. Following this period, U.S. military bases in Panama were also closed, saving the U.S. a lot of money. Panama has a democratically elected government today and is an ally to the U.S. I would deem the strategy and results in this action to have been successful.

Chalk another one up for limited, strategic engagement... (that's 3)

D. **The First Gulf War [Jan 16 – April 6, 1991]:** I draw your attention to the duration of the first Gulf War. President George Herbert Walker Bush, an experienced service veteran, diplomat, and former head of the CIA, and arguably one of the most qualified and well-prepared Presidents in recent U.S. history, believed strongly in his philosophies about the use of the military. If he was clear about anything, it was his belief that the use of military force had to have defined goals and objectives and once those objectives were met and the goals attained, that the military should be withdrawn. I believe the wisdom of his philosophy has been borne-out.

We accomplished in the first Gulf War, precisely what we set out to accomplish. We left Saddam Hussein a toothless, crippled tiger, who for the most part, could be controlled. We did not spend years there trying to nation-build. I would deem this strategy and the results in this case as successful. I'm sure many would disagree with me in this, since we went back in, but since I am not one of those who felt it was necessary to attack Iraq after 911 and since it is clear they had no WMD's and that Saddam was still a toothless tiger at the time we invaded Iraq, I feel confident in my position and conclusion on this. One cannot hold the father (George H.W. Bush) responsible for the sins of the son (George W. Bush).

Chalk another one up for limited, strategic engagement... (that's 4)

E. **Kosovo-Serbia/Yugoslavia [March 1998-June 1999]:** From March 1998 to June 1999, NATO forces attacked Yugoslavia in an admittedly, very controversial war, supported by then U.S. President Bill Clinton. Relative autonomy for Kosovo was achieved and the immediate objectives of NATO were met. This occurred in a climate where many powerful nations then, and to this day, do not agree and have not necessarily accepted that Kosovo should be independent from Serbia. Russia, China,

India and others, to name a few, count themselves amongst this group of dissenting nations. However, what I would like to point out is that the U.S., through NATO, went in with a limited, well-defined objective and achieved it, and relative peace has ensued since. By all appearances, tensions continue to percolate. But without occupying the area solely with U.S. troops and in conjunction with our allies, the immediate objective was achieved. We did **not** have to put a massive, U.S. military presence in place and support that for ten years, in order to achieve the objectives. Regardless of whether you agree with the political reasons for going in, or not (which is not the subject of this topic I am discussing), I would still deem the strategy and results in this action to have been successful, since they met the limited objectives.

Chalk another one up for limited, strategic engagement... (that's 5)

F. **East Berlin [June 12, 1987-Nov. 9, 1989: Leadership, Courage, Truth and Diplomacy...**

On June 12th, 1987, President Ronald Reagan gave, what I believe, will go down in history as one of the most famous, courageous, visionary and successful speeches by a U.S. President, demonstrating, in my opinion, the type of leadership and statesmanship that was the hallmark of his Presidency. On that afternoon in West Berlin, he challenged Soviet President Mikhail Gorbachev in a way no one else in the world had:

"We welcome change and openness; for we believe that freedom and security go together, that the advance of human liberty can only strengthen the cause of world peace. There is one sign the Soviets can make that would be unmistakable, that would advance dramatically the cause of

*freedom and peace. General Secretary Gorbachev, if you seek peace, if you seek prosperity for the Soviet Union and Eastern Europe, if you seek liberalization, come here to this gate. Mr. Gorbachev, open this gate. Mr. Gorbachev, **TEAR DOWN THIS WALL!**"*

Later in the speech, Reagan went on to say:

"As I looked out a moment ago from the Reichstag, that embodiment of German unity, I noticed words crudely spray-painted upon the wall, perhaps by a young Berliner, 'This wall will fall. Beliefs become reality.' Yes, across Europe, this wall will fall. For it cannot withstand faith; it cannot withstand truth. The wall cannot withstand freedom."

Without sending in our citizen-soldiers and putting them in harm's way, Ronald Reagan, by the exercise of leadership, statesmanship, vision, and an economic strategy of bleeding the Soviet Union nearly dry, combined with his own brand of diplomacy, accomplished what many thought could never be accomplished, except through armed conflict, which most all people thought would result in nuclear cataclysm. *The Iron Curtain fell.*

This was perhaps the most dramatic and important political and social development of our time, since World War II. I include this in this section, because it must be made clear that there are more means to a just end than armed conflict and sending our citizen-soldiers into harm's way to nation-build. This is an example of multiple stratagems being employed to achieve a just-end, over a period of years, combined with a little help from the political winds-of-change, which can present themselves at certain times in history. Maybe if our more current politicians were as creative, intelligent and strategic-minded as President Reagan and his team, we might not send our citizen-soldiers into harm's way, quite so often.

While you may disagree, I'm going to chalk another one up for limited, strategic, diplomatic and economic engagement... (that's 6)

MY PERSONAL CONCLUSIONS FROM THE EXAMINATION OF THE EXAMPLES LISTED ABOVE, AND A MORAL DILEMMA, AS WELL...

The point of my outlining these various armed conflicts and political moments in history, is to make the point that, by the accounting above, it appears to me (the average American from middle-income, middle-class America), that strategic, limited engagement, with defined objectives and goals and a clear exit strategy, combined with visionary diplomacy, statesmanship, patience and a plan, can accomplish much more, in less time, with less investment of tax dollars and most importantly, without the wasting of precious American lives (over periods of years), than the protracted invasion and nation-building efforts we have seen to date, at least in my lifetime, so far.

I don't know about you, but when I review the above and look at Iraq and Afghanistan, I am not filled with confidence about our chances there for long-term success, employing the current strategies. In fact, I feel that the continued investment of the lives of our citizen-soldiers and our tax dollars is absolutely the wrong thing to do.

After having thought about it at some length, I believe in the alternative. The alternative consists of arming and aiding those who will fight against the Taliban for their own freedom. It means aiding those same forces with limited intelligence and limited military Special Forces support (e.g. training) and perhaps even drone strikes in key situations. It also means educating those who want something better for their country, their people, and their children, and letting them fight for it themselves, with our assistance. Helping those who want freedom for themselves to achieve it themselves, is the right thing to do and the more noble thing to do, when considering the interests of both the people of that country AND the interests of our citizen-soldiers.

I further believe, as I stated previously, that freedom and democracy cannot be imposed. It must be fought for and won and the battle must be waged by those to whom the country belongs, not by our citizen-soldiers. I don't know about you, but I have a bit of a moral dilemma telling our servicemen and women that they have to lay down their lives for people of a country who are reluctant to fight for freedom for themselves and their families and who our citizen-soldiers must continuously worry about, not knowing whether some of the people they are fighting for and laying down their lives for will betray them, and thereby be the direct, or indirect cause of their death.

FINALLY, IF IT WASN'T WMD'S, 911 AND TERRORIST TRAINING CAMPS, THEN WHAT WAS THE END-GAME THAT PRESIDENT GEORGE W. BUSH HAD IN MIND IN INVADING IRAQ FOR A SECOND TIME?

Sorry, but I can't leave this subject without at least giving you my opinion, because it's an opinion I've held since prior to the invasion of Iraq.

I was traveling on routine business in Latin America about two months or so before George W. Bush invaded Iraq. The talk in Latin America at the time was whether or not Bush would actually invade. I was incessantly being asked my opinion about this in my travels. Now, my opinion and 50 cents would have bought you a cup of coffee [at least in Latin America]. But people in Latin America had a genuine interest and definite opinions about it.

A HARD LOOK IN THE MIRROR

After being asked a few times, I actually spent a fair amount of time thinking about it. I thought about the WMD concerns. I thought about possible involvement of Saddam Hussein's regime in allowing terrorist training camps to exist in Iraq, which may have aided those involved in the 911 bombing. I thought about a lot of things. But the evidence was very thin about the WMD's, as well as any involvement of Hussein's regime in 911, and even in the existence of terrorist training camps in Iraq. I kept thinking and thinking, waiting for a light to click-on in my head, but it just wouldn't. I kept telling myself that, if it's not WMD's and it's not 911, then the end-game I'm not seeing must absolutely huge for Bush to take such a gi-normous and monumental gamble, which could potentially cast him in the same light as the parade of Presidents responsible for Vietnam. Nothing I could think of was a big enough payoff or reward for such huge political risk, given the American lives that would surely be lost and the huge economic cost of the war and any aftermath.

Then one day, about a month before the invasion began, a light finally clicked on in my mind. I don't know if it was, or is the right one, but at that time, when asked once again about what I thought, I actually did have something to say that I felt conviction about. Here's what I told people who asked me, from that point forward:

A. If Bush does invade, there has to be a potentially huge economic, political, and security payoff that would put the U.S. in such a strong, strategic position that it would be almost impossible for Bush to resist the gamble. The strategic benefits that would accrue to the U.S. would have to be huge and success would have to lead to securing a prominent place in history for President Bush, should the war and the post-war results prove successful.

B. It has to be monumentally huge, because the downside risk is equally huge, and failure would result in Bush being ostracized, criticized and relegated to the scrap-heap of history, considering the human and economic cost of failure, short or long-term.

C. In my opinion, Bush was out to achieve four primary goals, if successful.

  1. First, Bush would establish a U.S.-friendly government, smack-in-the-middle of the hotbed of the Arab-Muslim world and their oil fields, where troops could be stationed and from which military and intelligence assets could operate.

  2. Second, Bush would establish a pluralistic democracy of some sort in the middle of the Arab-Muslim world and their oil fields, where none has existed in any legitimate sense before (including Iran and Egypt, which I do not consider pluralistic democracies in the least, despite the attempts at window-dressing).

  3. Third, Bush would establish a friendly relationship with a government that controlled the second-largest oil reserves in the Middle East [note that Iran adjusted its reserve estimates higher than Iraq to give them larger reserves and the no. 1 position, but reliability of their estimates is highly questionable and was thought to be done for political reasons].

  4. Such a relationship with a major petroleum producer and powerful OPEC member could prove valuable. I will get back to this point.

A HARD LOOK IN THE MIRROR

D. In achieving the first three primary goals (above), the U.S. could accomplish much, I thought:

1. With a successful outcome (which is not assured), the most threatening weapon that the U.S. could hold in our hands and wield against other countries in that part of the world, I thought, including against Saudi Arabia, would be the establishment and operation of a true, functioning democracy. Saudi Arabia, Kuwait and others would certainly see this as a threat to their functioning Kingdoms and way of government and way of life (which also meant that they would be in no hurry to see it succeed and would likely work against it, where they surreptitiously could).

    I thought that success in this area would have other Arab countries (particularly the Kingdoms), literally shaking in their sandals, thus providing leverage to the United States and Bush, or his successors, by essentially putting them in a position to say to selected Arab countries (without actually coming out and saying it), something like this...

[Please allow me now to have some fun and speculate how President Bush might have put it...and yes, I know he was educated at Yale... which also means he doesn't have to care what people think about how he might express himself]:

President Bush to the Arab countries, Kingdoms, et al:

"Now just listen-up, y'all, if ya don't keep them oil prices stable and if y'all don't give the U.S. a little priority in sales of your "all" (translated: "oil"), you know, instead of China and them other folks...well, we might just decide to use our CIA and our relationship with this-here friendly Iraqi government, to export some of this-here freedom and democracy stuff, right-on-over to your Kingdoms and see how your people like the taste and feel of it.

Now, O'course, we find that people eventually develop a hankerin to it, which may not be the best dang thing for the monarchy's and dictatorships y'all maintain today. Now, O'course, we might just start quietly shipping some-a-that-there freedom and democracy propaganda over your way...in Arabic of course, so's it looks like it's bein written by their brothers and countrymen; ohhh...I dunno, maybe we'll do it just enough to start a little movement over yonder in your neck of the woods. Now, I hear-tell that that sort of stuff can be kind of destabilizing to a monarchy and kingdoms and such. Have y'all heard that too?

Well, shucks, now we don't REALLY want to have to do that and, you know, as friends, we wouldn't want to interfere with your way of life and government, as long as y'all treat us like friends, as y'all should...heh, heh, heh...

O'course, we've seen that this freedom and democracy stuff just kinda has a way of creepin out on its own sometimes, and damn, ya know, once that stuff's out, well, it's just like some kind of ol renegade genie. Once that ol genie gets out of its lamp, it's real hard tryin to get that sucker back in, sure-as-shootin...why, I don't think Aladdin himself could get that ol genie back in there...heh, heh, heh..." Yep, best for y'all that it not get out of that ol lamp in the first place...heh, heh, heh..."

Right or wrong, that's my take on President Bush playing his hand with this. You get my drift now?

E. Another achievement that the U.S. would enjoy would be a military and intelligence presence and a friendship with an Arab ally in that hotbed of terrorism. This cannot be underestimated, in my view. The leverage this could provide to the U.S. could be almost inestimable; depending upon just how much of a presence could be achieved and tolerated by Iraq.

F. The aforementioned example I provided above, outlines the potential influence such an achievement could have on both the supply and price of oil and not only to the U.S. Stable oil supply and prices can mean only good things for the U.S. and global economies, in terms of stability.

The caveat to this, of course, are the veiled policies of President Obama, which appear to be fixed on intentionally increasing the price of oil to give him leverage in getting new taxes and bills through the congress to fund his alternative energy programs and his policies on energy efficient automobiles and such. Remember, Bush was an oil man, Obama is not.

G. Another achievement that could accrue is a better understanding of the U.S. and its people within Iraq, certainly, and within the Arab world, hopefully, if we don't conduct ourselves as we have on some past occasions, as the ugly Americans. Exchange of ideas and culture could bring positive developments between the U.S. and Arab world.

This has been my own pet-theory about President George W. Bush's tremendous gamble and adventure into Iraq, since before the invasion. Clearly, he was not able to accomplish it in his time in office, if indeed that was his plan. But regardless, if the experiment in Iraq does somehow accomplish some of these speculative goals, it should be interesting to watch.

By the way, this does not change my opinions at all, regarding when and for what purpose we should employ military force and commit our citizen-soldiers to battle. Even if these speculative goals I have outlined are deemed by some to be both important and even noble, which is very arguable, I do not believe that we should be using our troops to nation-build. I believe we should only ask our men and women in uniform to put themselves in harm's way for the purposes I outlined, previously.

WAR, NATION-BUILDING AND THE ECONOMY

Now, as a person from middle-class America, I may not be an expert on the economy, nor the effects of defense and military-related spending on it. I can only use my own common sense, such that it is, to determine for myself whether it is something that is hurting us or not. I would consider that, in the short-term, war spending is a shot-in-the-arm to our economy; creating more goods and services and therefore more jobs, thereby creating more taxpaying workers and more tax revenue from defense-related companies. These workers are then, theoretically, spending their money on more goods and services and the result would be more payroll tax revenues and more and higher taxable transactions in the economy, thus putting some level of the spending right back into the revenue pockets of the government.

Aside from the businesses directly getting the government contracts, there are those that are supplying underlying goods and services to those primary contractors. So, it would logically follow that these businesses would also benefit and that businesses in general would benefit (e.g. supermarkets, retailers, auto manufacturers, gas stations, etc.) from simply having more people employed than might otherwise be, without this spending (e.g. the in the short-term, we're better off with the spending, than without it, I'd think).

This said, I would think that it will also increase our deficits over time and I can't see that the above-mentioned revenues that do make it back into the economy and into the government coffers, can ever completely balance out the deficits we incur to maintain the long-term, nation-building-type wars that go on, literally for years (e.g. Iraq and Afghanistan).

Further, I would also logically think that such spending and deficits allocate government spending away from such things as infrastructure building and maintenance, and social spending (e.g. entitlements, education, etc.). I don't think that anyone would argue that we shouldn't do what's necessary to maintain our security, our national infrastructure, or to educate our children properly, or protect and maintain our natural resources, or to maintain those regulatory agencies that do serve the public interest and actually deliver results. And while I've never been big on unnecessary, wasteful social spending, **prudent, directed** social spending is necessary and in our best interest as a country and people, in addition to creating or maintaining safety nets for certain unfortunate members of our society, who do truly need it, and for spending on programs that actually do work and deliver value to us as a country.

I think that investment in alternative energy strategies is also important, since not a single American I know is in love with the idea of us being so utterly dependent upon the whims of the various kingdoms and governments today, who control much of the world's oil supply, such as Saudi Arabia, Iran, Venezuela, Russia, Mexico, Nigeria, Angola, Algeria, Iraq and others. I would further argue that being so utterly dependent upon some of these sources of supply, has been a big part of the critical considerations that have caused us to go to war twice in Iraq, in the first place. These considerations were certainly a major factor in the first Gulf War and I believe were also a major factor in the second, even though significantly understated in the explanations from President George W. Bush.

So the opportunity cost of these long, protracted wars, I believe, is great. We forego spending on other, potentially valuable uses of our country's capital, to spend on nation-building in other countries such as Iraq and Afghanistan, including bribing and making rich, certain corrupt political leaders in those countries, simply as an accepted cost of engaging in the "nation-building business" (which is grossly distasteful, in and of itself).

I ask you, in retrospect, does anyone argue, really, that the space program of the 50's, 60's and 70's didn't leap-frog our technology advantage over the rest of the world by more than a decade, and possibly significantly more than that? Didn't we enjoy a huge technological gold-rush from the fruits of those labors and that spending? People in opposition to the space program back then, pointed to the "moon rocks" and suggested we spent billions of dollars to collect a lot of rocks, rather than helping our own people in need. Hell, everyone knows the moon rocks weren't the gold "in them thar hills"...the gold was the technology explosion that resulted from it and catapulted this country into a leadership position that we still enjoy to this day (arguably).

What would happen if we put this kind of money into a NASA-type program to become 30% less energy dependent upon petroleum before this next decade is done (say by 2020)? Just asking... We went to the moon in 1969 and no one would have dreamed of that in 1959. Even those in leadership positions within the space program itself were extremely dubious about our being able to accomplish it...and they were the experts!

A HARD LOOK IN THE MIRROR

What would happen if we put part of this money into a research and testing program to reform our K-12 public education system to put us back into a leadership position in the world in education? I don't think anyone would argue that our education system needs a complete overhaul. Nor do I believe that anyone would argue about the value and the payoff to our children, and therefore to our nation, in the long-run. Maybe we wouldn't have to import so much intellectual capital from overseas and could give the high-paying, high-demand jobs to our own citizenry. We just need to get out of this short-term thinking and focus, and stop being the policemen of the world. Consider the following:

1. What would happen if we put part of this money into safety nets for the profoundly handicapped and the chronically and mentally ill people in our society, so that they can have proper, publicly funded, lifelong healthcare (if necessary) and so that we wouldn't continue to place our mentally ill citizens in prisons, rather than hospitals, which is a shameful, under-publicized scandal in our society today?

2. What would happen if we put part of this money into an interim healthcare safety-net program for people who have lost their jobs and are temporarily out of work, so that they can have at least basic healthcare options for their family that are cheap and affordable, during such crises? After all, this type of crisis is normally experienced by almost every family at one time or another. This would be my preference, as opposed to Obama-Care, which will turn into a complete fiasco for our citizens and our country as a whole. I personally believe that it will collapse under its own weight, waste, mismanagement and cost.

These I think are preferable, and in most cases, limited safety-net programs are much more desirable than having our government hobgoblins taking over the entire healthcare system for literally everyone in our society, to be run by a chronically and profoundly inefficient government bureaucracy. I ask you, has anyone known any government-run system to work efficiently, responsively and professionally on a consistent basis, because I haven't?

Now, these are admittedly just a few, random observations from a middle-class, middle-America-type citizen. So I'm sure a lot of people may poke holes in what I've expressed. But by the same token, I'd bet a lot of Americans feel the same way I do, at least in principle.

If you do, then you, like me, don't want our citizen-soldiers lives, our citizen's money (tax dollars), and our representatives in government, supporting nation-building wars that involve years of death, dollars and heartache, when similar ends can be achieved by empowering those whom we are trying to help, letting them fight their own wars and letting them set up their own governments, that are in-line with their culture, mores and values (rather than having us come in from the outside and impose our own version, which will never work in the long run). Meanwhile, we can use our own military to conduct limited, targeted operations when necessary, which I believe I have shown (in the past) to be more effective, more efficient, and much lower in cost in lives and dollars, than these conventional wars, invasions and extravaganzas. In addition, we more effectively protect the lives of our citizen-soldiers, keeping them out of the nation-building business and we put the money to much better use, toward **Life, Liberty and the Pursuit of Happiness**, for example!

If we must go to war, please refer back to the criteria I laid out earlier and see, once again, if you agree or not. Limited war for the purposes I outlined, that directly threaten our interests, our liberty and way of life are one thing. Nation-building is entirely another and, I'm sorry, but if a nation needs building, then let the people of that nation do it for themselves and we will be more than happy, if it's a just-cause, in-line with our foundational principles, to assist them economically and technically to do that.

But for any true nation-building to really work and take hold, it needs to come from the people of those nations themselves, and the stakes need to be so high and their passion for freedom and liberty so great and so deeply felt, that they need to be willing to risk and lay down their own lives and spill their own blood and that of their sons and daughters to achieve it, just as our country's patriots have since 1776, in all of the wars we have fought to maintain our freedom and liberty. Sending our citizen-soldiers over to fight another people's war for the purpose of nation-building, when the people of that country are not willing to fight for themselves, is nothing short of immoral towards our own citizen-soldiers, in my humble opinion.

CHAPTER 13

THE ABOLISHMENT OF DON'T ASK, DON'T TELL; GAY RIGHTS IN THE MILITARY – IT'S NOT ABOUT SEXUAL PREFERENCE, IT'S ABOUT CHARACTER...

Well, in the last election, President Obama and several members of congress had made it a point to make this a topic of discussion and action during the election year.

I believe that, historically, the military has been a proud leader and a solid example of social progress and social justice, in helping and supporting our society and nation in moving forward and accelerating the civil rights and equal rights movements, and that it has played a significant and important role in advancing our progress farther and faster than it might have moved otherwise, thanks to our former President Harry S. Truman, having made the correct and right decision to fully integrate the military through Executive Order 9981.

In my view, this was a significant and important milestone in helping us to change our perspective and our culture as a people, and in essence, helped us as a nation to "put our money where our mouth is", continuing to embrace and advance this Great Experiment in freedom and liberty for all. It was the right thing to do then and the courageous thing to do for any politician of the time and makes us, as Americans, proud of our past political leadership, proud of our military, and proud of our nation. Had this not occurred, we might not have had the great, collective lump-in-our-throats in November of 2008 and the overwhelming feeling of pride in our country, in our people, and in our collective American culture and values, when our first black President of the United States was elected and gave that most inspiring speech on election night, when the results became clear.

Now, I come from a military family, in that my father was a pilot in the Air Force for twenty-five years, before retiring and starting a second career in the private sector. I also had a nephew serving on active-duty in the military. As for me, I had intended on enlisting in the Navy to become a pilot, myself. Unfortunately, my eyesight betrayed me. Having grown up a military-brat and having had the desire to enter the military myself, however, does not give me insight that soldiers and military personnel, in or out of combat have.

I recall at the time of the last election, having read several different polls, both military polls and independent polls of citizens on the street. What I had concluded from these polls was that the results for me were inconclusive. There were so many contradictory interpretations of these polls and so much depended upon how the questions were framed and asked, that there was no way that I could determine the clear and current state of opinion of the citizen-soldiers themselves, nor of the American people (at the time).

I can tell you this, however; regardless of policy, the American people as a whole clearly support the gay and lesbian soldiers currently in the military and the fact that they are gay or lesbian, does not diminish the support of the American people in their respective roles, in my view. The key issue, of course, was whether or not they would be allowed to "serve openly" in the military.

The policy of "don't ask, don't tell" (DADT), didn't allow them to openly reveal their sexual orientation. Essentially, it called upon them to suppress it and not discuss it. As I understood the policy, should any gay person have discussed their sexual orientation openly while serving, or should their behavior have led to their being investigated, then depending upon the results of that investigation, they could have been discharged from the military (honorably, so long as no other compounding violations or conduct required otherwise). Therefore, by definition, in order to walk the safest possible course so as to avoid discharge under the DADT policy, they had to hide or suppress their sexual orientation, if it varied from heterosexual. Now, one may argue semantics, or if I have interpreted anything incorrectly, then tell me I'm wrong, but this is how I read it. So, for the purposes of this discussion, this is how I will frame my conversation and examination of it.

Now that gay, lesbian, and transgender soldiers can serve openly in the military, I do believe that the greatest weight in this whole discussion should be given to active-duty citizen-soldiers. Only they can know the rigors of combat and the effect of the current policy on unity within a unit. I think that the call, to a large degree, should be theirs. But of course, this is the military we're talking about and it never has been and never will be a democracy; nor should it ever be one.

Therefore, we have to rely on our civilian leadership, our Commander-in-Chief, to do the right things by them and to make the right calls; not for political popularity or political gains, not in this arena, where the stakes are life and death and the well-being of our armed forces and our ability to defend our country effectively. Harry Truman did the right thing in ordering the desegregation of the military and it took a lot of guts, vision and self-examination for him to do it at the time he did. He had to think about our history, our values as a country, our moral standing with ourselves and with God, and our duty to each other, as unified

A HARD LOOK IN THE MIRROR

Americans. He had to make a decision, which at the time was not popular...and of course, he did the right thing.

Now, based upon my stated view, one may logically ask if desegregation of the military under President Truman, through Executive Order 9981, should have instead been left up to a vote by those serving in the military at the time. God knows what the results would have been and the answer of course is no. In my estimation, and I'm sure in most everyone's estimation, the segregation that existed in our society and in our military at the time, represented a violation and contradiction of our own principles, laid-out by our own Founding Fathers, and made clear in our foundational documents; the Declaration of Independence, the Constitution, and the Bill of Rights. President Truman saw the injustice that needed to be addressed and demonstrated admirable leadership to right that wrong.

This said, we are getting a taste of that contradiction here in this question. I think we can only trust that our President Obama made the decision on the same basis as Harry Truman, and that he considered very similar questions and came to an answer in a similar way. Because if he did it for any other reasons, or if he considered what was politically popular, or expedient, rather than what is morally and ethically the right thing to do for our military and for the country, then we are in very deep trouble on several different levels; for then we would have serious issues with the character and integrity of the man holding the most important job in the country and arguably, in the world; a position of trust that the American people hold dear, going all the way back to George Washington.

I choose to believe that he did make the decision based upon similar reflections as Harry Truman, for similar reasons. I choose to believe that he made the decision based upon what he felt were the right moral reasons and in the best interests of our military, our country, and our people. I don't know if he was right and truth be told, I might have felt more comfortable leaving DADT in place a bit longer, given the wars we were fighting at the time and are still engaged in, at different levels. I didn't think our servicemen and women needed the distraction in the middle of two wars. But he's the President and I respect that. I continue to sincerely hope it works out okay and that we can one day look back and history will say that our President Obama showed the same guts and conviction as Harry Truman did, and did the right thing for the right reasons, and that we are a better country and a better people for it.

Personally, I don't ask people what their sexual orientation is and I don't care what it is. In my business, I evaluate people and promote people on the basis on one thing and one thing only...***DEMONSTRATED PERFORMANCE***. Race, gender, ethnic origin and sexual orientation don't matter to me. In business, being the best means having the best people around you, and the minute you start evaluating and promoting people on anything other than demonstrated performance, you're doomed, because you won't have the best performers in leadership roles, or in roles that make a difference, and you won't perform as well as you can and should, you won't set the right example, you won't be respected for your decisions, and if you're the right kind of person or leader, you wouldn't be able to look at yourself in the mirror each day. Furthermore, if you do the wrong things in this regard, you're results will ultimately demonstrate the consequences of your ethical and leadership failure.

Should the military be any different? Well, I don't live in close quarters with the people I work with and my very life doesn't depend upon a failure caused by a problem related to lack of unity. Some think a lack of cohesiveness, unity and teamwork could have been created by the elimination of DADT. Certainly we have gay, lesbian, and transgender servicemen and women and I'd say it's a fair bet that, even with DADT, their straight brother and sister soldiers knew, or suspected some of those who are gay, lesbian, or transgender, and yet still actively counted on them and depended upon them for unity within the combat unit and for the faithful and professional execution of their duties to protect the unit and their collective lives.

So I suspect that we are in the midst of a process, slowly playing itself out today in the battlefields and support units in places like Iraq and Afghanistan, under the most severe conditions. The process I speak of is that of acclimation. The more that gays, lesbians and transgender soldiers in the military demonstrate to their brother and sister soldiers that sexual orientation is *not* a factor in the professional execution of their duties and in their professional role and relationship with their brother and sister soldiers, and likewise that it does *not* negatively affect team unity, and that their behavior "at work" is not materially different than any other professional soldier, the more the issue will become a non-issue and over time, will disappear altogether, probably exiting with a whimper, rather than a bang.

Then and now, there are still divided opinions on the matter.

In the big picture, it is behavior, attitude, professionalism and performance that must be managed in business, and even more so in the military. Professional, competent behavior and execution is rewarded, while unprofessional, incompetent behavior is addressed through disciplinary measures or termination in business, and through discharge in the military.

As it took time for the military and for this country to work through its racial discrimination and prejudices, it will likely take some time to deal with this issue in the military. As people's understanding grows and as confidence builds through professional, consistent execution of one's duties, issues like this hopefully become non-issues. This said, the opposite is also true. Not hiding ones sexual orientation in the military and the successful, long-term elimination of DADT can only be as successful as the gay, lesbian and transgender soldiers make it. Really, it is up to them, as individuals, no different than it is in the workplace. The primary difference is that the stakes, of course, are so very much higher. After all, we're talking about life and death in this arena, not to mention victory and defeat on the battlefield, and the implications this has for our country's policies, goals and place in the world.

So, as I have given you my middle-America, middle-class insights, above, and indeed, as I have more formally worked through my own thought-process on the issues (in the writing of these passages), I find that I am more firmly *not* in favor of the past DADT (Don't Ask, Don't Tell) policy, as an independent citizen. I cannot of course speak for our soldiers on the battlefield. I do believe that there is a process that we must work through (and are working through as a society), however, and I don't think that when it comes to the military, the acclimation process can be rushed. There is simply too much at stake. So while some may believe that President Obama was premature and rushed things, by the same token, I also sincerely hope not, in my heart-of-hearts. For I want success for him, for our servicemen and women, and for our country, in this and in all things, aside from my disagreements with several of the President's other policies mentioned in this book.

I personally believe that our gay, lesbian and transgender soldiers simply need to understand that they are the Jackie Robinsons of the military right now, and that their service and professionalism will go a long way toward the old DADT policy fading into the past, forever, as these military conflicts in Iraq and Afghanistan hopefully come to a close. I don't know what our servicemen and women think today, now that the new policy has been in effect for a time. If we could put out a fair survey to them to understand their current thinking and what they've experienced, from each unique perspective and as a whole, I'd really be interested in knowing.

I personally believe that, as long as soldiers conduct themselves like soldiers, it shouldn't be an issue. Like the workplace, I don't care what anyone's sexual orientation is and what anyone does after work hours is of none of my business. I respect the people I work with for the quality of the job that they do, the type of team-players that they are, and the commitment and integrity they demonstrate. This said, being a soldier when one is on active combat duty, is 24/7. So taking a little more time to carefully implement the current policy with appropriate discussion, training and acclimation, at the field level, wouldn't necessarily have been such a bad thing, in my view. I saw this as a process of evolution that, if rushed, could result in a certain amount of chaos in dangerous places, where we don't need anymore chaos. But I also believed that, as its history has shown, our military would meet the challenge and figure out a way to work through this successfully and improvise where necessary, within their own community, in ways that make sense for them.

So while my own sense of caution, relative to battlefield rollout, might have been to move more slowly and order the military leadership to put forward their own plan and timeline to address the issue, frankly, I still trust the military to handle this in an objective, fair and even-handed way. They handled integration of the armed forces professionally and, I think, reasonably well, despite the difficulties and setbacks experienced by some individual soldiers. I believe they will handle things well here. Here were the views of a couple of past military leaders on the subject.

Regarding "Don't Ask, Don't Tell":

PATRICK F. WALSH

Former Chairman of the Joint Chiefs of Staff Gen. John Shalikashvili (Ret.) and former Senator and Secretary of Defense William Cohen spoke against the [DADT] policy publicly in January 2007:

"I now believe that if gay men and lesbians served openly in the United States military, they would not undermine the efficacy of the armed forces."

General Shalikashvili wrote.

"Our military has been stretched thin by our deployments in the Middle East, and we must welcome the service of any American who is willing and able to do the job."

I don't know about you, but for me, if General Shalikashvili, a lifetime member of the armed forces community and a former Chairman of the Joint Chiefs of Staff, as well as William Cohen, former Secretary of Defense, both believe it should not be an issue, then at the very least, I believe that should give us confidence in our servicemen and women to handle these changes professionally and with unity and esprit de corps.

I'm certain many will disagree with my views and recommendations on this subject. But in frank honesty, I found that at the outset of this discussion, I was somewhat hesitant to fully embrace the speed and manner in which the new policy was put in place and DADT eliminated, to the degree that I felt that the politics of the situation might have bred recklessness, which could damage the long-term success of the new policy, which I believe is the correct policy in the long-term. Yet, as I thought my way through the logic of my position, vis-à-vis my own life experience and my practical beliefs about this subject, relative to the business world and relative to my own, personal leadership style in my own job, I found that my concerns relative to the military and the battlefield arena lessened. Instead, my everyday, business world and social view became dominant and just as applicable in my mind, essentially, **that like any-thing else, it is not a person's sexual preference that is at issue, but rather the quality of a person's character, as embodied by their per-sonal integrity, professionalism, conduct and commitment, in under-standing the critical requirements and consequences involved and applying their own good judgment and sense of integrity to the over-all situation...a la Jackie Robinson...**

Therefore, I do hope that that I President Obama is right about it. I would be very pleased to see the most important qualities a person pos-sesses, come bursting through closed doors and speak loudly to ques-tions of character, professionalism, integrity and civil rights.

CHAPTER 14

911, THE LOUD MUSLIM SILENCE & THE GROUND-ZERO MOSQUE... THE DUMBING-DOWN OF THE AMERICAN PEOPLE, OR OF THE AMERICAN MEDIA?

"HELLO, HELLO...ANYBODY HOME?...THINK McFLY, THINK!"
[Quote from the wonderfully infamous Biff Tannen
in the 1985 movie, "Back to the Future"]

Honestly my brother and sister Americans of every race and gender, do they really think we're all nothing more than modern-day versions of George McFly, of "Back to the Future" fame? Do they think we are all a pack of dim-witted, mind-numbed George McFly or Gomer Pyle-types who run around saying "shazam" every time we have a single moment of mental clarity in our otherwise dullard existence? Do they picture themselves as Biff Tannen, above, running around, smacking us on the top of the head, saying "Hello, hello, anybody home?", whenever we deign to think for ourselves and be infuriated, angered and appalled at the downright gall of other people to insult our intelligence to our face, while expecting us not only to accept the slap-in-the-face as a people, but to also expect us to be ashamed of ourselves and apologize to them for not accepting the insult graciously and agreeing with them?

Do they expect us to allow them to use their irrational and specious logic against us, as they try to make a ridiculous argument that would have them illogically use our own constitution against us and actually attempt to use this hallowed document and the hallowed principles that it espouses, to prostitute our values, our common-sense, and our unity as a people and try to turn us against each other, as they tell us to repent?

God forbid we should use our minds, or listen to what our collective "gut" is telling us, even screaming at us at times.

Who are they? Well, let me count the imbeciles, whose right I absolutely defend to be imbecilic...:

1.   Ground Zero Mosque Islamic cleric Imam Feisal Abdul Rauf.
2.   Former BP CEO Tony Hayward
3.   Various MSNBC news commentators
4.   Bill Maher (was against the mosque, as he believes all religions are fairy tales, but for their right to build it under the first amendment).
5.   The Usual Suspects in the Liberal Media elite.

AN OBJECT LESSON: THE PAST CONTROVERSY AND RAGE OVER THE GROUND-ZERO MOSQUE, IMAM RAUF, AND THE BELIEF THAT WE AMERICANS WERE BORN YESTERDAY AND WILL SWALLOW ALMOST ANYTHING, IF SLICKLY PACKAGED...

As an object lesson, let's first discuss the past ground zero mosque controversy and debate. The obvious question is, why would Imam Rauf have continued to pursue the building of this mosque near ground zero, when he clearly saw the pain, grief and emotional suffering both the idea and the debate were causing, which he clearly knew the building of the mosque would bring to so many Americans in the city of New York and around the country?

Why would he have sought to continue the project that many Americans (and especially New Yorkers), considered as adding insult to injury to our people, who suffered and endured through 911, rather than decide to build it elsewhere? Of course he knew then that if he had announced that, after due consideration, he had concluded that this was clearly a mistake and misjudgment on his part and that indeed, seeing the divisiveness and pain this had been causing New Yorker's and the American people, and the anti-Muslim sentiment it had been clearly engendering in many, that he had decided to build it elsewhere instead, out of appreciation and respect for this country and for the everyday New Yorker, then he would have garnered significant praise, respect, and a newfound appreciation from Americans, for himself as a Muslim leader (at the very least). The same positive sentiments would have accrued as well, to other Muslims taking such a public position of support, understanding and consideration towards America and Americans.

A HARD LOOK IN THE MIRROR

So since he knew this (because after all, this was not a stupid man), why would he have continued to pursue it so unrelentingly? The answer to this, when analyzed, is not as complicated as it is important to understand.

Rauf stated that his purpose in wanting to build the mosque near ground zero was as follows:

"Our initiative is intended to cultivate understanding among all religions and cultures.

Our broader mission — to strengthen relations between the Western and Muslim worlds and to help counter radical ideology — lies not in skirting the margins of issues that have polarized relations within the Muslim world and between non-Muslims and Muslims. It lies in confronting them as a joint multi-faith, multi-national effort."

It was crystal clear, I think, to most Americans like me, who are everyday working people from the middle class and who can understand logic better than the politicians would give us credit for. We knew that allowing this mosque to be built would achieve precisely the opposite of what Rauf's stated intentions would suggest.

Most middle-class, common-sense Americans like you and me can still look at the color black and say it's black, and we can still look at the color white and say it's white, and we are not trapped in the politician's and the Media Industrial Complex's world of grays, browns and ambers, where there is no defined white or black, or good or evil, or moral certainty. There is only green, the color of money in their world, and political correctness gone awry.

Any reasonable, thinking, logical American would have read or heard the Imam's statement above and immediately seen it for what it was. They'd have been enraged and probably would've let loose with a string of verbal epithets, resembling the seven words you can't say on TV; for the sheer audacity and arrogance he demonstrated in essentially telling us that he considers us no smarter than a band of village idiots, who cannot see through the thinly-veiled endeavor to build a monument to the terrorists on the hallowed ground where thousands of Americans had their lives suddenly and viciously taken from them and from their families. Others of us would've sadly laughed at the preposterousness of it and the sheer audacity it took to say it. **Of course, those of us with such a reaction also noticed that not a single direct condemnation of the terrorists, or the terrorist act itself, came from Imam Rauf with the statement above. Curious? No, not really curious for those of us with a functioning mind.**

Reasonable, thinking, logical Americans, especially New Yorker's, recognize when someone is both trying to screw them and then wants to be thanked for doing so. By his actions and by his failure to directly condemn the terrorists and the terrorist act, Rauf showed himself for what he was (and is), an evil man who was trying to put one over on the American people, and we, the public, saw him coming from a mile away. Why didn't our leaders and politicians, the purveyors of political correctness and graft, see what he was doing and call him out? Answer: They did and they just didn't care. They cared more about political correctness and the color green. They showed little concern for the victims and their families in New York (their constituents), and little concern for the sensibilities of the American people, and they needed to be voted out of office.

The problem illustrated here, is the lack of values and decisiveness demonstrated by our so-called political leaders. In fact, it is much more serious and much sadder, with greater implications than an Imam in New York imitating a used-car salesman and trying to flimflam the American people. I think most common-sense Americans saw it exactly for what it was. **He and his supporters were, in fact, trying to use our values and our constitution against us, to build a monument to death, destruction and to what he and other Muslim's saw as a victorious band of Jihadists, who struck the Americans hard and achieved, in their minds, a great victory.**

Of course, it would also be a grand monument to graft, gross political negligence, insensitivity, ineptitude, and failure of leadership in the U.S. and in New York, on a significant scale. It would, in addition, create a monument to political corruption and stupidity, aside from the tragic sadness of it all. Our politicians ran for cover by saying that the Mosque represented a victory for American values of fairness and non-discrimination. This, while We The People, the American Public, saw it for exactly what it was and burned with anger, resentment, and righteous indignation for the colossal betrayal by our failed political leadership...once again, as they too took us all for village idiots.

So, if most common-sense Americans agreed with me, that the building of the Mosque would achieve precisely the opposite of what Rauf's stated objectives were, then why was he doing it? Why was he hell-bent on continuing the fight, knowing as he did (and as I outlined above), that a magnanimous retreat, based upon understanding and consideration for the feelings and sensitivities of the American people, would have brought him and the tolerant Muslims he purported to represent, a wave of appreciation and even respect from the American people? Why was he hell-bent on continuing this, when he knew that to retreat for the reasons I mentioned, would likely also have vaulted him into a position as a recognized Muslim leader of moderation, tolerance and understanding in this country and put him in the position of someone who could potentially move to try and broker meaningful understanding between the Muslim world and the West, at least in some limited way?

Well, as a famous writer used to say (I'm paraphrasing): Contradictions do not exist. Whenever you think you are facing a contradiction, check your premise (your basis and foundation for why you believe a contradiction exists) and you'll find that one of your premises is wrong. BINGO!

A. There was NO contradiction with my middle-class, middle-America explanation of why Rauf was building this and was hell-bent on continuing his fight. I repeat it here for clarity and emphasis:

"He and his supporters were, in fact, trying to use our values and our constitution against us, to build a monument to death, destruction, and to what he and other Muslim's saw as a victorious band of Jihadists, who struck the Americans hard and achieved, in their minds, a great victory."

The reason I outline above, would be in agreement with the premise I outline. No contradiction.

B. Meanwhile, there is a huge contradiction with Imam Rauf's explanation of why he was building the mosque...er...so-called "community center" and was hell-bent on continuing his fight. I repeat his stated reasons here, for clarity and emphasis:

"Our initiative is intended to cultivate understanding among all religions and cultures. Our broader mission — to strengthen relations between the Western and Muslim worlds and to help counter radical ideology — lies not in skirting the margins of issues that have polarized relations within the Muslim world and between non-Muslims and Muslims. It lies in confronting them as a joint multi-faith, multinational effort."

A HARD LOOK IN THE MIRROR

As I've stated, this would and did foment divisiveness, lack of understanding, lack of sensitivity and generated a backlash by New Yorkers at the time, requiring 24/7 police protection on the site of the project. They saw it as an arrogant, insensitive, slap-in-the-face, designed to humiliate, if not commemorate and celebrate the Jihadist attackers.

The reasons provided by Rauf are in contradiction to his premises, in my view, and the contradiction is both obvious and transparent.

Has Imam Rauf ever condemned the 911 hijackers individually and collectively in clear and certain terms and condemned the branch of Islam that embraces and promotes intolerance and jihad?

Not anywhere that I can find. He's called it a tragedy and he's even suggested that we are to blame, when he said:

'We tend to forget in the West, that the United States has more Muslim blood on its hands than Al Qaeda has on its hands of innocent non-Muslims.'

He has also suggested that to reverse the decision and to have built the mosque elsewhere could have resulted in a violent backlash from the Muslim world.

My reaction to that was and is to tell him that he can take his "violent backlash" and stick it in his ear (although I was actually thinking of a different, more appropriate anatomical location for it) and then plant a nice big kiss on my middle-income, middle-class, middle-American ass, and I'd bet that there are a majority of Americans and particularly New Yorkers, who told him and would tell him today, the very same thing. And they would do so with extraordinary passion, albeit using much more colorful and creative language than I.

PATRICK F. WALSH

HEY, SO WHO WAS LOOKING OUT FOR THE INTERESTS, THE SENSITIVITIES AND THE SENSIBILITIES OF THE CITIZEN'S OF NEW YORK AND THE AMERICAN PEOPLE?

Let me first say that the Media Industrial Complex of the liberal media elite was saying at the time that the building the mosque was looking out for the interests of the American people, in reaffirming our constitutional values of freedom and tolerance. Ok, that's certainly what I'd expect them to say and it's an argument and position I've evaluated and given a lot of consideration to (for about 5 seconds). In an isolated, strictly academic discussion, with no feelings that would give-way to perspective, or to matters of heart, soul, mind, and the fabric of the American spirit and its people, I would agree.

However, let me ask you if, during World War II, soon after the attack on Pearl Harbor, an organization calling itself the Japanese Society for Peace were to have proposed to build an Admiral Yamamoto "Community Center" for Mutual Understanding on the site of the attack at Pearl Harbor, for the stated purpose of promoting tolerance and understanding following the attack (while never clearly and directly condemning the attack or the attackers, I might add), would we expect that this should have been supported by our political representatives and our people? Well sure, if we were raving mad, dressed in straight-jackets daily and were confined to padded cells. So no, I think not.

Now, by the letter of the law, the Imam may have been fully entitled to go through the process and build this mosque. But I ask you, where was the President in all of this? Where was the Mayor of New York? Where was the Governor of New York and the State Representatives?

There is still such a thing as right and wrong and offending the American people and the citizen's of New York and their long-suffering families.

226

A HARD LOOK IN THE MIRROR

Could anyone have imagined George Bush supporting this as President Obama did? Where was the leadership, the shared sense of sadness and loss, not to mention outrage? Where was the demonstration by the American leadership I have mentioned, of shared understanding of the feelings, sensibilities, and the profound question of right and wrong involved in this issue and the basic compassion for the citizens of this country and most especially of New York, who lost so many loved-ones at the hands of the Muslim Jihadists?

Where also, was the elected leadership of our country and of New York, whose first response should have been to call upon the Imam to clearly and vocally condemn, in no uncertain terms, both the Muslim attackers and their terrorist acts committed against the U.S. on 911? Why were they not insisting, loudly and clearly, that he condemn this branch of Islamic believers and all who pervert their religion by such horrific acts (if indeed it is a perversion of their religion)? Could this be a premise that may again contradict? Hmmm, I wonder...?

From my perspective, based upon the overwhelming silence from the Muslim world (and from the Imam) in condemning the 911 attack and attackers, I begin to think that maybe it's not a perversion. Given their silence, what else can I reasonably and logically think? I only say that, because if it were a perversion of their faith, I would think that many in the Muslim world, from Muslim leaders, to Imams, to practitioners the world over, would have joined in a loud and united outcry, condemning the 911 attacks in the clearest and loudest of terms, calling the terrorists just what they were, TERRORISTS AND MURDERERS.

Now, I know this isn't politically correct to be so blunt and I don't know about anyone else, but I'm still waiting to see and hear that. Of course, Rauf never demonstrated that he condemned it in this way. Now, I know the vast majority of Americans felt then (and still feel today), the same way I do. Where was and where is the condemnation? It's been more than a decade and we're still waiting. **The loudest sound you'll hear <u>is</u> <u>the silence</u>! That continued silence, my brother and sister Americans of every race and gender, continues to speak volumes!**

Furthermore my fellow Americans, don't hold your breath. It's never going to come! Do you know why? Check your premise...there is no contradiction. You heard and still hear no outcry from the Muslim world, because they did not then, and still do not today, consider this a crime or a perversion of their religion. This was an outrage, a murdering of innocent people, this attack upon Americans. They clearly did not and do not consider it to be in contradiction with their goals, their beliefs, and their agenda. If they did, there **would** have been an outcry by Muslims the world over. But there was not, and that has been a very consistent theme over these many years. **Again, there are no contradictions...if there seems to be one, check your premise...**

SO WHAT SHOULD HAVE HAPPENED?

There are many ways that this could have been defeated, procedurally and legally, I'm certain. From denying a building permit, to a zoning board resolution, to a resolution by congress, to an executive order from the President (if you wish), who seems to issue executive orders for almost anything he wants done or wants stopped these days, without the inconvenient necessity going through Congress. Any one of these options (or name another), should have been employed.

The President and the Representatives should have behaved as if they actually cared about the sensibilities of the people they represented and represent, and about basic issues of right and wrong, and it's as simple as that. No reasonable American would have thought that such an act would have perverted our constitution or our legal system for all time.

It simply would have been the right thing to do, in an isolated situation, for the right reasons, and the only reason it wasn't done, is because our leaders had (and have) a shortage of courage, fortitude, conscience, and ultimately leadership.

SO, SHOULD WE GIVE-IN TO TERRORIST ORGANIZATIONS, WITHDRAW FROM THE WORLD AND OUR RESPONSIBILITIES AND BECOME AN ISOLATIONIST NATION?

To the latter part of the question, I would respond, clearly no. We do not benefit from becoming isolationists. Our interests in a growing, global economy are wide-ranging, complex and vast, and to think that we can suddenly pack up our SUV and go home and close the garage door behind us and the outside world will leave us alone and everything will be peachy, is sophistry and it's dangerous. Indeed, the practical concept of the global economy, in my middle-class, middle-American opinion, was originated by the earliest conquerors who strove to dominate the geopolitical world of their times. Whether you want to talk about Alexander the Great, the Roman Empire, or the British Empire (at one time, "The Empire on which the sun never set", as it were), all sought to benefit from and dominate the global economy of their times and indeed, they did, at least for as long as they could sustain their dominion's over their respective Empires.

Our U.S. economic interests have been global in nature and scale since just after World War I. It is well documented that, prior to World War I, foreign investment in the U.S. exceeded U.S. investment in foreign Countries. After World War I, the ratio did an about-face and the opposite was true. The U.S. investment in foreign countries significantly exceeded foreign investment in the U.S. With each succeeding year, our investment in business in foreign countries continued to dramatically grow.

PATRICK F. WALSH

By the time the 1920's rolled around, America produced more essential commodities than the wealthiest foreign nations and our gross national product was greater than that of Canada, France, Great Britain, Japan and others, combined. We were, in fact, the world's number one economic power. We didn't do this by closing our doors and contracting our economy. We did it through the means of production and economic global expansion and this only increased for decades.

Our economic strength and involvement in the global economy also helped to shape our policies towards foreign governments. Our economic strength and involvement in the global economy also shaped foreign governments policies towards us, since most wanted to encourage a healthy working relationship with the world's economic superpower. Had we not reached our economic hands outward to expand opportunities for our country's businesses and undergirded our commitment to an orderly, growing global presence with investment in our armed forces to defend and protect some of those interests (where geo-political threats may have jeopardized Americans, American businesses, or American allies and trading partners), we could not have become a global economic/business superpower.

Make no mistake about it, the American people and the American economy have benefitted greatly from this natural, global nature of American Capitalism and if we're smart, we'll continue to reap those benefits by staying aggressive, not by walling ourselves off from the rest of the world, due to the threat of terrorism. We just need to be intelligent and strategic in how we go about it, how we spend our money, and in how we correctly and with integrity, employ the use of our armed forces, as outlined earlier in the chapter on military strategy.

CHAPTER 15

POLITICAL CORRECTNESS... JUAN WILLIAMS TELLS DON CORLEONE WHERE TO STICK THE OFFER HE CAN'T REFUSE!

Let me preface this by saying that I am sorry for anyone who loses their job for reasons other than misconduct, negligence, or poor performance and I was sorry for Juan Williams when he lost his job at National Public Radio. Juan Williams, although also a contributor to Fox News, was and is a well known left of center writer and commentator. He has led a distinguished life and career, in my humble opinion (based upon what I know and have read), and although I may have differences of political opinion and perhaps some philosophical differences with him, I respect him as a man, and as a professional, accomplished and dedicated journalist and writer.

From what I know and have read of him, he has demonstrated professionalism and commitment in his endeavors and, from my own observations, it appears to me that his views (over time) have moderated from his younger days. Certainly, this is a man who has seen some of the best and worst of our culture and who has paid his dues in his chosen profession, and whether you agree with him or not, he certainly has done what it takes to earn respect as a committed professional in his field, in achieving the success he has.

For those who may live in a Unabomber-style shack out in central Montana, or who may not recall, Mr. Williams was terminated from his job at National Public Radio by Vivian Schiller, his boss, for making the following statement during an appearance on the O'Reilly Factor on Fox News:

"Political correctness can lead to some kind of paralysis where you don't address reality. I mean, look, Bill, I'm not a bigot. You know the kind of books I've written about the civil rights movement in this country. But when I get on the plane, I got to tell you, if I see people who are in Muslim garb and I think, you know, they are identifying themselves first and foremost as Muslims, I get worried. I get nervous. Now, I remember also that when the Times Square bomber was at court, I think this was just last week. He said the war with Muslims, America's war is just beginning, first drop of blood. I don't think there's any way to get away from these facts."

"But I think there are people who want to somehow remind us all as President Bush did after 9/11, it's not a war against Islam. ... Bill, here's a caution point. The other day in New York, some guy cuts a Muslim cabby's neck and says he's attacking him or you think about the protest at the mosque near Ground Zero ... I don't know what is in that guy's head. But I'm saying, we don't want in America, people to have their rights violated to be attacked on the street because they heard a rhetoric from Bill O'Reilly and they act crazy. We've got to say to people as Bill was saying tonight, that guy is a nut."

Now, Juan Williams had worked for NPR since 1999. After so many years of committed service to that organization, Schiller, apparently, did not feel that he had earned the privilege of even a meeting with her to discuss the circumstances and the context of what he had said in the Fox News discussion, which she apparently felt was so egregious and severe in its violation of NPR policy, that she decided to judge him, pronounce sentence, and then professionally and publicly execute him, all in the light and glare of the public media, which seemed to me to suggest that she also fully intended to publicly humiliate this honorable man. Indeed, Schiller did not even demonstrate the professionalism, or the common decency, to meet with Williams to discuss what he had said, nor did she provide him with a fair opportunity to present a different perspective.

Now, I've worked in the private sector my entire career and I must say that this is right up there with some of the coldest treatment that I have seen, even in frigid Corporate America, where the climate of private industry can be punishing and impersonal. Even there, you at least (normally) get a face-to-face meeting with your executioner, for goodness sake.

Instead, Schiller and her messenger, NPR's Ellen Weiss, decided to dump him, not like a faithful 10 or 11 year employee, who in Schiller's mind had erred (supposedly), but rather, she dumped him like a bad first date that she didn't want to go out with a 2nd time. She actually had her corporate messenger, Ellen Weiss, phone him and tell him he was through and then she went on the air and proceeded to personally insult this honorable man. I'll tell you, private industry and frigid Corporate America has nothing on NPR. At least when we're put out of a job in the [true] private sector, our boss doesn't add insult to injury by going on the nightly news to advertise it and then top it off by suggesting that we're crazy, making comments that suggest that we need to see a psychiatrist.

Schiller, NPR's CEO, said that Williams' comments should have been "between him and his psychiatrist or his publicist", thereby suggesting in the public's mind that Williams was either seeing a psychiatrist, or that he *should* see a psychiatrist. If you ask me, Schiller's own conduct screams for psychiatric help...*for her*...not to mention a lawsuit!

Prior to his firing, I had slowly watched his views moderate over time (again, my interpretation, only). I wondered occasionally if the more left-leaning sector of the media establishment's Media Industrial Complex might begin to take notice and either begin to draw him back into the fold, either through subtle intimidation or subtle threats of exclusion, or perhaps toss him completely "out of the club". Coincidentally enough, just as I'd been thinking about this, which is normally when I see him appear on Fox News, (on those occasions when I still happen to watch it), it actually happened.

It seemed clear that the media elite's Media Industrial Complex cadre on the left, must have effectively made Williams an offer he couldn't refuse; essentially, either return to the far-left-fold, OR ELSE!

Now, if I were a betting man, I'd say that he had probably been getting at least subtle warning shots fired over his head for some time, indicating that it would be best for his left-of-center reputation and credentials, to fully return to the fold at NPR and shun Fox News, even though, oddly enough, he normally provided the view from the left, challenging Fox's traditionally conservative positions in his appearances on that network.

I also surmised that, as his views appeared to moderate over time (normally a sign of intelligence and maturity in people like you and me, whether we started out on the left or the right), he was probably subtly, or even not so subtly told by NPR **(al la Don Corleone)**, that figuratively, either his signature or his brains would be on that agreement to return to the liberal media fold.

I suspect that, being a mature and thinking person, he probably tried to walk a fine line, as his journey through moderation seemed to apparently continue. I would suppose that the media elite of the left, not hearing a forthcoming "zeig-heil", accompanied by an immediate about-face and double-quick goose-step back to the liberal media wolfpack, then saw a thinly-veiled opportunity arise on Fox (with Williams' comments) to pull the trigger on him and complete the execution of sentence.

So, without so much as a meeting, the liberal media mob immediately did a "Don Corleone" on Juan Williams and publicly executed him (in the professional sense…or so they thought), without even observing the normal, accepted custom of first placing a warm, bloody horse-head between his bed sheets as a final warning. If nothing else, it was certainly bad form. If you're going to force someone to bend to your will "Corleone Style", the "severed horse-head-warning" is obligatory I'm afraid, so that there's absolutely no mistaking the message and what's coming, and it is considered a breach of professional mob etiquette if you bypass it.

Instead, they decided to rush the process forward and send a clear and public message to the other "soldiers in their family", who might dare consider committing a similar "omerta". But, if you're going to behave like the mob, then you'd better know what you're doing and you'd better at least heed Don Corleone's clear warning…

> *"I spent my life trying not to be careless. Women and children can be careless, but not men.".… [Or media-elite-amateur types like NPR, who tries to use mob tactics]*

> *- Don Corleone*

So, as it happened, they were careless. As a result, what they figured would be a pretty clean hit on Juan Williams, instead turned very messy for them. They should have listened to the advice of Sollozzo, when he told Tom Hagen; "I'm a businessman, Tom. Blood is a big expense". A big expense indeed for NPR, as it turned out.

Now, as it happened, Frankie Pentangeli...er...Juan Williams, had some life left in him after the attempted hit, and immediately began to turn state's evidence, going to the Feds for protection (Fox News). The Feds (Fox News) immediately put him in witness protection. Thereupon followed a series of televised hearings on Fox News and other Fox outlets, where Pentangeli...er...Williams, began to sing like a bird, and eloquently and effectively bludgeoned his failed executioners into bloody submission.

Aside from some token resistance on their part, NPR went to the mattresses to wait-it-out until the hail of bullets stopped...and the hail of bullets was coming from more than just the conservative news outlets. The New York Times and others even found the attempted hit on Mr. Williams to be distasteful and unfair, or at least questionable at best... and it didn't stop there.

Mr. Williams, as it turned out, was no shrinking violet ready to fade quietly into the setting-sun. Nope, he had a lot of ammo and wasn't about to let the NPR mob come out from their mattresses and do what they did to Sonny, if he had anything to say about it. And it turns out, he had plenty to say. So he pulled his Tommy-gun out of its violin case and set it on full automatic and he kept his finger pressed firmly on the trigger, not for a few seconds, but for a matter of days (or perhaps a couple of weeks). It must have seemed like months to his former employers at NPR.

Make no mistake about it, they received the Juan Williams version of "shock and awe". You see, he correctly followed Clemenza's advice to Michael Corleone to "come out blasting" and as Clemenza told Mike..."don't worry...they'll be plenty scared". And you know what? They were...**for their jobs.** Juan Williams effectively turned the tables on them, at least for a time. But all serious-kidding aside, I was very happy for Juan Williams, to see him supported by prominent conservative and liberal defenders, alike. It was a real treat to see the Political Correctness Gang (on the left or the right), and the crooked practitioners of it, get their comeuppance. You see, I, like most of you, despise the Political Correctness Gang, whether it's from the left or the right.

Now, keep in mind, in my view, the far-right sector of the Media Industrial Complex's media-elite, is fully capable of, and has engaged in similar behavior. This particular case just happened to be both extraordinarily blatant and egregious.

So when viewed in this light, the question that I ask myself is, was this really political correctness, or was this nothing more than a professional hit, masked as political correctness? Does the distinction really matter? In the end, isn't it political correctness run amok, since the reason given for his dismissal are those comments he made, regardless of a secondary strategy, which in my humble opinion was almost assuredly in-play? And my answer is...?

It was clearly both. They used political correctness as an excuse to put the hit on Williams, which was probably in the works for some time. But it was indeed political correctness, since his statement was the reason given as the basis for the firing and, since this is so, and since it is most clearly and certainly political correctness run amok, this sector of the media industrial complex got precisely what it deserved from Juan Williams, the American people, as well as from several sectors of the left and right general media, and from people like Jessie Jackson and others. It got a swift kick in its huge behind and I'd have liked nothing better than to see it followed by a pie-in-the-face, in the form of a resignation or two at NPR.

Furthermore, the following statements made by Jessie Jackson, a man who has fought for civil rights most of his life and whose liberal credentials are well documented, certainly exemplified the Political Correctness phenomena collapsing-in on itself:

"NPR was wrong because they did not afford him freedom of speech,"
Jackson said. "They did it in a way that was unfair. The context was
he was arguing with Bill O'Reilly, saying why he should not be so
virulently anti-Muslim ... It reminded me so much of the case with
Shirley Sherrod. They jumped so quick."

"I think that some of this predisposition towards Fox was the rea-
son for the gotcha," Jackson said. "If they did not want his point of
view, they should have said, 'When your contract is over, you do
not fit into our scheme of things.' And then (he'd) go gracefully and
with dignity. But to fire him in that way, and then to suggest he
should see a psychiatrist, it was beneath the character and reputa-
tion of NPR."

[Excerpted from Jackson's comments made Wednesday, Oct. 27,
2010, during an extended interview with respected D.C. newsman
Bruce DePuyt on TBD's "Newstalk" program.]

The only disagreement that I have with Jackson is that I do not believe
it was beneath the character and reputation of NPR. I believe it was exactly in-line with the character and reputation of NPR, as unfortunate
as that may be for NPR and its followers.

Now, what we also had the extraordinary privilege to watch and potentially understand is that, once again, politics is not a flat-plane with a
right and a left. It is in fact, a circle. Go far enough to the left and you
are at the right again, and go far enough to the right and you are at the
left again. Please bear with me in this thought.

For those who are old enough to remember the **real** Cold-War between
the Soviet Union and the United States, what we saw in the Soviet Union
was the far left taken to its logical extreme; namely, complete and total

government control of its citizenry, of its public dialogue and discourse, and complete control of its press and media (not to mention the military and intelligence agencies, of course). It was, if you will, political correctness imposed by the government and taken to the furthest extremes possible, where a free exchange of thoughts, a free press, and freedom of speech were literally non-existent. You see, in my book and in its simplest terms, Political Correctness equals Censorship.

The Juan Williams case, admittedly, echoes far lower degrees of that type of control of free speech and thought, but surely it can serve to illustrate the point that, should we as American People support that type of Media Industrial Complex, either to the extreme left or the extreme right, we end up in the same extreme spot of that 360 degree circle, eventually. If we also allow "Trojan Horses" like the oft-discussed government proposed "Fairness Doctrine" to be implemented and foisted upon us, essentially to control the free exchange of ideas in the media, we will only be selling ourselves out and pushing our society closer to an extreme spot on that circle.

In my humble, middle-America, middle-income, middle-class view, there is the old Soviet Union style of society on one extreme side of the political spectrum and there is Adolph Hitler-type fascism on the other extreme side. Yet both, paradoxically, while viewed as being on opposite sides of the spectrum, are very close together on the aforementioned circle, in terms of the practical result, relative to their absolute control over society, the military, the media, and independent thought and dialogue, I think. And if they control all of that, then **they** control our freedom, and "WE THE PEOPLE" do not.

Acute political correctness, when allowed and supported by us (We the People), and when voluntarily engaged in by the media to support their own political agenda, stifles the true American Values of freedom of speech, liberty and independent thought, which our Founding Fathers and our brothers and sisters before us laid down their lives to preserve.

And at least in one prominent case, it demonstrated that, in exercising these freedoms in a supposedly free society, where NPR's political agenda controlled the freedom of speech of their employees, through a de-facto policy of "political-correctness-type-intimidation", it can result in a prominent, eminently qualified employee-journalist with a long track record of success, integrity and fairness, ruthlessly and unjustly getting fired from his job, for nothing more than doing his job and reasonably and professionally exercising his freedom of speech.

If you don't agree with me...just ask Juan Williams...

CHAPTER 16

GETTING IN TOUCH WITH OUR INNER DIRTY HARRY; THE POST OBAMA ELECTIONS – WHAT HAVE THE REPUBLICANS AND DEMOCRATS LEARNED?

Going back to the first mid-term elections, following President Obama's first term, if President Obama's post-election press conference from the White House was any indication, the answer to the question posed would seem to be that the President was in the midst of one of the most serious cases of political denial that I have witnessed, which in my view, continues to this day. The first questions asked of the President were very clear and very pointed. They basically asked if the President accepted the notion that the election results (the Democrats took a shellacking) reflected a repudiation and clear disagreement among the American people with his policy decisions and the path he was following. The President appeared to repeat over and over again, that the results reflected the American people's dissatisfaction with the **progress** achieved so far, **_not with the policies themselves_**.

Prior to those first midterm elections, poll after poll had demonstrated that a majority of the American people had a basic disagreement with the President's policies, from healthcare, to the bailout, to immigration, and the midterm elections reflected the American people simply taking the liberal side of the Democrat party out to the woodshed, to the degree that they ended up punch-drunk and out of a job. The only thing preventing the President from the same fate was timing. Had he been up for re-election back then, he most likely would have joined the rest of the liberal Democrats on their journey to the woodshed and possibly been handed a similar fate.

It's not possible that he was oblivious to this. Therefore, it's clear that he chose to be in public denial. I also believe that the President's selective tunnel-vision, his ego, and scarier still, his core beliefs, had him combining his state of denial with an attitude of "damn the torpedoes, full speed ahead". You see, he has demonstrated a habit of making extraordinary efforts to say the things he's required to say in order to at least sound somewhat prudent, while then going on to essentially ignore what he has said to pursue his agenda, regardless of the practical or financial consequences, and regardless of any clear messages sent by the American people regarding their preferences.

Back then, for example, he spoke about his post mid-term election reflections and his deigning to consider working with Republicans across the aisle, with a greater spirit of unity and cooperation. But in the end, it's clear that his ego and his core-beliefs wouldn't allow him to deviate in any material way from the path he had set for his administration and this country, and I didn't think it would matter what the people had said through the midterm election results, and I didn't think it would matter what the Republicans said, moving forward from that. I had hoped I was wrong, but that was my sense of it. It turns out, sadly for America, that I was correct.

So that you can get a taste for yourself, have a look at the first two sets of questions asked at the post mid-term elections press conference at the White House, following the President's first term, and the President's responses. Pay particular attention to the portions I have bolded for emphasis. If you find the reading too tedious, just skip down to the end of the comments (where it says UNQUOTE), and you can pick up on my reaction to it and the fear we should all have about the President's answers. You can then refer back to his answers, if you desire.

QUOTE

Question: Thank you, Mr. President. Are you willing to concede at all that what happened last night was not just an expression of frustration about the economy, but a fundamental rejection of your agenda? And given the results, who do you think speaks to the true voice of the American people right now: you or John Boehner?

THE PRESIDENT: I think that there is no doubt that people's number-one concern is the economy. And what they were expressing great frustration about is the fact that we haven't made enough progress on the economy. We've stabilized the economy. We've got job growth in the private sectors. But people all across America aren't feeling that progress. They don't see it. And they understand that I'm the President of the United States, and that my core responsibility is making sure that we've got an economy that's growing, a middle class that feels secure, that jobs are being created. **And so I think I've got to take direct responsibility for the fact that we have not made as much progress as we need to make.**

Now, moving forward, I think the question is going to be can Democrats and Republicans sit down together and come up with a set of ideas that address those core concerns. I'm confident that we can.

I think that there are some areas where it's going to be very difficult for us to agree on, but I think there are going to be a whole bunch of areas where we can agree on. *I don't think there's anybody in America who thinks that we've got an energy policy that works the way it needs to; that thinks that we shouldn't be working on energy independence. And that gives opportunities for Democrats and Republicans to come together and think about,* **whether it's natural gas or energy efficiency or how we can build electric cars in this country, how do we move forward on that agenda.**

I think everybody in this country thinks that we've got to make sure our kids are equipped in terms of their education, their science background, their math backgrounds, to compete in this new global economy. And that's going to be an area where I think there's potential common ground.

So on a whole range of issues, there are going to be areas where we disagree. I think the overwhelming message that I hear from the voters is that we want everybody to act responsibly in Washington. We want you to work harder to arrive at consensus. We want you to focus completely on jobs and the economy and growing it, so that we're ensuring a better future for our children and our grandchildren.

And I think that there's no doubt that as I reflect on the results of the election, it underscores for me that I've got to do a better job, just like everybody else in Washington does.

Savannah Guthrie.

*Q Just following up on what Ben just talked about, **you don't seem to be reflecting or second-guessing any of the policy decisions you've made, instead saying the message the voters were sending was about frustration with the economy or maybe even chalking it up to a failure on your part to communicate effectively. If you're not reflecting on your policy agenda, is it possible voters can conclude you're still not getting it?***

*THE PRESIDENT: Well, Savannah that was just the first question, so we're going to have a few more here. I'm doing a whole lot of reflecting and I think that there are going to be areas in policy where we're going to have to do a better job. I think that over the last two years, we have made a series of very tough decisions, **but decisions that were right in terms of moving the country forward** in an emergency situation where we had the risk of slipping into a second Great Depression.*

A HARD LOOK IN THE MIRROR

But what is absolutely true is that with all that stuff coming at folks fast and furious -- a recovery package, what we had to do with respect to the banks, what we had to do with respect to the auto companies -- **I think people started looking at all this and it felt as if government was getting much more intrusive into people's lives than they were accustomed to.**

Now, the reason was it was an emergency situation. But I think it's understandable that folks said to themselves, you know, maybe this is the agenda, as opposed to a response to an emergency. And that's something that I think everybody in the White House understood was a danger. We thought it was necessary, but I'm sympathetic to folks who looked at it and said this is looking like potential overreach.

In addition, there were a bunch of price tags that went with that. **And so, even though these were emergency situations, people rightly said, gosh, we already have all this debt, we already have these big deficits; this is potentially going to compound it, and at what point are we going to get back to a situation where we're doing what families all around the country do, which is make sure that if you spend something you know how to pay for it -- as opposed to racking up the credit card for the next generation.**

And I think that the other thing that happened is that when I won election in 2008, one of the reasons I think that people were excited about the campaign was the prospect that we would change how business is done in Washington. And we were in such a hurry to get things done that we didn't change how things got done. And I think that frustrated people.

I'm a strong believer that the earmarking process in Congress isn't what the American people really want to see when it comes to making tough decisions about how taxpayer dollars are spent. And I, in the rush to get things done, had to sign a bunch of bills that had earmarks in them, which was contrary to what I had talked about. And I think folks look at that and they said, gosh, this *feels like the same partisan squabbling, this seems like the same ways of doing business as happened before.*

And so one of the things that I've got to take responsibility for is not having moved enough on those fronts. *And I think there is an opportunity to move forward on some of those issues. My understanding is Eric Cantor today said that he wanted to see a moratorium on earmarks continuing. That's something I think we can -- we can work on together.*

Q Would you still resist the notion that voters rejected the policy choices you made?

THE PRESIDENT: Well, Savannah, **I think that what I think is absolutely true is voters are not satisfied with the outcomes.** *If right now we had 5 percent unemployment instead of 9.6 percent unemployment, then people would have more confidence in those policy choices.* **The fact is, is that for most folks, proof of whether they work or not is has the economy gotten back to where it needs to be. And it hasn't...**

And ultimately, I'll be judged as President as to the bottom line, results.

UNQUOTE

Ok, I don't know about you, but the reaction I had to the above was to be afraid...very afraid. The President seemed clearly determined NOT to accept the message sent to him by the American people, through the elections results. So, let me be clear about what I believe the message was that the American people sent to the President and to the government in Washington, and to the country at-large:

A. Mr. President, we absolutely take great issue with many of your policies and disagree with them.

A HARD LOOK IN THE MIRROR

B. We are not saying we disagree with only the outcomes so far, Mr. President. We disagree with the policies themselves. It's as simple as that and you need to start changing them, as we've now clearly told you how we feel and what we think.

C. We noticed in your comments during the press conference (above), Mr. President, that you basically acknowledged that the American people were in disagreement with the deficit spending (e.g. Bailout), when there was (and still is) no plan outlined to pay for it.

Yet you simply leave that statement hanging out there in the air, Mr. President, and you never address it and we, the American people, know very well why that is, even though you and much of Washington may think that we (the American people) are the walking, talking, reality version of "Dumb and Dumber"...**It's because you have no plan whatsoever about how to pay for it, Mr. President, nor did the Democrat Congress that supported it. So we threw them out...gave them their walking papers...we fired them Mr. President, because we needed to remind all of you that you work for us, the American people, which all of you seemed to forget**.

The fact is that this gi-normous debt is the elephant in the room that you just don't want to talk about or address, Mr President. You just ignore it and you ignore us when we ask you for answers about it and we know that if we, the American people, don't take action ourselves to do something about it, that you are going to continue to ignore the elephant, continue to spend our money wastefully and profligately, and you will indeed let future generations deal with the repercussions of what amounts to the greatest "rip-off" of a people and a country in the history of the world, and the biggest transfer of wealth from that "rip-off", carried out by the government bagmen in the Treasury and Fed, to millionaire and billionaire Wall Street banks and bankers. These are the same people who made bad investments and bad business decisions, and who were never forced to take full responsibility by having to deal with the consequences of their actions, as demanded by our Capitalist system, not to mention our regulatory agencies, who apparently were given instructions by those in power in the government, *not* **to prosecute anyone.**

Essentially, the self-correcting justice of our Capitalist system and self-correcting mechanism of our capital markets was rigged. It was fixed and jimmied by you, Mr. President, aided by your cronies in Congress, as well as by George Bush and his cronies, who share this responsibility with you, as does Mr. Barney Frank. And if you want to see the *true* reality version of "Dumb and Dumber", go to one of the most highly educated states in the union...Massachusetts...where they subsequently re-elected Barney "flimflam" Frank to another term in the midst of the crisis; he, the Director of the Fannie Mae and Freddie Mac housing bubble disaster flick (the Producers were, of course, the Wall Street banking concerns and the Treasury Secretary).

So, we may ask ourselves, what should the President, the remaining Democrats and the Republicans have learned from those first midterm election results?

Answer? That they were sitting on a volatile keg of explosive voters who had adopted a "Dirty Harry" approach and mindset, because then and now, we've seen more corruption and dirty-dealing and politics-as-usual, than we would care to see in a lifetime. We've had our pockets picked clean with the Bailout and with continued profligate spending, and we've seen our jobs shipped overseas and unemployment high. We've seen the government growing out-of-control and we've seen little difference between the actions of Republicans and Democrats, regardless of what their rhetoric and platforms may say. "We the People" were and are angry and in that election, we had the 44 magnum loaded (in the form of ballots), and we had a very itchy trigger-finger, and we used it on one group of political hacks. **The message to the ones that remained...and to the incoming ones was clear..."Do you feel lucky?"...**

Pictured: "We the People" getting in touch with our inner Dirty Harry during the last mid-term elections...

While the above may sound a bit "over-the-top" and exaggerated, I assure you, as a middle-income, middle-class working stiff, it is not. If you are reading this and think that the mood of the American people, then or now, has softened that much, then you are either:

A. A Politician
B. An "Inside-the-Beltway" Gadfly

C. A Member of the Media Industrial Complex/media elite [either of the left-leaning variety, or the big-spending right-leaning variety (who agreed with the spending habits of President George W. Bush)].

As long as I'm on the subject of telling it like I think it is for most of my fellow middle-income, middle-class working stiffs of every race and gender, let me continue my rant:

1. We don't want you politicians in Washington continuing to pick our pockets clean, so that you can all continue to grow the government. Not a single one of us believes that Washington bureaucrats, state bureaucrats, or county bureaucrats can do anything efficiently. You are all simply there to carry out our wishes, not your own.

   We've all dealt with the drivers' license bureaus, the courts, city government offices, state government offices, and federal government offices. We've all seen the extreme waste and fraud in government contracts and Medicare. We've all seen the millions paid out to fraudulent government contractors. At one time or another, we've all been treated like peons by these government agencies, acting as if they were doing us a favor by providing us with any service or information whatsoever, and treating us with a mix of arrogance, dismissiveness, and inefficiency, basically telling us by their attitude and demeanor, **"You'll take my attitude and inefficiency and you'll like it!"** When, in fact, they work for us, the American people, and we pay their salaries. So we want less government, not more government in our lives. We want smaller government, not bigger government. The more of you there are in government, the more money it costs us and the more inefficient we as a country become, and the more our pockets are picked clean.

2. We've watched you bankrupt Social Security, grow the federal deficit to astronomical proportions never before seen in the history of the country, or the world. We've been watching you print money to purchase bonds on the open market, which will devalue our currency in the long-run.

3. We may not trust private industry, but frankly, we trust you even less with our money. At least with private industry, they have a certain level of efficiency and competency they must deliver, because they, unlike the government, have competition and can be out of a job if they don't perform. That doesn't suggest they shouldn't have regulatory oversight. Heck, if privatizing Social Security will give us control of our money and some level of efficiency and prevent you, the politicians, from going in and misappropriating those funds for your pet-projects and political payoffs, then guess what? We're for it. Better the devil-you-know. At least they have stockholders to answer to, so at least we know they will be efficient and will be audited and the bad ones will be excised like a cancer cell by the market. And guess what? It's our money anyway, not yours! We're paying into it. Let me repeat...it's our money, not yours...! (Sorry, I'm getting emotional...).

4. You've talked about increasing our taxes, Mr. Obama, you and our esteemed Democrats and liberal media elite...You talk about taking more from the so-called rich, who are the ones who invest in companies that keep us middle-income, middle-class Americans employed! You say they should pay more and we should pay more. In your first term, you wanted to discontinue

the Bush tax cuts, or at least minimize them. You wanted to have us pay capital gains and you talked about a value-added tax (VAT), on top of our income taxes. Guess what? We didn't want the Bush tax cuts to go away. We want to keep more of our money and spend it on...**surprise...ourselves and our families** and we're proud to say so!

And by the way...who gave you the right to re-distribute our income and tell any of us who should pay more taxes and thereby divide the classes and set us Americans against each other, and cause our wealthy to want to take their money out of the country, along with their business interests (e.g. setting up their head-quarters offices overseas to avoid high taxation here, as they have been doing)?

5. Here's a news-flash from all of us middle-income, middle-class American citizens of every race and gender, who are marginalized and disrespected by Washington!

When we, in our own households, don't have the money to spend, we don't spend it! How about all of you doing the same when it comes to our tax dollars and our children's future? Rather than spending the money on bailing out billionaire bankers and their banks, and spending it on pork-barrel projects and earmarks, how about concentrating on education, defense, fixing social security and infrastructure, and cut out all of the other waste and B.S.?

How about cutting the size of government and government spending? Cut expenses and first spend only on those things that will directly serve the American people at the most basic, important levels (education, defense, a repaired and effective social security and infrastructure).

6. How about sending the illegal aliens in our jails, who have committed crimes against us (excluding the most serious crimes), back to their countries, instead of us supporting them in those jails? How about using our school funds and our medical care funding on Americans and on people and visitors here legally, not on illegal aliens? Because, guess what? We just don't have the money to support them and we shouldn't have to support them. We didn't sign on for that.

   Let them follow the laws of our country, as we did, or as our parents and those before us did, who entered this country legally from foreign lands, just as many law abiding citizen-hopefuls from other countries do today. **Enforce the damn laws!** There must be organization, orderliness and a high level of efficiency, fairness and lawfulness. We have to do what is in this country's citizen's and taxpayer's best interests.

7. The political shills, with the two bailouts and profligate spending, have set us and our children up with the biggest debt ever incurred in the history of the world. You must know that there is no possibility to tax the American people and American business to the degree required to ever pay it off, without bankrupting the country.

   If they are allowed to tax to do this, they will impose the taxes, and businesses will contract and more unemployment will ensue, and more people will be on the public/government dole, and more programs will be added or extended, and their costs will increase and deficits will increase, and they will then try to tax some more, and more of the same will result. It will be a never ending spiral downward, feeding constantly on itself, until the house-of-cards collapses completely and our currency is valueless.

8. The magnitude of the debt today, and the debt that continues to build tomorrow, is so very great that the Fed has been printing money to buy bonds on the open market, which will result in a continuing devaluation of our currency over time and will eventually create a spiral of inflation, if my college economics courses were accurate, and if I understood them correctly.

9. In my view, the only engine that has any hope of getting us out of these economic crises and the greater, looming economic crisis, is the great engine of American productivity and commerce.

10. The only way out of the grim economic future, which will result from the economic policies that have been put in place and followed, is...and will be...to expand the economy on a large enough scale to produce a sustained economic recovery (and dare I say, prosperity and tax revenues) that will allow us to pay down our debt and get our financial house in order. To achieve a sustained economic recovery and long-term financial stability, we must have in place the *sustained* economic policies necessary to support it.

11. The only proven way to get such results, which many of the current politicians will not support (including liberal Democrats and big-spending Republicans, along with the left-leaning Media Industrial Complex), is to introduce a dramatic series of tax cuts on businesses and on consumers, which go well-beyond the Bush tax cuts. These tax cuts must be significant and must be guaranteed for a minimum period of 5 years, with an opportunity to extend them. Why?

12. When you immediately put more money into the American people's pockets, what do they do? They spend some and save some

and pay down some debt. By cutting taxes, this has the immediate effect of people having more money in their pockets, by having less taken out of their paychecks, and thereby more disposable income. They will behave predictably. They will spend more in the economy, buying goods and services. This will create more demand, more jobs, and a sustained recovery, putting people back to work to support that recovery.

13. When you cut taxes on businesses and leave more money in their pockets, what do they do? They replace plant and equipment, they invest in R&D, they expand production, they hire people, which supports all of the forgoing, which is supported by the market demand stimulated in point #11, above. This creates an upward economic spiral. I've personally seen this at work, so don't try saying that the greedy American businesses will simply put it into the pockets of their executives. That's not how it works. May some of it go back to stockholders in the form of dividends? Yes, maybe in some cases that's a reality. But there's nothing wrong with that. Many working Americans have a 401k plan of some kind. As stockholders themselves, they will never complain about a dividend, I think (increasing the value of their plan).

But the overriding reality is that businesses have to expand and have to gain market share and deliver profits, or their management gets fired. They can't grow and expand if they don't reinvest in their businesses, and trust me, after 25+ years in corporate America (from the management ranks), I have seen how businesses behave. When they grow and expand, they hire people and spend money in the economy, on real estate (office space/production space), plant and equipment, computers and technology, office furniture, logistics and transportation...you name it. This creates demand and therefore jobs in many sectors. This is good for Americans because it's good for the economy.

14. But let me ask you a question? What do people do if they know the tax cuts will only last one year, while the economic present is bad and the economic future uncertain? Answer? They spend almost none of it. They save and pay down debt. They put very little extra spending into the economy, because of the uncertainty and the expectations that dictate such behavior. The thinking goes something like this...since it's only temporary, bad times will probably continue or return and I'd better put money away and pay off debt, because I could be laid-off next month or next year.

15. What do businesses do if they know the tax cuts will only last one year? Answer? They will pocket the cash and hold it, uncertain about consumer demand and the economy, and they will hang on to it for future needs and against a rainy day. This is why the tax cuts must be guaranteed and sustained for at least 5 years, or it will not have the appropriate stimulating effect or desired result on the behavior of people and businesses. I'm only a middle-income, middle-class working stiff and I know this. How come our brilliant politicians in Washington don't?

16. Now, here's a dirty little secret I suspect they keep...**They do know!** They have the historical facts, figures and statistics to demonstrate clearly what happens to the economy when instituting such policies. When given sufficient time to work, government revenues grow...they do not decline, once the economy's version of a Saturn V rocket is fully lit by this type of stimulus. And this is a true stimulus...not a "let's pay off our billionaire

bankers and banks on Wall Street-type stimulus"...which is of course, a fake stimulus, which was pulled-off by the greatest "flimflam" artists the world has ever seen. I say this because no one has ever pulled-off a greater "flimflam" job than the great stimulus packages of 2008, by President Bush, and 2009, by President Obama.

So why don't they want to give us back more of our money? It's because *they* want to control more of it. They clearly want more control, not less. They want the people and the people's pocketbook under their thumbs, and they want American business under their thumbs. You see, it's about power and control, most importantly. It's about income re-distribution and ideology, more than it is about other considerations. That's the only answer, in light of the facts they have at their disposal and their reluctance to take the type of corrective action that has been proven to work repeatedly in the past.

Additionally, that which I propose above is economic action which does not directly add to our national debt, through increased spending (e.g. it's not a Bailout).

17. The only hope that we and our children have now, to get out from under this universe of debt on our shoulders, is to unleash the greatest economic engine that the world has ever known and we can only do that with tax cuts, the same vehicle that has proven its value and impact in the past. Due to the magnitude of the debt burden we carry, we will need to make the magnitude of the tax cuts large enough to unchain our great economic engine, in order to dramatically expand the economy, thereby creating demand, supply, jobs, and tax revenues, in that order.

18. The message from us middle-class and middle-income Americans? Cut the spending and cut the taxes and free this great economy to do what you, the politicians, will never accomplish by raising taxes, re-distributing income, or executing bailouts...

19. What party or politicians will do this? Answer? The smart ones... the ones that want to stay in office or get into office...the ones that have the hearts and the guts of our Founding Fathers.

20. ...And by the way, if you really want to cut spending and do the right thing, then get our brother and sister Americans, our sons and daughters, the hell out of Afghanistan and Iraq. If the citizens of those countries want and value freedom as badly as Americans do, they will fight for it like we did. Fund them, send them weapons, let them earn it, but let's get our brother and sister Americans, our sons and daughters, the hell out of there as soon as possible. Enough already!

21. **...and also, by the way...if you hadn't realized it by now, we want term limits put in place, immediately, and we want the earmark process eliminated.**

Should you politicians choose not to heed these messages, then you should definitely begin thinking about your answer to the 64-dollar question mentioned earlier, posed originally by the famous and infamous Inspector Harry Callahan (Mr. Dirty Harry himself)...**"Do I feel lucky? ...Well do ya, punk?"**

Ok, well, now I feel better. I've been in touch with my inner "Dirty Harry" and I feel somewhat unburdened, having said what I've wanted to say for a very long time to the nimrod Politicians. Everyone should get in touch with their inner "Dirty Harry" now and then, especially when contemplating our current crop of politicians (Democrat and Republican).

Now, I don't have to ask if my fellow middle-income, middle-class brothers and sisters of every ethnicity agree. I believe they mostly do. They understand the promise of America as I do. Further, if they are recently arrived to this country, or are first generation arrivals to this country, as legal American citizens, then they know the promise of this country, perhaps better than anyone, because they came here for opportunity, for freedom from oppression, and to enjoy true economic, spiritual, and political freedom, and they don't like the flimflam artists in Washington any more than I do, because in many cases, that is what they were, in- part, experiencing to a much greater degree and escaping from, leaving the countries from whence they came. Furthermore, they had enough respect for this country, and their now fellow Americans, to come here in the right way, respecting our laws and respecting our people and respecting themselves as law-abiding individuals.

So, it will be interesting to see if the politicians have been reading the American people and the political climate correctly and if they behave accordingly. So far, they have not. I believe the lack of integrity and leadership in government (Democrat and Republican) is worse today, in 2014, than it ever has been in my lifetime. I believe that the majority of the American people feel the same way I do. If the politicians don't read the citizens correctly, there will of course be another political change at the polls in these upcoming mid-term elections, and the American People will, in-turn, fire the current group of political weasels.

But do not forget and do not lose sight of the fact that it is "We the People" who are fully responsible and must make the changes in leadership that are necessary. My own consistent view has been that we need to throw the current crop of bums out of office through our power at the ballot box, if we want change. If we don't, we will get more of the same and we will only have ourselves to blame!

For you see, it's not the right or the left that will eventually take back the country. It is "WE THE PEOPLE" who will take back the country, in the manner that our Founding Fathers and citizens fought and died and risked everything for...We'll take it back peacefully, orderly, honorably, and in the precise manner our Founding Fathers proscribed in this great American Experiment, which was born of revolution, courage and sacrifice, and which is still alive and well in these United States. We'll take it back together, inclusively, in brotherhood and sisterhood with each other, through the free and peaceful exercise of our will as a people and as a nation; *THROUGH OUR VOTE...!*

To me, there is no greater expression of the success of this great American Experiment and no greater tribute to the vision, courage and sacrifice of our Founding Fathers and our citizens, through all of the wars fought since 1776.

CHAPTER 17

FROM REVOLUTION TO EVOLUTION – AMERICA CONTINUES TO MATURE AND REDEFINE ITSELF, CONSISTENT WITH THE PRINCIPLES OF THE FOUNDING FATHERS...

THE TEA PARTY, IF NOTHING ELSE, IS A HEALTHY SIGN THAT THE REVOLUTIONARY SPIRIT AND THE PRINCIPLES OF OUR FOUNDING FATHERS ARE STILL ALIVE WITHIN THE FABRIC OF AMERICA AND THE HEARTS OF THE AMERICAN PEOPLE.

We, the American people, are not who the Media Industrial Complex tries to tell us we are and tries to marginalize us into becoming. What they don't yet realize is that we, the American people, of every gender, color, preference, national origin and ethnicity have reached a level of perspective and maturity in this continuing revolution and evolution, to better understand what we have, how proud we are of it, and how special it is in the world we live in, as well as how quickly it can be lost. We have reached a point in our history and evolution where "WE THE PEOPLE" now better appreciate each other and more deeply appreciate what this country stands for, as we elected our first African-American President and as we all felt great pride in our country and in our people at that defining moment in our history, whether we voted for President Obama, or not.

Today, we as Americans of every race, gender, sexual orientation and national origin, perhaps more clearly than ever before, embrace what this country stands for and we realize that TOGETHER, we *are* the fabric of this country and **together**, we make that fabric ever-stronger. We as a people, have our *own* identity. **Together**, we believe in the values and principles of this country and we know we are not who the Media Industrial Complex and the people on the right or the left tell us we are (much to their chagrin).

Today's Media Industrial Complex, in my view, tends to believe that *they* set the political trends today and likewise shape the discussion and the agenda. Now, I would go so far as to say that they certainly do influence it more so than in the past. But by and large, the media still reports developments and trends and comments upon them, after they have already developed. The truth still is that "WE THE PEOPLE" define the political landscape and the direction of the country. What the media does not yet seem to understand completely, is that "WE THE PEOPLE" embrace and encompass (in a manner of speaking) the Michael Moore's **and** the Bill Maher's; the William F. Buckley's **and** the Rush Limbaugh's of this country, and everything in-between, **and there is no contradiction in this**.

What today's media elite may not grasp, or perhaps may not wish to accept, is that "WE THE PEOPLE" can listen to the view from the right **and** the view from the left, evaluate the arguments and yet agree with none. *For you see, WE are neither...and yet we are both...and this is what makes our country and this great American Experiment so very unique and so very special in all the world.*

A HARD LOOK IN THE MIRROR

We are free to have the opportunity to have a society so diverse and so rich in thought and in freedom, that we can listen to all points of view and agree, or disagree, even vehemently disagree, but peacefully...and yet still appreciate and wonder at the miracle of what we have, what this great country represents, and what our Founding Fathers and generations of Americans have fought and died for.

The question now is, are we still worthy of it? Well, I'll tell you. I saw a small news item not too long ago, which indicated that Hispanic businesses in California grew at a rate of 47% in what had been a down and sluggish, very slow recovering economy, showing me that freedom, Capitalism, independence and entrepreneurship are principles well-known and embraced by many of our Latino brother and sister Americans. You may notice I do not say Latino-Americans. Only when absolutely necessary to make a specific point, do I use such descriptions of ethnicity of any kind. As previously mentioned, the reason for this is that I dislike such distinctions and labels between Americans and only use them sparingly.

I also look at the commitment and dedication of our troops in Afghanistan and in Iraq and around the world, and am encouraged that we are reaffirming each day that we are worthy custodians and participants in our shared heritage, regardless of the argument of whether or not we should be there.

I look at our elected President, Barack Hussein Obama, and feel great pride as an American in this. By the way, although I did not vote for President Obama, I use his full name, above, not as a means of implied disparagement of the man, as was done during his first primaries by the right-wing, but instead as a source of great pride that our society, our people, could look beyond the labels and the cultural origins of his name and beyond the color of his skin and focus instead upon the **content of his character**, thereby fulfilling in many ways, the dream of a great American and peace-loving freedom fighter, the Rev. Dr. Martin Luther King Jr. And although I didn't vote for President Obama and do disagree with many of his policies, I believed then and I believe today, that this man's heart is in the right place, that he is a good man, that he does love America, and that he is doing what he believes in his heart to be right for the country, no matter how misguided I believe his economic policies to be.

You see, I believe that his election to the highest office in the land reflects our evolution as a people and reflects our heartfelt understanding of our shared American heritage, in its purest and most idealistic sense. And if it shows us and the world nothing else, it surely demonstrates that we are indeed worthy of our heritage and the sacrifices of our Founding Fathers, along with the sacrifices of all the men and women in all of our wars. It shows that we understand and embrace what they fought for and in many cases died for, and that we are slowly but surely continuing to fulfill the promise of the Declaration of Independence, the Revolution, and the tremendous sacrifices made, even as the elements of the media-elite and the opportunistic, self-absorbed politicians in Washington continue to demonstrate that they just don't get it, as they endeavor to sow seeds of descent to polarize us from one another.

You see, as they try for self-serving reasons to divide us into economic factions on the left and the right, and factions of ethnicity or color (for political reasons, or for ratings in the case of the media elite), we instead continue to evolve as a people and as an electorate and once again we remind them just who is in charge; not conservatives, not liberals...nope... just Americans...

A HARD LOOK IN THE MIRROR

So what does the emergence of the Tea Party mean? Is this the emergence of a bunch of right-wing, conservative rednecks trying to turn the clock backward?

Well, I think that this is clearly what the Media Industrial Complex would like us to think and believe...and it's not restricted to the left or the right side of the Media Industrial Complex, either. Both are threatened by the emergence of the Tea Party. Just look at MSNBC, CNN, ABC, CBS and Fox News' Bill O'Reilly. The emergence of the Tea Party takes votes away from the left and the right (but clearly more from the right); therefore, they both dislike it (excepting Glenn Beck, of course). And, I also think the jury is still out on the Tea Party. We have to watch its development and evolution to really see what emerges.

From what I have observed as a middle-class, middle-income working stiff, it seems that the Media Industrial Complex has tried to pigeonhole the Tea Party as a bunch of rednecks, yahoos and bigots on the right, who are trying to impose their own brand of right-wing government on the country. The Media Industrial Complex on the left and the right have worked hard at minimizing and marginalizing the Tea Party. But their efforts have not been as effective as they would have liked. The Tea Party continues to be relevant and they continue to maintain their numbers and even grow their base of support. They couldn't do this if they were, in fact, a bunch of rednecks, yahoos and bigots on the right. The fact is that they have at least a fair amount of support from citizens who cross racial and ethnic lines, who evidently believe in a good portion of their fiscally conservative approach to spending and the economy.

How do I see the Tea Party? Well, I'll be the first to admit I don't know as much about it as I should. Based upon what I do know, they seem to be focused on sound economic principles that happen to be conservative in nature. Now, here's a secret...well, maybe not so secret...When it is suggested that the government should manage its finances more like a household must manage its finances, meaning don't spend more than you make and don't let your credit cards get out of control and take control of your life...and don't conduct your financial life irresponsibly, so that you become a burden to your children...well, that's labeled "Conservative Economic Thinking", in the world of the left-leaning side of the Media Industrial Complex. Most people would simply call it "Responsible Thinking", "Logical Thinking", or "Responsible Behavior and Management" of one's finances (and dare I say the country's finances). In business, we call it "good business" and managing effectively to your budget.

When people talk about tax cuts to stimulate the economy and to let people keep more of what they make so that they can save some, spend some, and unleash the marketplace to create jobs through spending in the economy...well, that's called "Conservative Economic Thinking" by most talking heads. I just call it common-sense and a set of economic principles that have proven themselves through President Kennedy's administration, President Reagan's administration and in George W. Bush's administration (before Bush began spending us into oblivion). So in fact, it has been practiced by the Democrats and the Republicans.

It is my understanding that the Tea Party embraces these principles, as well, and as I've outlined previously in this book, so do I and I have embraced these principles since the late 1970's and more importantly, it has been demonstrated that they work, as long as they are accompanied by an Administration and Congress that reins-in and controls spending at the same time, so as not to irresponsibly generate tax revenues with right hand and spend it all with the left.

A HARD LOOK IN THE MIRROR

So from an economic perspective, I appear to be in agreement with the Tea Party's stance, insofar as they embrace these principles, and I have always believed that we should be prudent with our money, as a country, and that we should balance our budget each year.

From a social perspective, I'm not really clear about what the Tea Party believes or embraces. However, I will take some license here and tell you as a middle-income, middle-class working stiff, what I would like to see the Tea Party do to get my vote and fulfill the promise that a viable third party could bring to this nation and to our people.

Personally, I have never understood why being economically conservative and socially mid-stream are characterized as mutually exclusive, in that the media and the politicians would program us to believe you can't be both. As a businessperson and having an accounting background, you CAN of course be both.

It seems pretty straight forward to me that, if you have the right vision, business plan, managerial oversight and committed management team (read governance) in place and operate in a highly disciplined and efficient manner and within the budget targets you establish, you can accomplish most goals you set, as long as you are prepared to work within the economic and market realities that present themselves, and as long as you are prepared to adjust your plan to deal with those realities.

This said, personally, I would like to see the Tea Party, or any third party come out and operate with a fiscally conservative economic platform and agenda and a mid-stream, moderate, social policy agenda that will operate by embracing the following principles:

1. Always operate with a balanced budget and adhere to this discipline, always.

2. Eliminate all the earmarks and political payola bills, programs and projects and adopt the real-world economic operating policies of a business that is accountable to its stockholders...The American People!

3. Adopt the flat-tax/VAT Tax (not both) structure, which I proposed earlier, and instead of grossly scaling back the IRS (which would be possible under such a system), re-define its role beyond collecting tax revenue alone (which would now be much simpler and less complicated), to include being an aggressive investigative arm of the U.S. Government, working in conjunction with law enforcement, to go aggressively after and eliminate waste, fraud and corruption in Medicare, Medicaid, and all government entitlement programs, and in government contracting operations, wherever our federal tax dollars are spent (differentiated from the G.A.O., which is strictly an audit arm).

   I don't know about you, but this is my money and your money... not the government's money, and I want an independent arm in the government that is going to work for me to nail all the corrupt politicians, contractors, and purveyors of fraud, who are bilking you and me and the rest of us citizens. We are the ones who are really paying these bills...and who better to aggressively go after these crooks than the IRS?

4. Enhance and revamp our laws to make fraud and ripping-off the Government (read-The American People...you and me), so severe and draconian that no one in their right mind would take such risks, due to the punishment and mandatory incarceration times involved.

5. As outlined in another chapter, get our military out of the business of nation-building and stop spending money we don't have in overseas, foreign adventures and extravaganzas and use our military as outlined in that chapter. This should allow us to preserve our security, be a pain in the neck to those terrorist organizations that are threatening us (while helping those nations who truly want freedom and a Democratic system of government) and should allow us to save billions and billions in tax dollars in the process.

6. Prioritize our tax dollars to go towards Defense, Education (see Chapter 4), fixing and making social security efficient and effective, Infrastructure (roads, bridges, general infrastructure maintenance and building/re-building, and our environment), and to our other truly necessary and truly beneficial social programs.

7. Social Programs: Social programs should be prioritized to identify most to least important to our citizens. With the above steps in place, more money, not less money should be available, I think, and we should not look to simply spend it all. Our most important needs and priorities and the budget we set to remain within, should drive our decisions.

   A. We certainly don't need a complete government healthcare program to cover everyone, as I've outlined (see Chapter 5 and others). We simply need to eliminate the waste, investigate vigorously and enhance our laws and criminal penalties, so that they are so severe (as mentioned above), that to even contemplate committing fraud and stealing from you and me (the American People), a person would have to be considered mentally incompetent, given the severe jail time involved (e.g. make the minimum penalty, imprisonment for 10 years with no time off and no parole possible...or hell, make it 15 years minimum...).

B. Leave the private insurers alone. They do a pretty good job and are more efficient than anything the government is capable of running...sorry, but let's be real about this.

   1. Then create a healthcare safety net, as I've described before, which will reflect our values as Americans, to take care of the elderly in our society who are uninsured (a society that does not take care of its elderly who are ill, needs to ask itself just how civilized it really is, after all).

   2. Within this safety net should also fall those people who are between jobs (e.g. fired, laid-off) and who need insurance for a temporary period of time to cover themselves and their families, while they are seeking employment. We are brother and sister Americans after all and we have to look out for each other. I've been in this dilemma myself once before and it's a real problem. I know a high percentage of Americans have, as well.

   3. We must also have a program for those in our society who are medically unable to take care of themselves, or to provide for themselves, as a result of mental deficiency or physical impairment or other profound medical condition that makes them unable to function in society and provide for themselves. These days, we have moved towards an unspoken policy of turning many of these fellow Americans over to the criminal justice system to rot

in jail, in order to avoid the economic challenges they present to us. **This is an OUTRAGE and a SCANDAL.** If we're a civilized society that cares about our brother and sister Americans who cannot take care of themselves, through no fault of their own, then we **MUST** take care of our own, **PERIOD**!

4. There should also be a program that covers abandoned or parentless children who cannot provide for themselves. This goes without saying. Foster care programs have been problematic and inconsistent.

5. We must fix Social Security once and for all. We must fund it effectively, eliminate the fraud and keep government's hands out of the till and make the program effective and efficient.

In my personal view, these are some of the areas that we as a people, I think, should want to spend our tax dollars in, if we are as good and caring a people as we believe we are. You get the picture.

As I am a middle-class, middle-income working stiff, I know that there's nothing that drives me crazier than seeing our money spent on programs designed to provide millions to build "bridges to nowhere", to study things such as "why people who eat more get fat"...or "the mating habits of the Brazilian Tree Frog", or the infamous $500.00 ball-peen hammers that the defense department buys...**CUT ALL THAT %$@! OUT...STOP IT, ALREADY. We're tapped out and we're changing direction and we ARE going to manage our government budget like a business and we will live within our means and we will not burden our children with insurmountable debt!**

Give me and the American people a viable 3rd Party that will represent our true values and behave fiscally/economically responsible and will treat and use our military correctly and honorably. Give me and the American people a viable 3rd Party that will behave in a manner consistent with working for us, while keeping ever-present in their minds the shared commitment they have to staying true to the principles, the sacrifices, the honor and the integrity of the Founding Fathers, and of all of those who have died in all of the wars representing and defending our country, as well as the commitment they bear to the Declaration of Independence, the U.S. Constitution, the Bill of Rights and to us, the American People. Give us a viable 3rd Party like this, and it will be popular and unstoppable.

CHAPTER 18

CONCLUSION: BECAUSE...OR "BE-THE- CAUSE"...IT'S YOUR DECISION...AND IT'S OUR DECISION!

You know, I recently had the opportunity to attend some training that my employer was kind enough to send me to. In my middle-income, middle-America job, I finally took a training class that fascinated me, instead of having me look longingly at the clock for it to move faster towards the next break, where I could down some coffee, stale doughnuts, or some strange, fruit-like pastries the hotel had left over from breakfast. It actually provided me with some thoughtful insights into life and how we approach it, think about it and live it.

To me, essentially, it said that life is not what your circumstances dictate it is, or even what your perceived options dictate it is. Your life and our life, is simply what our decisions and our actions, **or lack thereof**, make it, and when you think that there are no options and therefore no choices, think again, because there is always more than one option and we always have a choice, even when it may seem that is not the case.

Believe me, I'm not trying to get complicated or esoteric, but I am trying to make a point. I've covered a fair amount of ground so far and based upon what I've covered, we have some choices to make. In some cases we have several options and in some cases, few. But we have options, as the 2010 mid-term elections clearly demonstrated.

I've talked about politics, education, the economy, war, immigration, the upbringing of our children, the Media Industrial Complex and our responsibilities as Americans to each other, to our country, to our Founding Fathers and to all of those who have died in all of the wars our country has fought to preserve our freedom, protect our people and our way of life.

All of the things I've discussed and whether or not they will make any difference at all to you, my brother and sister Americans of every race, ethnicity, gender, preference, and income bracket, boils down to two things...

WILL YOU MAKE DECISIONS AND WILL YOU TAKE ACTION...?

Now, some may be inclined to say:

"Yes, I will make decisions and take action to bring about change, but I need to wait until after the end of [whenever], because I've got a lot on my plate at work and that's as soon as I can commit to reading the newspaper more, participating in the school board meetings, our local elections, and the rest of that stuff you talked about..."

Does this sound familiar?"

How about...

"Yes, I will take time to live in the moment with my family, pay more attention to my children and what's going on in their lives and in their school and with their schoolwork, and I will know more about what their teachers are teaching them, but it will have to wait until after I finish the project I'm working on at the office, because I'm just too busy and I've got very little extra time on my hands..."

A HARD LOOK IN THE MIRROR

Well, this training I went through stated that we ought to be aware of the little voice in our heads that manufactures these types of answers for us. Based upon what I learned, if I understood it correctly (which is always iffy in my case), we need to be very aware of the words "but" and "because". Why? Because everything that comes before "but" and after "because", is nothing but **BULLSHIT!** It's an excuse, an alibi, pure and simple and it's a way to prolong the status quo while sounding like we're actually going to act, when in fact, we will not, even though we think we may have intentions to do so. It is the voice inside of every one of our head's that allows us to cop-out on our commitments and best intentions to ourselves and to each other.

It's very important to be aware of that at work, at home, and in listening to the endless stream of bullshit coming out of the mouths of our Presidents, our Congress, our local representatives, our school board members, our friends, our business colleagues, our wives and husbands, our children, our other family members, *and most importantly... the bullshit that comes streaming out of our own mouths!* [Kindly excuse my repeated use of French in the last two paragraphs, but there is just no English translation of the word "bullshit", that conveys the meaning quite as well...]

We've got problems in this country, but not a single one of them is insurmountable. If Einstein could come up with great bagels...er...the Theory of Relativity...while also coming up with the recipe for some really good bagels...and if Robert Oppenheimer and the scientists at Los Alamos could split the atom...then we can overcome the challenges we face, which I've gone to some lengths to talk about and suggest solutions to, in these pages.

Now, while I'm no philosopher, I do believe that Voltaire said something that I felt was partially right. He said that:

PATRICK F. WALSH

"No problem can withstand the assault of sustained thinking."

I agree in-part with that, but I'd add to it:

No problem can withstand the assault of sustained thinking, coupled with committed, effective action.

After all, I don't think the United States of America would exist today, if our Founding Fathers had taken Thomas Jefferson's Declaration of Independence and simply said:

"Tommy boy, jolly good sustained thinking old man. With this Declaration, the problem we have with the British is well on its way to being solved. Now, let's post this Declaration of Independence around town, send a copy to King George and get copies out to the colonies. We'll have a drink of whiskey to celebrate and then let's all go home to our families. Our work here is finished and problem solved..."

Er...gentlemen! Uh...you're forgetting something. You took care of the sustained thinking part, but there's the little detail of fighting the actual War of Independence, fellows...you know, the "committed, effective action" part of the resolution!

"Oh, bollocks...! Why of course...you're right old man! How did we overlook that one? Can't have independence from Britain without fighting the war, eh? Uh...George, Tommy, Benny, round-up Hancock, Adams and the rest of the boys and let's get back to the meeting and have at the rest of this thing, shall we? There's a little detail of a Continental Army we have to deal with...and George Dubya, if you fall asleep again during the meeting, you may just find yourself voted in-charge of the Continental Army! Get them to bring us some tea. I think it's going to be a long night"

A HARD LOOK IN THE MIRROR

"Hey, Patrick old boy, thanks for reminding us about the effective action part. We would have looked bloody silly leaving that part out, eh?

Yep...With only sustained thinking, the job would not have gotten done. What brings about solutions and change is participation and committed action by individuals and by groups of people. This is what gives our nation its vitality and this is why the people of our nation, those families here since 1776; those families here since 2014, and every new, legal arrival of people from other countries to our shores, adds to that vitality and makes our country stronger and makes us stronger, as a nation and as a people. And, as I learned, participation in our way of life and in our communities and most importantly, within our families, is the source of **unlimited vitality**.

The question is, **are you participating in your own life? Are you participating in the life of your family and in the lives of your family members? Are you participating in the life of your community? Are you participating in the life of your state and of your country?**

If not, then choose the things you will give time to and participate in, and give 100% of yourself to those people and those activities. After all, if you want heat out of your fireplace, are you going to put 50% of the wood required in it? Will you get an effective result with that? Of course not. Now, notice that I did not say give 100% of your **time** to each thing you do. That would be mathematically impossible. Just give 100% of **yourself** to each thing you choose to do and choose to give of yourself to your family, to your community, to your school board, and to educating yourself about our problems locally, and as a nation, and educate yourself about the candidates and what they stand for. It simply requires a decision and effective, committed action.

Give of yourself to go out and vote as an informed American, who understands that this is the minimum of what is expected of each of us as Americans of every race, gender, preference and religion, if we are going to fulfill our obligations to our Founding Fathers, to our fellow Americans, to our families, to our communities, and to those who fought in and those who died in all the wars defending our way of life and our freedoms.

Embrace your religious values (whatever faith you hold) and embrace our nation's values, and work to re-instill good family values. Assert yourselves as parents, whether you're a traditional family or a blended family, and take the actions necessary to protect and guide your children and allow them **the *right not* to grow up too fast**, having to be exposed to sex, drugs, violence, and a world that is short on values and morals. **Do your job** and protect them and shield them and draw lines in the sand about behavior and values and attitude and the value of education for its own sake, and the value of hard work for its own sake... **AND BE FIRM ABOUT IT!** They will thank you later, believe me.

Remember, you were not put on this earth to be your child's best friend. They have kids their own age for that. You were put on this earth to be your child's PARENT(s), a much more important role and responsibility, and that requires hard work, diligence, discipline, faith, patience and courage, and it is not a popularity contest that you are trying to win, despite what you may see on the reality shows (God forbid-and stop watching them). Kids still need limits, now more than ever to protect them and their sensibilities, in a seemingly limitless world that can take them in the wrong direction in the blink of an eye. Be the GROWN-UP.

We know that some adults try to remain perpetually young by acting like overgrown adolescents. Well...**grow up for God's sake!** Or if not for God's sake, then for your children's sake and for your own sake. Start behaving like adult parents and you will become adult parents! I see too many parents out there, too worried about their own convenience and not about doing their primary job...**being parents**. And make no mistake about it...**being a parent is a job**. Just ask my wife...My wife is the workhorse on the kid's side of things, while I am brought in as the disciplinarian...the heavy! In each family, there has to be at least one parent willing to be the fair disciplinarian and the heavy, in my humble opinion.

Also remember, when you are fulfilling your role as a parent, setting the example and engaging your children as a parent and giving 100% of your-self in those moments, you're making things happen, even if only in the most subtle of ways. In those moments, you're helping to shape them as people and influencing them, for good or bad. What you convey and how you convey it is most important and each interaction is an opportunity to teach and to set an example. And as I learned in the training, know this and keep it at the forefront of your awareness...**When you demonstrate interest in someone, you automatically become interesting to them**, as well. Demonstrate that you care about them and about their concerns. Don't take them for granted. Talk straight to them and ask questions. If you do this, you can make things happen in your life and in theirs. Otherwise, you're just letting things happen, to them and to you. If you take that hands-off approach, the problems inevitably come. When they do, **instead of making things happen, you'll be asking yourself, "What the hell happened?"** You don't want to be in this category.

Talk to your wife (or husband, or partner, as the case may be) and your kids about important values **and don't apologize for them...it's not the 60's anymore and you see where that got our mores**! And hey, don't ask me to flash my credentials, either...I grew up as a young kid in the 60's and saw both the good and the bad of it...and there are clearly both, good and bad! Some want to characterize the 60's as if it were the dawn of the enlightenment...OH BROTHER!

Now, don't get me wrong, some good things came out of the 60's...some very good things that we should be very proud of. But like every other age, some not-so-very-good things came out of the 60's, too. I'm not going to enumerate them here, but anyone who knew the 60's, knows very well what I'm referring to. All of the former flower-children who lived it and who still live in a state of denial about there being any bad that came out of those years, is either out of touch with reality, or still smoking weed (or worse), and perhaps did so in their house and around their kids, as their kids grew up...in which case, don't even try to relate to what I'm saying, because it will be a waste of your time...and mine... you're living in the past and have lost touch with both awareness and self-awareness.

Additionally, our Congress, our President, and our local governments and school boards, as well as our teachers and parents, need to understand that *"grown-ups" can delegate accountability, but can never delegate responsibility*. We assign accountability for our children's education to the educational systems in our states and local counties. But as parents, *responsibility* for our children's education remains with **us**! This is a very important distinction. If you don't like the education your child is getting, you can't throw your hands up and say, it's not my responsibility. *It absolutely is your responsibility*! You may have temporarily assigned accountability to the public school system, but once they fail, **the responsibility is *yours*, *it's ours*.** Now that it is failing, what are **"We the Parents"** going to do about it?

Remember what I said about the training I took and about always having choices and options? Well, we have choices and options, whether we admit it or not, and we need to act upon them for our children and for ourselves. For example, you can put your child in good private school if you wish; one that reflects your values and standards, and you can make the financial sacrifice to do that, again, if you can and should you wish to.

A HARD LOOK IN THE MIRROR

You can put your child in parochial school, a cheaper option, generally, and make the sacrifice to do that. You can get involved with the public school system through the school board and through the school board elections, as well as through involvement and participation with the PTA and your local school. Change can only come when you actively work for it and participate in that change, personally.

It's your tax dollars after all that support the public school system! They work for us, the taxpayers and parents. Shouldn't you have a serious say? Of course you should, but only if you'll act and demand that say.

What about our elected officials? Guys like Barney Frank made the case that he and his committee were not responsible for what happened to Fanny Mae and Freddie Mac and the collapse of the housing market... not even a little responsible. He said others were responsible. Well, Sir, my response is that if you allowed others to act in irresponsible ways because you delegated your authority, or allowed irresponsible behavior to take place on your watch, then you entrusted accountability to the wrong people. **But you can't delegate responsibility for the mistakes.** You were responsible for the decisions you made from a policy standpoint and from a delegation of accountability standpoint. You still bear responsibility for the failures of those institutions, based upon your poor decision-making. But sadly and expectedly, you tried ever-so-hard to slough-it-off by your normal bluster and your cock and bull rhetoric, as a politician so typically does.

Let me illustrate this point that you can't delegate responsibility with just one more example...the BP-Gulf of Mexico disaster. Tony Hayward, former CEO of BP, first tried to say that the platform operator, Trans-Ocean was responsible. Then he tried to say that a division of Halliburton was responsible for a shoddy job with the cement seal (according to reports,

BP had actually altered the formula for the cement without testing the formula)...If you listened to Hayward, anybody and everybody but BP was responsible. Of course, he was hoping no one would notice the 800 lb. gorilla in the room. BP was of course **responsible** for the entire operation and chose those sub-contractors and vendors.

If you choose to make someone else on your team *accountable* for results, it does not allow you to disavow *responsibility* when things fail. You chose to make those other people/entities accountable for certain results, but if you chose the wrong people or interfered with their operations, or didn't INSPECT what you EXPECT, then you can't say you're not responsible. *So, you can delegate accountability, but never responsibility.*

Our members of Congress and our President need to remember this. They are responsible for the results. If they delegate accountability to others, it still comes back to them, when it comes to who is responsible for the results, good or bad. We as Americans must always remember this and hold them responsible and never let them slip off the hook with their deceptions and verbal misdirection strategies (a la Mssrs. Frank and Hayward).

I would also like to touch on a couple of other points as I wrap up my thoughts in this book. You know, America is still one of the most powerful and influential nations in the world and might still be the most powerful and influential nation, globally. With this, I think, should come a fair amount of reflection, soul-searching, and dare I say, **humility**.

Now, we venture off into Middle-Eastern wars to fight terrorists, who we believe are hell-bent on our destruction and we then, at some point, decide to engage in nation-building as a by-product (I don't know about you, but I never knew that we signed on for nation-building as a part of the retaliation for 911). Now, as I've mentioned in earlier chapters, I believe we were right to engage in retaliation for 911 and I would have taken specific, limited strategic action with a defined policy for getting in and getting out, as President George Bush (Sr.) did in the first Gulf War. I would not have engaged in any adventure involving nation-building.

We go into these countries to achieve our strategic goals and we supposedly bring along with us the ideals of Freedom, Justice, and American values to their shores. As you know from previous chapters, rather than nation-building, risking the lives of our young citizen-soldiers, I instead believe that people should have to fight for their own freedom for it to really take effective root, for the reasons I've previously outlined. I don't believe that us imposing freedom on people works in the long-term. I believe that just as **we** did in 1776, people have to want freedom passionately enough to fight for it and be prepared to make the ultimate sacrifice for it, and they have to forge their "founding documents and principles", based upon the beliefs, mores and values of their own cultures. Hopefully they are the right beliefs, mores and values, but let's face it, there are no guarantees in war, or their outcomes.

Meanwhile, through this exposure to America, we hope that they have an opportunity to reflect on America's own struggle for freedom during our own Revolutionary War, as well as our values and principles, which constantly seek liberty, equality, and fairness for our citizens. We hope that what they see in our people, in our soldiers who are there, in our culture, our society and our values, may have a positive influence in what they may want for themselves, as they struggle for their freedom and self-determination (e.g. Iraq).

This said, we did engage in nation-building in Iraq and who knows if we're done? But being a just people of values, and I hope, reflection, I would challenge all of us to put ourselves in the other person's shoes for just a moment.

PATRICK F. WALSH

What I worry about, is what they may see in our society today and how they may interpret it and view it, since they may have only a limited frame of reference in many cases. If we reflect candidly for a moment upon how peoples of other countries, like those in the Middle East, may interpret the societal values and mores they may see coming out of our country these days, as opposed to 50 or 60 years ago, we may learn something important from that reflection.

Today, people in other countries and in the Middle East in particular, may look at America today and see many of the things I've outlined in this book, such as:

1. Decline in moral values.

2. They see that we have become one of the world's largest purveyors of pornography, even child pornography.

3. They see we have serious problems with drug use and drug addiction in our society, particularly amongst our young.

4. They see serious problems with teenage pregnancy and sexual freedom run amok, amongst our young and adults, alike.

5. They see divorce rates amongst the highest in the world.

6. They see deterioration of family values.

7. They see disintegration of the family unit and family's imploding, as divorce, drugs, and failures in parenting take their toll on our society.

8. They see alcohol addiction at high levels in our country, amongst young and old.

9. They see college campuses as being dens of iniquity, and aside from declining educational standards in our country; they see these as places where drugs, pornography, sex (all types with all types of partners) are also learned and run rampant.

10. They see TV programming from the U.S. (e.g. when they travel), which includes the likes of "Jersey Shore", "Real Housewives of Beverly Hills, Miami, Atlanta, et al", various and sundry nauseating, base and demeaning reality shows...you get the picture. All of which demonstrate the very lowest and most vile behavior, which is antithetical to what were once considered "Traditional American Values", and that must be shocking to many peoples of the Middle East when/if they view it.

11. They observe the mortgaging of our future through the mismanagement of our economy by our corrupt politicians, many of whom are in the pockets of Wall Street (as I've outlined), as we citizens allow the building of a gigantic debt burden for our children and grandchildren to bear, which is an impossible burden and challenges our very values and morals as citizens, parents, and responsible Americans, **as we allow that to happen**.

12. They also see our citizens, so fixated and focused on material wealth and appearances that they are living on credit, well beyond their means.

13. They see the political corruption in our country running rampant.

Given all of the above, if I were a moderate political leader in the Middle East, following an admittedly strict, and by U.S. standards, very restrictive set of religious rules, that on the one hand supported some form of traditional family values, but on the other hand deprived my people, particularly women, of many of their freedoms and rights enjoyed by the West...well, I just might not be so keen as you might think to embrace Western Culture and all that goes with it.

For example, if I had a U.S. diplomat coming over and telling me that I needed to embrace and follow the U.S. example of freedom, liberty, justice and human rights, and that I needed to change things in my country, well, I'm sure I would give the U.S. diplomat's perspective a fair amount of consideration.

After giving it due consideration, I might then surprise the U.S. diplomat by saying something like:

"Mr. U.S. Diplomat, you have given me deep pause for thought. While I understand and respect what you say and the values you say your country embraces and promotes, you must understand that what you speak of and what we observe, do not appear to us to be one in the same. Now please excuse me, for my country is a small, simple country by your standards, made up of simple people. Certainly, we are not as sophisticated and educated as yours, perhaps. But in saying this, I must point out some of our observations...

Now honored Sir, from my admittedly limited observations and those of my countrymen, which of course may be wrong, since I am a simple man; well, I must consider that my country does not have the levels of moral, spiritual, and family decay in some areas, that your country appears to us to have. For you see, we do not have drug problems running rampant amongst our young here, due to the severe punishment of drug traffickers in my country and the strict upbringing of our young. Nor do we have many of our families disintegrating before our very eyes; nor do we have our women exploited as sex objects (er…we go to Europe for that…); nor are we degrading our women by putting them in pornographic films; nor do we have our children in moral and substance abuse chaos, strung out on drugs and in rehab clinics and having all kinds of sex with all kinds of partners; nor is our television polluted with the likes of the programming your country sees fit to expose your children and society to; nor are our common people consumed by material concerns on which we focus most of our energy; nor when we educate our children to the degree we are able, which is admittedly modest by your standards, do we have to worry about them being overcome by abuse of drugs or alcohol in their schools or on their campuses, or having to pass through metal detectors to check for weapons that might be brought in by other children to kill them.

It is true that our colleges are few, but they are not dens where orgies take place, drugs are plentiful, or alcohol is grossly abused. We also don't have high rates of teen pregnancy and abortion in our simple country, honored Sir. So, while we may be a very backward country in many ways, and while some of the countries in our part of the world may be ruled by families, tyrants, or so-called religious fanatics, and while we certainly don't have the freedoms that your great society enjoys and certainly not the economic power, we also, in a very modest way, con-sider ourselves fortunate in some respects, that we don't have much of what we see as the growing moral depravity that goes with what your mighty country offers us by example.

You may see us as less civilized and certainly several of our governments in vari-ous countries within our region are indeed abusive and corrupt and indeed less civilized, in abusing their own people the way they do at times, Mr. U.S. Diplomat. But as your government freely criticizes our societies and in many cases, our way of life, I look at your country, honored Sir, and I must say that a biblical expres-sion from your own Judeo-Christian Bible comes to mind, when I hear the arro-gant manner of your government's criticisms, their lack of any genuine attempt at appreciation or understanding of our culture, and the way you clearly look down your noses at us as if we are far less civilized than yourselves, despite our culture having a rich history as a bedrock of civilization, culture, learning, and religion, going back centuries before your country or your culture existed. The biblical expression I refer to goes like this..."

"You hypocrite, first take the plank out of your own eye, and then you will see clearly to remove the splinter from your brother's eye."

- Matthew 7:5

Now please think about the above for a few seconds, because while admittedly it may not appear fair or balanced and must be taken with a large grain of salt, this is nevertheless the feedback that I received from someone who lived many, many years in the Middle East, in several countries ranging from Iraq, to Kuwait, to Dubai, to Saudi Arabia, to Jordan. I had not really thought about it from the Middle Easterner's perspective, until I heard this. The gentleman, a naturalized American who was educated in our University system, indicated that this is an amalgamation of what people from the Middle East said to him, frequently, when talking about the U.S.

At first I was a little put-off by the statements and was a bit salty in my initial response, being a proud and prideful American and coming from a middle-class, middle-income, military family and having family members in the military, both past and present, serving our country and trying to bring the ideals of freedom to foreign shores. But as I considered it, I also thought, reluctantly, that there is a certain measure of truth to be considered in the perspective and perhaps something meaningful to be learned from it, if we are willing to sincerely reflect upon it and look at ourselves in the mirror, as a country and as Americans of every race and gender.

A HARD LOOK IN THE MIRROR

Admittedly there are atrocities committed every day around the world, in many countries, including in some countries in the Middle East. As revolution slowly moves across the region, I don't think that in today's world, considering the state of our own society, that we can be going around telling other people and other cultures that we are the prime example to follow in every respect, except insofar as to suggest that they take the good and leave out the bad. Focus on the principles of freedom, equality, liberty and justice, outlined by our Founding Fathers and our Founding Documents, but figure the rest out for yourselves folks, in harmony with your respective histories and cultures. Incorporate what works into your culture.

Sorry to say this, but if we're frank with each other, our country and our society appear to be degenerating a little more each year. We seem to take one step forward in knowledge, technology, and merchandising (yes, I'm being facetious with the last one), and two steps back in moral gravitas, civility, social discipline and mores, and education of our young (to name just a few). We seem, in some parallel respects, to be going the way of the old Roman Empire, as they experienced progress in knowledge, mathematics, philosophy, and technology, while they simultaneously experienced a dramatic decline in their moral foundation, values, discipline, etc.

Cannot the same be said of us here in the U.S.? Extend what I have mentioned to the way we raise and educate our young, the unlimited and unending smut we expose them to (without their consent), as well as the corrupt and morally flawed way we administer the business of our country, through crooked politicians on the take, peddling their influence to the highest bidder and looking to control **our money**, in any way they can and to take more of it, any way they can, ignoring regularly what is in our best interests.

Now, this may all sound pretty depressing, and make no mistake about it, it is and should be. But we have to see and admit the truth to ourselves as Americans, if we're going to start to turn things around. **We have to take a hard look in the mirror!** I hope it will spur all of us to action, similar to the action we took in the November mid-term elections of 2010. We need to be angry and frustrated, because this encourages both self-examination and examination of those around us, including our family, our neighbors, our school boards, the teachers in our educational system, our politicians, our judges and others, as well as ourselves. It is only this type of self-examination that will spur real change and get us into the right conversations, asking ourselves the right questions. We need this type of shock to the system in order to get back in touch with our values, our morals, our heritage and our birthright as Americans of all colors, races, genders and preferences.

We need to shut off Sports Center, Real Housewives of New York (et al), and Jersey Shore, glorifying its sluts, punks and lowlifes of every description; Reality Programming in general, and start being selective about which people from the Media Industrial Complex we let into our homes; because that's what it amounts to. *Realize that whatever we have tuned-in on that TV is the equivalent of who we have just invited into our home to influence our children and our family. Would you invite sluts, drug dealers, punks and lowlifes in to spend time with your children and family? If you would, you deserve what you get!*

We need to pull together as Americans and demand better. We need to demand more and better accountability and we need to get involved and stay involved in our communities, our school boards, and our elections, and most of all, our own homes and families.

Again, we need to re-instill values into our young by BEING examples to them and staying away from the things that titillate and instead embrace the things that reflect solid values and have valuable messages to convey. We need to stop trying to be their best friends and focus on being their parents, instilling values and living those values and standing firm about what is and what is not acceptable conduct and behavior. We need to get closer to God and embrace the values reflected by that relationship and teach our children the value of that relationship.

TO BORROW AND MODIFY A CONCEPT FROM OUR LATE PRESIDENT JOHN F. KENNEDY, WE NEED TO STOP DOING WHAT'S EASY AND DO WHAT'S HARD!

We've done what's hard, many times before. Americans have sacrificed their lives and the lives of family members to do what's hard, fighting for freedom and true American Values. Our forefathers did the same and gave us the example and the roadmap. We simply need to reconnect with them and with each other as American brothers and sisters, whether we've been citizens all our lives, or only for the last few days. We are brothers and sisters in this journey, together. We need to do what's in our best interests as people and as a society and take our country back from the corrupt politicians. I've outlined my thoughts about how to do this and why we need to do it and I hope you can agree, or at least reflect fairly upon what I've said.

Now, I'm just a middle-class, middle-America working-stiff. But you know what? I've heard a lot of highly educated, highly paid politicians say a lot. But I haven't yet heard them deliver a message that resonated with me and the things I believe. And since I believe that most of you agree with a lot of what I've said in these pages, even if grudgingly at times, then I believe that maybe one needs to be a middle-class, middle-America working-stiff, in order to really understand what changes we're looking for, why we're looking for them and what such desired changes will require from each of us.

What do I mean by that? I mean that in order to achieve the changes we want in our society, we need to take a hard look at our own behavior, attitude and actions and make whatever changes are required there, first, before we can expect them of our elected representatives, our courts, our school boards, etc.

If this book has been about anything, it's been about taking ownership, which means taking a frank and hard look at ourselves first, and at our society as a whole, and understanding that it is a reflection of us and that if we don't like what we see in that reflection and we don't like what we are experiencing, then we'd better make some changes in our behaviors and attitudes, by re-ordering our priorities to get back in touch with God, Family, Traditional American Values and what's really important, and relegate our focus on money, material concerns, reality shows and titillation to lower orders of priority and invest the time, effort and focus on the important priorities and take action on those priorities, accordingly. Only then can we effectively communicate our priorities and our resolve to our children, to our families, to each other, and to our elected officials.

It's about taking ownership and getting back in touch with the values that made our country and our society great, and that allowed us to continually work on and change those things about our country and our society that needed changing (e.g. slavery, civil-rights atrocities, discrimination, etc.).

I believe we are still a society that possesses the basic DNA of our Founding Fathers, and I believe that all of the elements of those values and that greatness are still there, as evidenced by so many of the wonderful qualities we still possess and the leadership we still demonstrate, as evidenced by our election of our first African-American President, which again, demonstrated to ourselves and to the world that we continue to grow and evolve and put our past prejudices and weaknesses behind us as a people and as a country.

We still have much to be very proud of and we must continue to work on being good parents, good and moral people, and good and moral citizens (whatever sexual preference we may hold, which in my view should have zero to do with the points I make in this book, because this is inclusive of all of us, together). We should all work together to change those things about our society that threaten our family values, our children, and the very fabric of our society, and we, every brother and sister American of every ethnicity, color, sexual preference and religion, must get focused again on the basics, the fundamentals, and what is important.

What I've written in these pages is the equivalent of my love letter to my country and to all of my brother and sister Americans, inclusively and without exception, as I have described above, and encompasses my deepest hopes that we will carry on the dream of this GREAT AMERICAN EXPERIMENT and be worthy of the enormous gamble taken by our Founding Fathers and our brothers and sisters in 1776, putting their hopes, their dreams and their lives in the balance. It is my hope and my dream that we will recapture and continue to improve and build upon that dream and the ideals expressed in our Declaration of Independence, our Constitution, and our Bill of Rights and what they stand for.

I believe that The American Revolution and the hopes and dreams represented by it, are very much alive in the hearts of all Americans, inclusively.

I wrote this book because I love this country and because I am one of those people who still tear-up at the sound of the Star Spangled Banner, because it evokes in me the emotions of the great vision, courage, determination and sacrifice demonstrated in the founding of our country and the great, tumultuous and courageous journey this country and our citizens have made, including all that it has stood for and still stands for. We can re-commit ourselves to these Traditional American Values and recapture and maintain all the things we're so very proud of about our country, our people and our commitment to each other as brother and sister Americans.

WE NEED ONLY DEMONSTRATE THE VISION, COURAGE AND DETERMINATION TO TAKE OWNERSHIP AND TAKE ACTION, TOGETHER!

ABOUT THE AUTHOR

Patrick F. Walsh

[For additional information visit: patrickfwalsh.com]

Patrick Walsh is a Vice-President with one of the world's largest companies within the Global Logistics Industry. He has had a 20+ year career as an international transportation and logistics executive with top-tier, global organizations. He has traveled the world and met people of many cultures, beliefs and ways of life and considers himself to have a well-rounded perspective on issues.

He is a working American, having progressed within his industry, to the point of leading and managing various geographic regions for the companies he has and continues to work for. He is in touch with the working men and women in today's America and experiences and understands the economic, social and political challenges we are seeing in our society. He deals with the same concerns and struggles we all face. With his unique background, experience and education, he identifies that which ails America, our political leaders and our citizens and speaks directly to his brother and sister Americans of every race, gender and orientation, about the issues concerning us all. His results-oriented business and financial experience allows him to get directly to the heart of the issues, call-out those accountable, and offer logical, well-considered solutions that he is able to articulate in a style and with a level of clarity that is straight-forward and uncomplicated.

His years of management and leadership experience in small, medium and large global organizations, positions him to understand the financial, competitive and management challenges that business owners and working men and women and their families face and to recommend solutions needed to fix America, socially and economically.

He is an effective speaker and has experience in public speaking and in presenting to large groups and diverse audiences.

Originally from the Washington, D.C. area, he has lived in South Florida for more than twenty years and has traveled overseas extensively in his career. He appreciates and enjoys working in a diverse, multicultural environment.

Patrick is married to his wife of 27 years, Awilda, and they have two children, Jessica and Sean.

Education/Licenses: Patrick holds a Bachelor of Science Degree in Accounting/Business Administration from George Mason University in Fairfax, VA. He is also a past Registered Representative, having held a Series 7 Securities License from the NASD/NYSE and a Series 66 Securities License from the state of Florida.